W9-BPP-307

iPAD® FOR SENIORS
QuickSteps®

About the Author

Marty Matthews "played" with some of the first mainframe computers, the ones that took up half a football field and still used vacuum tubes, and from those to the latest iPad, he has never lost his fascination with computers. He has been everything from a programmer to a software company president and many steps in between. Throughout he has worked to bring others along with him and help them make the best use of all that computers can do. Toward that end, he has written 80 books on software and computing subjects, with many becoming bestsellers and receiving many accolades.

His recent books include *Computing for Seniors QuickSteps®*, *Windows 7 for Seniors QuickSteps®*, and *Windows 8 QuickSteps®*.

Marty and his wife Carole, also a writer, are the co-creators of the QuickSteps® books and live on an island northwest of Seattle, Washington.

About the Technical Editor

Anne Dotson's passions are technology and education. She was an early PC adopter and is constantly exploring new software. She is a Google Certified Teacher, a Google Apps Certified Trainer, and a Microsoft Innovative Educator. Long before most people were aware of computers, Anne took computer science courses, and a very early course on the Internet and HTML put on by NASA. Most of Anne's professional career has been as a teacher, from elementary education, to home economics, to high school English and special programs. She pioneered two separate high school programs: one in character education, where she wrote three books on the subject, and the other in critical thinking, where she established a new program to teach and test the subject. Most recently, Anne has married her two passions by working as the Technology Integration Specialist in her local school district where she introduced the iPod and iPad into the school program and brought the district teachers and staff up to speed on the subject. She is never very far from her iPad, and when she is on the move, which is most of the time, her iPad is under her arm.

iPAD® FOR SENIORS
QuickSteps®

Marty Matthews

McGraw Hill Education

New York   Chicago   San Francisco
Athens   London   Madrid   Mexico
City   Milan   New Delhi   Singapore
Sydney   Toronto

Cataloging-in-Publication Data is on file with the Library of Congress

iPad® for Seniors QuickSteps®

1234567890   QVS/QVS   109876543

ISBN   978-0-07-182150-6
MHID   0-07-182150-3

SPONSORING EDITOR / Roger Stewart

EDITORIAL SUPERVISOR / Patty Mon

PROJECT MANAGER / Vastavikta Sharma, Cenveo® Publisher Services

ACQUISITIONS COORDINATOR / Amanda Russell

TECHNICAL EDITOR / Anne Dotson

COPY EDITOR / Lisa McCoy

PROOFREADER / Paul Tyler

INDEXER / Valerie Haynes Perry

PRODUCTION SUPERVISOR / Jean Bodeaux

COMPOSITION / Cenveo Publisher Services

ILLUSTRATION / Erin Johnson

ART DIRECTOR, COVER / Jeff Weeks

COVER DESIGNER / Pattie Lee

SERIES CREATORS / Marty and Carole Matthews

SERIES DESIGN / Mary McKeon

Carole, thank you for your constant support and love, and for being a full partner with me. You make my sun shine!

I love you, Marty

Contents at a Glance

Contents

1

2

5

6

7

8   Chapter 8   **Working with Photos and Videos** 203

9   Chapter 9   **Socializing and Playing Games** 233

10   Chapter 10   **Accessing, Securing, and Maintaining Your iPad** 267

Acknowledgments

The author of a book is just the beginning of what it takes to produce one. The team for this book is especially accomplished and added greatly to making the book all that it is. I am most appreciative for all that they did. I particularly want to acknowledge

Anne Dotson, technical editor, who corrected many errors, added many notes and points, and did so with much enthusiasm and many kind and supportive words. Thanks, Anne!

Patty Mon, editorial supervisor, who often rolled up her sleeves and did much of the editorial heavy lifting throughout the project. Thanks, Patty!

Vastavikta Sharma, senior project manager, who was very patient with me and made sure that all the pieces and roles came together to produce the book. Thanks, Vas!

Lisa McCoy, copy editor, who is so very good at making my words readable without changing my voice. Thanks, Lisa!

Valerie Haynes Perry, indexer, who adds so much to the usability of book and does so with such grace. Thanks, Valerie!

Paul Tyler, proofreader, who made sure that the words and illustrations actually work to tell a story that makes sense. Thanks, Paul!

Amanda Russell, editorial coordinator, who tried hard to keep us on schedule with all the chapters and illustrations accounted for, an almost herculean task with this book. Thanks, Amanda!

Roger Stewart, editorial director, who is responsible for making this book a reality for us. He has worked with us for over 25 years and never lost faith, although I'm sure he questioned it more than once. In the process, he has become a valued friend. Thanks, Roger!

I am also fortunate to live in a very supportive community that includes our local telephone, Internet, and broadband supplier **Whidbey Telecom** and its co-president **George Henny**, who provided assistance in a number of ways, not the least of which was to cheer me on. Thanks, George!

Introduction

The iPad is the ultimate computing device for seniors. It is small, light, very portable, and very capable, allowing seniors to have in their hands at all times the means for doing email, messaging, scheduling, getting news and information, working with photos and videos, socializing, reading, listening to music, and watching movies. I believe that every senior should have an iPad, and it is my objective to make that assimilation as easy as possible with the end result being the fullest possible use of the iPad.

Most of my friends and acquaintances are seniors, as I am, and I have spent a fair amount of time helping them get comfortable with computers in general and the iPad in particular. This book is written for them in a voice without jargon using relevant examples in clear, step-by-step instructions. This book zeroes in on only the most important topics and uses brief instructions in plain language, with many color visuals to clearly lead the reader through the steps necessary to perform a task. In addition, a group of fellow seniors, one in each chapter, have added their comments in "QuickQuotes" about what they think of the iPad and how they use it.

QuickSteps® books are recipe books for computer users. They answer the question "how do I…" by providing a quick set of steps to accomplish the most common tasks with, in this case, an iPad and iOS 7.

The sets of steps are the central focus of the book. QuickFacts provide information that, while outside the primary discussion, is important to understand for the overall use of the iPad. Notes, Tips, and Cautions augment the steps with concepts and thoughts that the reader needs to be aware of. The introductions are minimal, and other narrative is kept brief. Numerous full-color illustrations and figures, some with callouts, support the steps.

You can easily find the tasks you want to perform through

- The table of contents, which lists the functional areas (chapters) and tasks in the order they are presented

- A QuickSteps® To list of tasks on the opening page of each chapter

- The index, which provides an alphabetical list of the terms that are used to describe the functions and tasks

- Color-coded tabs for each chapter or functional area, with an index to the tabs in the Contents at a Glance (just before the table of contents)

Conventions Used in This Book

iPad for Seniors QuickSteps® uses several conventions designed to make the book easier for you to follow:

- A ● in the table of contents references a QuickFacts sidebar in a chapter.

- A ● in chapter sidebars shows a QuickQuotes by a contributing iPad senior.

- **Bold type** is used for words on the screen that you are to do something with, like "…tap **Settings**, and tap **Calendar**."

- *Italic* type is used for a word or phrase that is being defined or otherwise deserves special emphasis.

- <u>Underlined</u> type is used for text that you are to type from the keyboard.

- SMALL CAPITAL LETTERS are used for keys on the keyboard, such as ENTER and SHIFT.

- When there are several commands in a row with the same verb, for example, tap **Settings**, tap **General**, tap **Siri**, tap **On/Off**, it becomes long and hard to follow. To simplify that, I have replaced the comma and repeated verb with the | vertical line or pipe character, so the example becomes tap **Settings | General | Siri | On/Off**.

QuickSteps to...

Chapter 1

Becoming Familiar with Your iPad

Welcome to your iPad! It is one of the foremost information devices ever created. Information in the form of sound, such as music and speech; images in either still photos or video; and text in books, magazines, newspapers, and other forms of media are all available to you on your iPad. It allows you to create, access, and exchange this information on the Internet; through email, notes, or documents you write; through photos or video you take; and through appointment calendars, maps, and games that you use. Your iPad even provides a built-in voice-activated assistant to help you use it and its information. In addition to what you see on the screen when you first start your iPad, there are currently over 475,000 "apps" (applications) that you can download from the App Store and run on your device.

The iPad is a tablet computer. In terms of what you can do with it, an iPad is a fully capable computer, every bit as capable as a desktop or laptop computer. The major difference is in the size and shape of the computer. The iPad is a tablet with all of its components built into a smaller, thin screen, as compared with the larger screen and keyboard of a laptop computer, or still larger screen, separate computer case, and separate keyboard of a desktop computer. While there are some limitations due to the tablet size, such as its smaller screen and less memory, this is more than made up for by its cameras, its global positioning system (GPS) in cellular models, its ability to use cellular as well as a Wi-Fi Internet connection, and its considerable portability.

How you make use of your iPad and its capability is up to you. This book will help you get started and show you how to use much of what is available, but it is up to you to try out and become familiar with the iPad. Set aside your fear and uncertainty and begin to explore the many things that you can do with the iPad. Follow the steps in this book to see how to start using the features that interest you and then challenge yourself to master these areas while using this book to explore additional areas. Set a pace for yourself by exploring a new area every day, week, or month, whatever is comfortable for you, but don't stop until you have covered every feature in this book that you are interested in, and then use the links that are mentioned here to explore new apps and new ways to use existing apps.

In this chapter you'll explore the external features of the iPad, see how to plug it in, charge its battery, turn it on and off, put it to sleep, and wake it up. You'll then go through the iPad setup to get an Apple ID and activate your iPad and set up its basic services. Finally, you'll take a look at some of the accessories that are available for the iPad.

> **TIP** Sign up for AppleCare+ two-year extended warranty in the first 30 days and get two instances of accidental damage coverage, plus two years of telephone support versus no accidental damage coverage and 90 days phone support in the basic one-year warranty. The extended warranty currently costs $99 over the one-year basic warranty that comes with the product for no additional charge.

EXPLORE YOUR IPAD

Take a moment to explore the physical iPad and what you got when you purchased it. Later in this chapter you'll see how to activate your iPad, begin setting it up, and get started using it. In future chapters you'll explore what is on the iPad screen and how to use those elements.

Review What's in the Box

The contents of the attractive box that the iPad comes in depend on whether you got one for use with a cellular service or not. The iPad and the iPad Mini come with the following:

- A 12-watt Universal Serial Bus (USB) power adapter to plug into a wall socket. This is different from the smaller 5-watt USB power adapter that comes with an iPhone or iPod. The iPhone power adapter will not work with the iPad.

- A 3.5-foot USB cable with Apple's connector to the iPad on one end and a standard flat USB connector on the other end.

- A small white folder containing a feature identification and instruction card, and a sheet with two Apple decals (the intended use of which is uncertain).

In addition, iPads with cellular service have the following:

- A cellular service subscriber identity module (SIM) card, which may be preinstalled.

- A device that looks like a paperclip, and that can be replaced with a paperclip, to open the SIM card tray. If the SIM card is preinstalled, you may not ever need to use this device.

Look at the Physical Features of the iPad

Your iPad has several controls, sockets, and features that allow it to perform its functions. These are located on both the front

App icons   Front camera   Status bar

Touch screen

Dock   Home button   Apps on the dock

Figure 1-1: **Front of the iPad 4th Generation (Courtesy of Apple Inc.)**

and back of the device. Figure 1-1 shows the front of the iPad, which contains these components:

- **Touch screen**, also called a "multitouch screen" or just the "screen," comprises the majority of the front face of the iPad. It allows you to view, select, and manipulate the contents displayed there.

- **App icons** represent the applications available on the iPad. You start out with apps that come standard with the iPad and in a standard layout. You can add icons, and you can rearrange

their layout on the screen, but you cannot delete the standard apps. (However, you can hide the standard apps by enabling Restrictions and turning off the apps you want hidden.)

- **Front camera**, called the "FaceTime" camera, has, on an iPad 4th Generation and iPad Mini, a 1.2MP resolution, face detection, and takes 720p high-definition (HD) video. It is used with FaceTime, the video-conferencing app that comes with the iPad, but can also be used with other apps. See Chapter 8 on how to use FaceTime.

- **Status bar** at the top of the screen provides information about the connectivity with both Wi-Fi and your cellular carrier, the current time of day, and the degree to which your battery is charged.

- **Home button** displays your Home screen from anywhere on your iPad. From the Home screen you can open or reopen any app and access the settings that control how the iPad behaves.

- **Dock** at the bottom of the screen provides a separate area to park your most heavily used apps so you can more easily reach them. You can move apps on and off the dock, but it is limited to 6 apps.

Figure 1-2 shows the back of the iPad. It contains these components:

- **On/Off – Sleep/Wake button** is the primary power controller for the iPad. Pushing it quickly puts the iPad in power-saving sleep mode. Pushing it quickly again or pushing the Home button wakes the iPad from sleep. Pushing and holding this button for about three seconds begins the process of shutting the power fully off. Pushing and holding this button for about three seconds when the iPad is powered off begins the process of powering up the iPad.

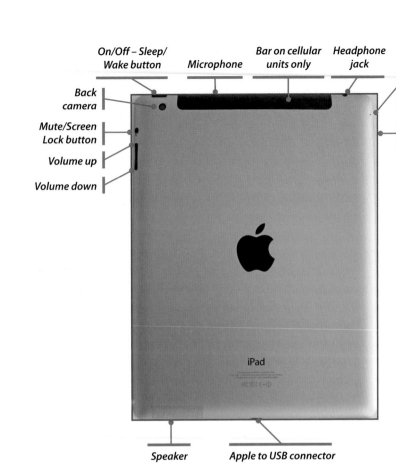

On/Off – Sleep/ Wake button — Microphone — Bar on cellular units only — Headphone jack

Back camera

Mute/Screen Lock button

Volume up

Volume down

SIM card release on cellular units only

SIM card tray on cellular units only

Speaker — Apple to USB connector

*Figure 1-2: **The back of the iPad 4th Generation***

- **Back camera**, called the "iSight" camera, has, on an iPad 4th Generation and iPad Mini, a 5MP resolution with autofocus and tap to focus, a five-element lens, face detection, and backside illumination. It can be used for either still pictures or videos with video stabilization and 1080p HD. See Chapter 8 for more information on using the camera.

- **Microphone** used to talk to Siri (the voice assistant) and used with Voice Memos, FaceTime, and other apps.

- **Headphone jack** into which you can plug headphones, earbuds, and earpods to listen to music and any other audio, including Siri, produced by your iPad. When a listening device is plugged in, the iPad's speaker is turned off.

- **SIM card** release hole and tray are only on iPad models that can connect to a cellular service. The release hole is used with the paperclip-like device—poke it in the hole to open the tray. The tray holds the SIM card, which normally comes already installed, so you probably will never need to open the tray.

- **Apple-USB connector** is used to plug in the iPad to both charge the battery and directly communicate with another computer.

- **Speaker** lets you hear Siri, music that is being played, and any other sound that is produced by your iPad.

- **Volume up/Volume down** changes the loudness in both the speaker and whatever is plugged into the headphone jack. Press the top of the rocker switch to increase the volume or press the bottom to reduce it.

- **Mute/Screen Lock button** performs one of two functions based on a setting in the iPad. The default is to mute all sound when this button is on so you can see a red dot. If you'd rather, you can use this button to lock the screen display in either vertical (portrait) or horizontal (landscape) orientation. If it is not locked, the screen orientation automatically changes depending on how you are holding the iPad. Normally, you want the orientation to automatically change, but if you are lying down and reading, you may want to lock the orientation so it doesn't change every time you move around. You can change how the switch works in iPad Settings, as explained in Chapter 2.

▷▷ Review the iPad You Have

As you use your iPad and read this book you will want to know which model you have and what its major features are. You basically want to know three items: the model, the memory size, and whether your iPad has cellular capability. There is a label on the back of the box that has all three pieces of information. In the top line you can see if it has cellular capability, the network it works on, and the amount of memory in gigabytes (GB). (Gigabyte or GB is a billion bytes, and a byte is roughly a character. You can think of 16GB of memory as enough space to store 16 billion characters of text.) On the third line down you can see the model number, which is also on the back of the computer. If you don't have the box, I'll show you how to find whether your iPad has cellular capability and its amount of memory later in this chapter.

Take a moment to better understand iPad memory and cellular vs. Wi-Fi communications.

Use of iPad Memory

Memory is used to store pictures, movies, videos, TV shows, music, books and magazines, mail, contacts, documents, and apps. Apps can also temporarily use some memory when they execute. No two people will have the same mix of these items, and there is no easy way to determine what your mix will be. And not all of any one item takes the same amount of storage. Remembering that last statement, here are some rough rules of thumb for the amount of memory used by various items (a kilobyte (KB) is 1,000 bytes, 1,000KB is a megabyte (MB), and 1,000MB is a GB, and a byte remember is roughly a character):

- Full-length commercial movies and TV shows are 1 to 3GB.
- Videos, depending on their length and their format, take from 500MB (.5GB) to 1.5GB.

- Music takes about 1MB per minute, or about 50MB for a CD.
- Magazines depend on length and the number of photographs, but generally range from 150MB to 500MB.
- Pictures, depending on their size and quality, take from 50KB to 2MB.
- Apps vary greatly, from 50KB to over 1GB for some games.
- Documents, mail, and contacts take relatively little space.

As you store information on your iPad, consider your mix of movies, TV shows, music, and games. If you are around a computer where you can store these items, it is very easy to transfer items back and forth from your iPad. You can also use iCloud for this purpose. Both of these processes are discussed at length in this book.

 TIP Store the bulk of your movies, videos, pictures, and music on your computer or on iCloud and only keep on your iPad what you know you will be using in the near term.

Understand Wi-Fi vs. Cellular

Both Wi-Fi and cellular service give the iPad the ability to connect to the Internet and through it to communicate with the hundreds of millions of people, businesses, organizations, and institutions that are connected to the Internet. This communication ability is foundational to both the use of the iPad and its operation. The iPad could not do what it does without this ability, and it is therefore critical to its success.

All iPads come with the ability to use Wi-Fi, which is a standard for wireless communication among computers. The term "Wi-Fi" originally comes from "wireless fidelity," but today it simply means wireless data exchange. If you don't already

Reviewing What You Need

To use your iPad, you will need or probably want the following:

- A connection to the Internet. You can do this through either a
  - Wi-Fi wireless network in a public space or with a Wi-Fi access point in your home or office.
  - Cellular telephone account from AT&T, Sprint, or Verizon in the United States.
- An Apple ID to register your iPad and download apps from Apple or to get iCloud or iTunes accounts. You will see how to get this later in this chapter.
- Access to another computer, either a Mac or a PC, and either a desktop or laptop that you can connect the iPad to using a USB 2.0 or later connection on the computer and the Apple-USB cable. If the computer is a Mac, it must be running OS X version 10.5.8 or later. If the computer is a PC, it must be running Windows XP (with Service Pack 3 or later) or either 32-bit or 64-bit Windows Vista, Windows 7, or Windows 8. On this computer, you'll need to have or download for free iTunes 10.6 or later (for iOS 7 you will need iTunes 11.1 or later).
- Access to a printer with wireless printing capability, such as Apple's AirPrint. In addition to Apple printers, HP, Epson, Cannon, Brother, Dell, and others all make wireless printers that work with the iPad. Some printers, in addition to Apple, use the iPad's built-in AirPrint capability; others use their own downloadable app. Some printers using AirPrint cannot access all printer features such as multiple paper trays and booklet printing.

have Wi-Fi service in your home and/or office, it is easy to get from your local telephone company, TV cable company, or an independent Internet service provider. Also, it is available for free in many public locations such as libraries, coffee shops, hotels, and airports.

PLUG IN AND START THE IPAD

When you first get your iPad, the temptation is to turn it on and start using it. The iPads are shipped from the factory with enough charge in their battery to do this, but unless you had your iPad set up at the store where you bought it, you must go through the activation and setup process. To make sure you have enough power to do all you want when you first turn it on, I recommend that you start by plugging in and charging your iPad; it should not take more than a couple of hours. After that, you can turn it on and begin the activation and setup process.

▷▷ Plug In and Charge Your iPad

Plugging in your iPad is not exactly rocket science, but there are two ways to do it, and there is a significant caveat with one of the ways. Here are the ways.

Plug into a Wall Socket

The simplest and surest way to plug in and charge your iPad is by using the 12-watt USB to AC adapter, plugging it into a wall socket, and plugging the Apple to USB cable into both the AC adapter and your iPad.

When you are successfully charging your iPad and have turned it on, you will see an icon in the upper-right corner of the iPad screen that looks like a battery with a lightning bolt in it as well as the percentage of charge 61% ⚡ .

Plug into a Computer

You can also use the Apple to USB cable to connect your iPad to a computer through a USB socket on the computer. This primarily allows you to transfer information between your computer and your iPad, as discussed later in this chapter and in Chapter 2.

On some recent desktop and laptop computers, you can also charge the battery by plugging the Apple to USB cable into them, but on the majority of computers, when you do that you get the message "Not Charging," telling you that the computer is not charging the iPad. You must use the AC adapter and plug into a wall socket to charge the iPad.

It does not hurt to try to charge the iPad from your computer, so you might as well try it to be sure. If you do, make sure your iPad is completely powered off, so nothing but the battery charging is using power.

Turn On and Set Up Your iPad

When your iPad battery is reasonably charged, it is time to turn on the iPad and begin the activation process. Begin by getting a Wi-Fi service, if you don't already have one.

Get Wi-Fi

Wherever you choose to start and activate your iPad, you must at least have Wi-Fi available and you must know the password to sign on to the wireless service. You must also have the time to complete the full activation—approximately 30 minutes. The best place, of course, is your home where your time and privacy are hopefully your own. If you don't have Wi-Fi in your home, you are probably going to want it. If you already have an Internet connection, you may already have Wi-Fi available or you may be able to easily turn it on. Call your Internet service provider (ISP) and ask them how you can get Wi-Fi if you don't already have it. If you don't have an Internet connection, call your local phone company or TV cable service provider (or both to compare them). Ask them if they can install Wi-Fi in your home and how much it costs per month. They may have several prices depending on the speed. For example, my

Package	Speed*	Price
1	Up to 6 Mbps** download, up to 1 Mbps upload	$29.95
2	Up to 12 Mbps download, up to 1 Mbps upload	$39.95
3	Up to 18 Mbps download, up to 1 Mbps upload	$44.95
4	Up to 30 Mbps download, up to 3 Mbps upload	$69.95

Table 1-1: An Example of a Local ISP's Levels of Service and Related Prices

* Speed is measured in terms of how fast information is transferred to your iPad, called *download* speed, and how fast information is transferred from it, or *upload* speed.
** Mbps, or megabits (million bits) per second, where there are eight bits per bytes, which are each approximately equal to a character.

local phone company offers four levels of Internet service with the prices, as of Summer 2013, shown in Table 1-1. Probably get rid of the slowest and fastest offerings and choose one in the middle. The second offering from my phone company is perfectly adequate for use with an iPad.

TIP Some Internet service providers, especially TV cable companies, offer a low introductory price for an initial number of months, only to increase it substantially after the initial months. Be sure to ask what the price is after the initial period.

Activate Your iPad

When you have Wi-Fi available to you, use these steps to start and activate your iPad:

Hold your iPad in portrait fashion where it is taller than it is wide with the Home button at the bottom. This will orientate the iPad for the instructions here.

1. Press the **Home** button. The screen should come on and display the word "Hello" in a number of languages.

   If the screen does not come on, press and hold the **On/Off – Sleep/Wake** button on the top right of the iPad for several seconds. The screen should display the Apple logo for several seconds as the iPad starts up ("boots up"). Finally, you should see the initial screen with the word "Hello," as shown in Figure 1-3.

2. At the bottom of the screen, use your finger to slide the words "Slide To Set Up" to the right.

3. Touch or *tap* the language you want to use and your country. For example, "English" and the "United States."

Figure 1-3: *The first screen that your iPad displays is only used when the iPad is not activated.*

4. If there are several Wi-Fi networks around you, you will see them listed. Tap the network that you want to use. If you don't see a network, then none is available where you are. If you think you have Wi-Fi, contact your Internet provider, or ask the business or organization that you think is providing the Wi-Fi.

5. You are asked to enter the password for that network, as shown in Figure 1-4. Use the onscreen keyboard that pops up to do this (see the "Using the Onscreen Keyboard" QuickFacts later in this chapter), and tap **Join**.

6. When a checkmark appears next to the network you want, tap **Next**.

7. Determine if you want to enable Location Services. This uses the iPad's GPS and/or Wi-Fi to determine your current location, and is valuable when you are asking Siri about the location of restaurants or with maps. It is especially valuable when you are getting driving directions. Also, Location Services must be enabled to use Find My iPad. On the other hand, apps can see where you are and use that information, which you may or may not want. I think that the benefits of Location Services outweigh the perceived loss of privacy. Based on your decision, tap either **Enable Location Services** or **Disable Location Services** and tap **Next**.

*Figure 1-4: **When you are asked to enter text, an onscreen keyboard will pop up.***

You'll need to have and use an Apple ID even for free apps and other free items. Apple doesn't charge for the ID itself, and there is no other way to work with Apple. Continue with these steps to set up your iPad:

1. If you have used an iPad in the past, you probably have a backup you can use to quickly set up a new iPad. In that case your first question is, do you want to set up as a new iPad or do you want to restore from an iCloud or iTunes backup? If you don't have a backup, you won't see this question. We assume you want to set up as a new iPad—we'll talk about restoring in Chapter 10. Tap **Set Up As New iPad** if you have the choice of restoring.

Set Up Your iPad

With your iPad started and connected to the Internet through Wi-Fi, you next need to connect to Apple to set up an Apple ID and register your iPad. Apple uses a common ID and password for Apple itself, the iTunes Store, the App Store, iCloud, the iBook Store, and the Mac App Store. This allows you to get accounts to download apps from Apple's App Store, or music and videos from the iTunes Store, and accessories from the Apple Store.

TIP You do not have to use a credit card to set up an Apple ID. Simply select "None" when you are asked for a payment type. You, of course, will not be able to buy anything that costs something (there are many free items on both the App Store and iTunes Store). Also, you can get a very limited credit card and use that for your Apple ID and other purchases on the Internet.

2. You are then asked to either sign in with an Apple ID or create a new one. Again, we'll assume you need to create a new one (if you have an Apple ID, enter it and skip to Step 11). Tap **Create A Free Apple ID**.

3. Select your birthday by using your finger to move the three calendar elements up or down, as shown in Figure 1-5. When you are done, tap **Next**.

4. Tap or type your first name using the keyboard at the bottom of the screen. See "Using the Onscreen Keyboard" QuickFacts later in this chapter to understand how to do that.

5. Tap **Return** to go to the next line and type your last name; then tap **Next**.

6. If you have an existing email address, accept that default, tap **Next**, and skip to Step 8. If you do not have an email address that you want to use, tap **Get A Free iCloud Email Address**, tap **Next**, and follow on to Step 7.

7. Type the first part of your new email address. For example, type <u>funnyclown</u> for an email address of funnyclown@icloud.com, and tap **Next**. You are asked if you are sure you want to use that email address. If so, tap **Create**.

8. Enter and verify a password at least eight characters long and containing a number and both uppercase and lowercase letters. Tap **Next** when you are done.

9. Choose three security questions, enter their answers, and tap **Next**. If you wish, and if you have one, enter another email address that can be used in case all else doesn't work. In any case, tap **Next**.

10. If you want email updates from Apple, leave the default ON and tap **Next**. If you do not want these updates, *swipe* (move your finger across) the **ON** button to turn it off, and then tap **Next**.

11. You are asked if you agree to Apple's terms and conditions. You can read them on your iPad or have them sent to you by email. If you don't agree, you will not be able to use your iPad, although if it is shortly (within 30 days) after you purchased it, Apple will allow you to return

Figure 1-5: *To enter your birthday, iPad gives you a set of three cylinders to spin.*

it with a full refund. When you are ready and do agree, tap **Agree** and then tap **Agree** again.

Terms and Conditions

I agree to the iOS, iCloud and Game Center Terms and Conditions and the Apple Privacy Policy.

Cancel   Agree

12. Next you are asked if you want to use iCloud, which is Apple's free Internet storage service for backing up the information on your iPad. If something happens to your iPad, you can recover your information from iCloud, and if you store your iPad information on iCloud, you can access that information on your iPhone, iPad touch, or Mac. I think it is a good idea, and the first 5GB are free. If you want this, tap **Use iCloud**; if not, tap its alternative, and then, in either case, tap **Next**.

13. You can use iCloud to automatically back up your iPad daily, which I also think is a good idea. The alternative is to back up to your computer, which is probably more vulnerable. Make your choice and tap **Next**.

14. Tap **Use Find My iPad**, which would be invaluable if you lose it or it is stolen, and tap **Next**. Find My iPad is good insurance, and I recommend that you activate this.

15. If you have used an iPad before, you will be asked if you want to let people contact you via iMessage and FaceTime, and your phone number and email address will be displayed and selected (with a checkmark). If you don't want to use either of those contacts, tap them to deselect them. In any case, tap **Next**.

16. Next you are asked if you want to create a passcode, which can be used whenever you start or wake up your iPad to protect it from unauthorized use. You don't have to use a passcode, so there would be nothing preventing someone from using your iPad, but I recommend you do use one. If you want that, follow the instructions to set it up. The standard passcode is four numbers, like the pin you might have at your bank. Enter your passcode, and then re-enter it for confirmation.

17. Tap **Use Siri** and tap **Next**. Siri is a voice-activated assistant to which you can ask questions like "What are the Greek restaurants in Bellevue?" or "Do I have an appointment next Tuesday?" I can't imagine someone not wanting Siri.

18. You can choose to help Apple by anonymously sending them information about how you are using your iPad, including your location. I believe that doing this helps all users, and so I recommend it. If you agree, tap **Automatically Send**; if not, tap **Don't Send**. In either case, tap **Next**.

✓ QuickFacts

Using the Onscreen Keyboard

When you need to enter text on your iPad, an onscreen keyboard is automatically displayed, such as the one you see here. Simply tap the keys you want to use. Here is how to use the other features of the onscreen keyboard:

- If you don't see a keyboard when a form or text entry box is displayed, simply tap the text box into which you want to place text.

- To make a letter uppercase, press the upward-pointing arrow or SHIFT key so the arrow itself darkens, ⬆ and then tap the letter. Uppercase will automatically be turned off after tapping the letter.

- To make a series of letters uppercase, *double-tap* (tap twice in rapid succession) the SHIFT key so the key, not the arrow, darkens, ⬆ and then tap the keys you want in uppercase. When you are done, tap the upward-pointing arrow again to turn it off.

- With the !, and ?. keys [! ?], press the SHIFT key and then press the desired key to get the character on top. (There are also additional choices with these keys. If you tap and hold the , key and slide your finger up you get the ' and the . gives you the ".)

- To correct an error, tap the BACKSPACE key ⌫ once for each letter you want to replace. Then tap the replacement key(s).

- To complete one line of type and go to the next line, tap the **RETURN** key. You may also tap the new line on the screen.

- To enter numbers and some of the special characters, tap the **.?123** key. If you don't see the special characters you want, tap the **#+=** key for additional characters. When you are done entering numbers and/or special characters, tap the **ABC** key to return to the original keyboard.

- When you are done using the keyboard, tap the miniature keyboard key ⌨ in the lower-right corner of the onscreen keyboard to put the keyboard away. Often when you finish entering text and complete a form, the onscreen keyboard automatically disappears.

19. Finally, you see "Welcome to iPad." Tap **Get Started**. The familiar iPad Home page is displayed, as shown in Figure 1-6.

⏩ Attach Your iPad to a Computer

If you have a recent (in the last five years) computer available to you, either a Mac or a PC, you can attach your iPad to it and transfer information between the two devices. To do that, you need to install Apple's iTunes on that computer if you haven't already. This is a particularly good approach if you have a lot of music or videos on the computer that you want on the iPad. See the "Reviewing What You Need" QuickFacts earlier in this chapter for the specifications of the computer that you need to use.

Figure 1-6: **The iPad's Home page is the starting point for the many things you can do with it.**

If you have iTunes already on the computer, make sure it is up to date. On a Mac, press the **Apple** key and click **Software Update**. On a PC, Windows 7 and before, click **Start**, click **All Programs**, and click **Apple Software Update**. On a Windows 8 PC, on the Start Screen, start typing Apple and click **Apple Software Update**. You will be told if iTunes is not up to date. If so, follow the instructions to update it.

Download and Install iTunes

If you do not already have iTunes, you can download it for free from Apple and install it on your computer.

1. On your computer, open a browser, type itunes.com in the address box, and press **ENTER**. The Apple iTunes download page will open, as you see in Figure 1-7.

2. Click **Download iTunes**, and then on the next page click **Down Now** (you don't have to enter your email address, and I uncheck the two email offers) and click **Run** at the bottom of the screen.

3. In the Welcome To iTunes dialog box that opens, click **Next**. Uncheck any of the options you don't want, and then click **Install** and click **Yes** to allow iTunes to make changes to your computer.

4. Finally, when you are told that iTunes has been installed, click **Finish**. iTunes will open on your desktop.

Connect Your iPad Through iTunes

Once you have iTunes installed and your iPad set up, it is time to connect the two.

1. Plug the Apple connector into your iPad and the USB connector into your computer. The iPad's screen will come on. Swipe the **Slide To Unlock** arrow left to right. Enter your Passcode, if you have one, and tap **Trust** in the Trust This Computer? dialog box that opens.

2. If it isn't already running on your computer, start iTunes. You should see your iPad appear in the left-hand column. If you don't have a left-hand column or *Sidebar*, click the **View** menu and click **Show Sidebar**. If you don't see a menu bar across the top, click the **Select** menu (the black and white rectangle) in the far upper-left corner, and click **Show Menu Bar**.

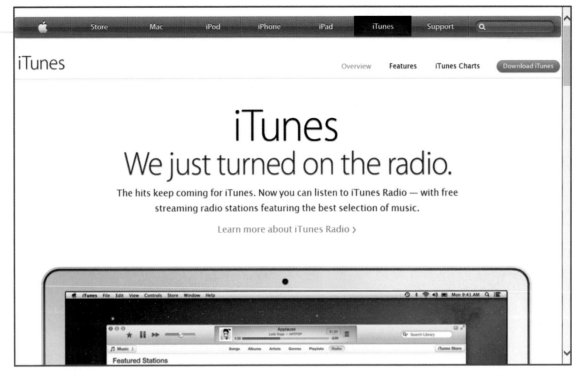

*Figure 1-7: **iTunes is a program to acquire, organize, and share music, movies, and TV shows. Apple also uses it to transfer information between a computer and an iPad, iPhone, or iPod.***

3. Click *your* **iPad** in the left column to open a pane on the right about your iPad, as you see in Figure 1-8.

4. If, when you set up your iPad as described earlier in the chapter, you selected to automatically back up on iCloud, it will be selected in iTunes, as you see in Figure 1-8.

5. You may additionally, or in lieu of iCloud, back up on the computer you are connected to. If so, click that option, if desired, click **Encrypt Local Backup**, enter and verify a password, and click **Back Up Now**.

You will see a lot more about syncing music, videos, and other media between iTunes and your iPad in later chapters of this book.

 NOTE Although you can back up your iPad to a computer, I recommend additionally or in lieu of the computer, backing up to iCloud. The computer can be destroyed by fire or be stolen; the iCloud cannot be. If you choose to back up both to your computer and to iCloud, I recommend that you leave the iCloud selected for automatic backup and manually back up to your computer.

Figure 1-8: iTunes not only allows you to transfer information, but also to control some aspects of your iPad.

⤷ Turn Your iPad On or Off and Put It to Sleep or Wake It

In going through the setup of your iPad, you have probably experienced the screen shutting itself off automatically after the iPad had been inactive for a period of time. This is the iPad's

sleep mode, a low-power condition that prolongs the battery life, but makes it immediately available to perform some task for you. This is one of three power modes:

- Fully powered on with the screen lit and the iPad is available at a single touch.

- In sleep mode with the screen dark, but the iPad is available by waking it.
- Fully powered off and not using any power. It must be turned on to be used.

Turn the iPad On or Off

When the iPad is fully powered off, you must start it up, or "boot it up," to turn it on. You know it is off if you press the **Home** key and nothing happens (given that your battery has a charge).

- **Turn off** your iPad:

  Press and hold the **On/Off – Sleep/Wake** button until the Power Off command appears, and then swipe that command from left to right.

- **Turn on** your iPad:

  Press and hold the **On/Off – Sleep/Wake** button until the Apple icon appears and then, when the Slide to Unlock command appears, swipe it from left to right. Enter your Passcode if you are using one.

Put Your iPad to Sleep or Wake It

By providing the sleep mode, Apple made your battery last a lot longer. Remember that when you get tired of your iPad often being asleep. You can adjust the period of time before your iPad goes to sleep, as you will see in Chapter 2.

- **Wake** your iPad. You can do this in two ways:
  - Press the **Home** button, swipe the Slide to Unlock command from left to right, and enter your passcode if you have one.
  - Press the **On/Off – Sleep/Wake** button and swipe the Slide to Unlock command from left to right, and enter your passcode if you have one.
- **Put your iPad to sleep**. Normally, your iPad will automatically go to sleep, but if you want, you can do it manually:
  - Press the **On/Off – Sleep/Wake** button.

⊳⊳ Get Accessories for Your iPad

A large number of accessories are available for your iPad from both Apple (apple.com/ipad/accessories; see Figure 1-9) and a number of retailers, including Amazon (go to amazon.com, and search for "iPad accessories"; see Figure 1-10). Here are some thoughts about a few of the accessories you can buy:

- **Cases and covers** come in many styles, colors, and materials, from aluminum, to leather, to polyurethane, to hard plastic. The most important function of a cover or case is to protect your iPad from dropping, being hit, or getting scratched. It is gut-wrenching to see a shattered screen on an iPad, especially if it is yours! The most

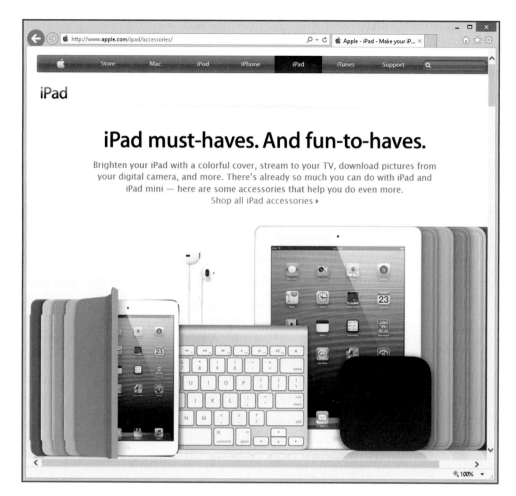

common is Apple's Smart Cover in five colors of polyurethane and leather, currently beginning at $39.00 for polyurethane and $69.00 for leather. It folds to provide a stand for viewing. The OtterBox Defender Series case

Courtesy of OtterBox

with an integral screen protector and stand provides some of the best protection, but it is a bit bulky, currently from Amazon for $59.99.

 TIP The most important thing to remember in buying a case is corner protection.

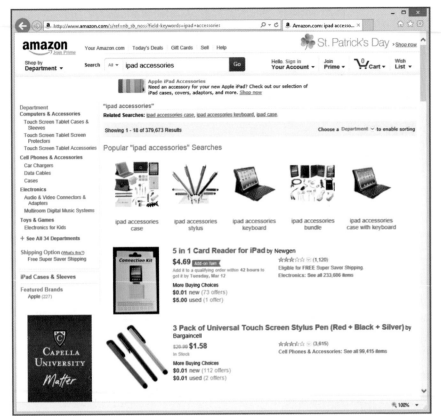

Figure 1-10: *Amazon offers many more iPad accessories at significantly reduced prices, but not always of high quality.*

- Keyboards come as stand-alone items or integrated in a case. If you do much typing on your iPad, a separate keyboard might be handy. Apple makes a stand-alone wireless keyboard with an aluminum case that uses Bluetooth technology to connect to the iPad. It is thin and attractive, but not very portable, at $69.00 from Apple. Logitech offers the Ultrathin Keyboard Cover that can be used as a stand and has a matching aluminum back to the iPad. It also uses Bluetooth to connect to the iPad, magnetism to hold on to

it, is very portable, and is currently available from Amazon at $84.47. (I have one of these and love it.)

Courtesy of Logitech

- **Screen protectors** are very thin plastic sheets that adhere to the iPad's screen and protect it from scratches, abrasions, and some lighter knocks. Some users swear by them, while others swear at them. They are hard to put on without leaving bubbles under them and may show fingerprints and dust more than the actual screen. Amazon offers a number of varieties in packets of two to four protectors currently from $2.23 to $13.98.

- **Cables** are primarily the Apple to USB cable used to connect iPad to a computer ("docking it") and to charge the iPad, but also include cables to connect the iPad to cameras and TVs. It is handy to have several of the Apple to USB cables so you can charge your iPad (and maybe an iPhone 5, which uses the same cable) in your car, office, and home. Apple offers a full selection of these, beginning with the Apple to USB cable in both one-meter and half-meter lengths currently for $19.00 for either one. Amazon offers many styles and lengths of the Apple to USB cable currently from $2.69 to $16.99. I have had some less-than-perfect experiences with the very inexpensive third-party cables.

- **Earpods and headphones** let you privately hear stereo sound in place of the single (monaural) not-too-great speaker in the iPad. Apple offers both in-the-ear earpods, with a remote mic and moderate sound quality, at currently $29.00, and in-the-ear headphones, with a remote mic and good sound quality, at currently $79.00. Amazon offers a number of earpod replacements currently beginning  at $2.23, as well as Apple's own earpods currently at $24.95. Amazon also offers a number of headphones, some wireless using Bluetooth, and some very high quality that currently go over $99.00.

 NOTE Several other sellers besides Apple and Amazon offer many other iPad accessories than what has been described here. You need to spend some time on both websites and do a Google search for "iPad accessories."

QuickQuotes

Anne Dotson **is the leader behind her school district getting iPads for all seventh and eighth graders and is the technical editor of this book.**

My iPad has to be my favorite device of any I have ever had. I do everything electronic on it. I have all my recipes stored in the Dropbox app and use that every day. I have all my mail forwarded to my mail account and check my mail on it. I use Facebook, Flipboard, and Pinterest daily. I have multiple Kindle books and books in Overdrive from the public library. I use the iPad to read books to me when I am driving on long trips. I take pictures and video with it and love the fact that I can access all my pictures from my iPhone on Photo Stream on my iPad. It is really my go-to device for answering any questions that arise, from what do I substitute for wine in this recipe to how many miles is it from one place to another. I use the ability to capture the screen as I teach others how to use the iPad. I try never to be without my iPad, at church, at home, at the beach, on the road.

Anne's Favorite Apps

Dropbox   Allows me to save all my recipes and share them with my daughters and access them wherever I am. It has become my recipe book.

Pinterest   Online pinboard of great ideas for almost anything imaginable. I have over 40 boards set up and spend some time each day looking at the sites that my followers are following and adding to my resources.

Flipboard   A combination magazine-like approach to social media that I am involved with. A great way to catch up fast. Customizable to your own interests.

Overdrive Media Library   Allows you to access library books and borrow them to read as they become available. Books are generally offered in epub, which must be read in Overdrive, or Kindle, which must be read in a Kindle app and downloaded from Amazon. However, the borrowing is done through Overdrive.

Facebook   Social site that allows me to stay in touch with my family, far and wide.

Diigo   Social bookmarking site that can be shared with others who are researching and saving sites of similar interest.

Maps   An awesome GPS system built right in to your iPad or iPhone.

Notes   Keep all your important information there that you need to access, like your kids' addresses, phone numbers, and Wi-Fi login information.

Chapter 2

Exploring and Customizing Your iPad

In Chapter 1 you reviewed the physical aspects of your iPad. In this chapter you'll explore the iPad's screen, how to manipulate the apps on it, what those apps do, and how to, in general, use them and how to navigate among them. Much of the rest of the book will be spent on how to use specific apps in detail. The balance of this chapter will be spent on how to customize your iPad to fit your particular use.

EXPLORE THE IPAD SCREEN

The screen is the central focus of the iPad, as shown in Figure 2-1, with the initial Home icons on it. The screen is used to both control the iPad and display everything that the iPad has available and does. Besides the few buttons along the edges or at the bottom front, the iPad is controlled on the screen. You do it with your fingers, often with just a touch, but there are other moves of your fingers that you need to know. With that knowledge, this section will then introduce the standard apps that are on the Home screen of new iPads. Most of these apps are described in more detail in later chapters. Finally, this section will describe how to start, pause, and leave apps as well as how to navigate among them.

Figure 2-1: *The Home screen provides the starting place for all that you do on the iPad.*

Let Your Fingers Do the Work

The principal control device for your iPad is your fingers. You don't have to remember to bring them along or learn how to use them, unlike a mouse, and their use is intuitive and simple.

Use One or Two Fingers

The principal commands used in this book can be performed with one or two fingers:

- **Tap**   Lightly touch and withdraw your hand once from an object on the screen to select it.

  - Tap an app on the Home screen to open or start the app.

  - Tap an item in a list, such as an option in a menu or a photo in an album, to select or display it.

- Tap an action in an app, like a previous or next arrow, to follow that action, for example, to return to the previous page in Safari.

- Tap a text box, as in the address bar in Safari or text line in Notes, to identify the line into which text you type will go.

- Tap a key on the onscreen keyboard to place its character on a selected text box or text line.

- Tap the status bar at the top of the screen when a webpage, an email message, or a list is displayed to quickly move to the top of the page, message, or list.

- **Double-tap**   Tap an object on the screen twice, such as a page in Safari or a map in Maps, to generally enlarge the content being displayed.

- **Flick** or **Swipe**   Quickly move one finger up or down, left or right, to

  - Scroll or move a webpage, an email message, or a list up or down or left or right

  - Turn the pages in a newspaper, magazine, or book

  - Open the Notification Center by flicking down from the top of the screen

  - Open the Control Center by swiping up from the bottom of the screen

- **Drag**   Press and hold a finger on an object until it is selected, or, in the case of the apps on the Home screen, until all apps wiggle and then drag the object to where you want to move it.

- **Pinch**   Bring together two fingers, often your thumb and forefinger, to zoom *out* and display more area in a webpage, email message, reading page, or a map.

- **Spread** Spread apart two fingers to zoom *in*, enlarge, and display less area in a webpage, email message, reading page, or a map.

Use Multiple Fingers with Multitasking

The iPad has three multifinger gestures, called "multitasking gestures" because they have to do with switching among apps you have used and are still running in the background. The iPad keeps track of the apps you used and what they were doing when you last used them. The multitasking gestures let you work with this set of recently used apps. As you'll see later in this chapter, you can turn multitasking gestures on and off in Settings. The multitasking gestures are as follows:

- **Double-press** the Home button to open multitasking view, showing the apps you have used and are still running. Tap any of the apps to switch to that app.

- **Swipe up** with four or five fingers to display the multitasking view, which is not easy to do.

- **Swipe from right or left** with four or five fingers to open one running app after the other when you are in one of them.

 NOTE In multitasking view, you can switch from one app to another with a single finger swipe from the right or left.

- **Pinch together** four or five fingers (your whole hand) to return to the Home screen from an app you are using.

- **Swipe up** with one finger on an app in multitasking view to close that app so it is no longer running.

- **Press** the Home button to close the multitasking view.

 TIP The four- or five-finger pinch is extremely useful and very intuitive. I find it the preferred way to return to the Home screen from an app.

▷▷ Review the Initial Home Screen Apps

On a new iPad there are 20 apps on the Home screen, as you saw in Figure 2-1 earlier in this chapter. The icons and their order can be different, depending on when you got your iPad, but here are the Home screen apps in the order they appear in iOS 7 in the fall of 2013:

 FaceTime Allows you to video-chat (conference) with anyone who has an iPhone, iPad, iPod touch, or a Mac computer for free if you are using Wi-Fi. FaceTime is discussed in Chapter 8.

 Calendar Allows you to enter and keep track of appointments and events; create reminders; and sync with Microsoft Outlook, Mac iCal, and Google or iCloud Calendar. Calendar is discussed in Chapter 5.

 Photos Stores, organizes, and displays photos that you have taken. Photos is discussed in Chapter 8.

 Camera Allows you to take both still and video images from either the front or rear camera. Camera is discussed in Chapter 8.

 Contacts Allows you to store names, addresses, email addresses, phone numbers, and notes about the people you want to keep track of. Contacts allows you to sync with the Mac Address Book, Microsoft Outlook, iCloud, Windows Live, and other PC and Mac applications. Contacts is discussed in Chapter 4.

 Clock Displays the time of day, temperature, and weather conditions in up to 12 locations around the world. The Alarm component of Clock is discussed in Chapter 5.

 Maps Displays maps and satellite views, gives driving direction, and shows you your current position, if you approve this. Maps is discussed in Chapter 7.

 Videos Provides the means to store, organize, and play movies, TV shows, and other videos that you have collected through the iTunes Store or in some other way downloaded. Videos is discussed in Chapter 8.

 Notes Allows you to jot down any thoughts you have, from a few words to several pages, and then save, email, print, and delete them. Notes is discussed in Chapter 6.

 Reminders Allows you to create and keep track of calendar-oriented to-do lists. It can sync with Microsoft Outlook, Mac iCal, and iCloud. Reminders is discussed in Chapter 5.

 Photo Booth Lets you play with images you are considering taking by allowing you to use one of nine special effects. Photo Booth is discussed in Chapter 8.

Game Center Provides a social networking site where you can find people to play with and get recognized for your ability to play a game. Game Center is discussed in Chapter 9.

Newsstand Provides a place to store, organize, and read magazines and newspapers that you have subscribed to. Newsstand is discussed in Chapter 7.

 iTunes Store Allows you to purchase, store, play, and sync music, pictures, movies, TV shows, and university courses across most of your computing devices. iTunes is discussed in Chapter 7.

 App Store Provides a place to search for, learn about, purchase, and download additional applications beyond the 20 that come standard with your iPad. App Store is discussed in further detail in this chapter and in many other chapters.

 Settings Allows you to change the settings for the iPad itself, as well as many of the apps. Settings is discussed further in this chapter, in many other chapters, and in Chapter 10.

 Messages Allows you to send text and media messages using iMessage to anyone who has an iPhone, iPad, iPod touch, or a Mac computer for free if you are using Wi-Fi. Messages are discussed in Chapter 4.

 Mail Provides an email program that allows you to send, receive, reply to, and forward email messages from one or more email accounts. Mail is discussed in Chapter 4.

 Safari Provides a web browser that allows you to search and surf the Internet and do anything you can do in a browser. Safari is discussed in Chapter 3.

 Music Provides the means to store, organize, and play music that you have collected through the iTunes Store or in some other way downloaded. It closely resembles the functioning of an iPod touch. Music is discussed in Chapter 7.

Understand the Status Bar

Along the top of the iPad's screen is the status bar that can contain a number of icons, as described in Table 2-1. The icons appear at various times depending on what the iPad or its apps are doing. Many of these icons are described in this and other chapters.

Navigate Within and Among Apps

You have seen that you can start an app by simply tapping its icon on the Home screen, but then what do you do? How do you get to other pages and parts of an app? When you are done using an app, what do you do with it? What if you want to temporarily leave an app to use another and then return to the original app? What happens when you have more apps than can fit on the Home screen? The iPad has techniques for handling all of these situations that include using your finger alone, the Home button, and the multitasking view.

 TIP When you start an app, especially one of the 20 basic apps, and then start another app, put the iPad to sleep, or even turn the iPad off, and then come back to the first app, it is still where you left it. In other words, when you leave an app by simply starting another app or by switching away from it, the original app remains "active"—the definition of "active" depends on the app. This is the multitasking that was discussed earlier in this chapter. In almost all cases, when you come back to the app, you will return to where you were and what you were doing when you left the app.

Table 2-1: The Meaning of Status Bar Icons

Status Icon	Indicates That:	Status Icon	Indicates That:
✈	Airplane Mode has been turned on and all cellular, Wi-Fi, and Bluetooth transmissions by the iPad have been turned off.	☼	There is some network activity going on, such as downloading or uploading a picture or a document to or from the Internet.
••••• Verizon	Your iPad is connected to the cellular carrier shown and has the signal strength indicated by the number of dots—the more the better.	VPN	Your iPad is connected to a network, often a corporate network, using VPN (virtual private networking).
LTE	Your iPad is connected to your cellular carrier using 4G LTE (Long Term Evolution, a high-speed cellular service).	🔒	Your iPad is locked. See Chapter 1 for information on locking and unlocking your iPad.
3G or 4G	Your iPad is connected to your cellular carrier using 3G (3rd Generation) or 4G (4th Generation) service.	🕐	An alarm has been set. See Chapter 5.
E	Your iPad is connected to your cellular carrier using EDGE (Enhanced Data rates for GSM Evolution, a cellular service before 3G).	↻	Screen rotation has been locked, as explained later in this chapter.
O	Your iPad is connected to your cellular carrier using GPRS (General Packet Radio Service, a cellular service between 2G and 3G).	➤	Location Services is being used by an app to determine your current location.
📶	Your iPad is connected to the Internet using a Wi-Fi network. The number of semicircles indicates the strength of the connection. The more the better.	▶	A song, podcast, or audio book is currently playing. See Chapter 7.
🌙	Do Not Disturb is currently turned on, silencing all notifications and alerts, including FaceTime calls, but letting alarms still sound. See Chapter 5.	✱	Bluetooth is paired with a device, such as a keyboard, and, if white, is being used to communicate. If gray, the paired device is off or asleep.
☍	Your iPad is using its cellular connection to provide a personal hotspot or Wi-Fi connection to the Internet for other Wi-Fi devices, such as other iPads, iPhones, and iPod touches.	🔋	The battery level of the battery in a paired Bluetooth device.
↻	Your iPad is syncing with iTunes on your Mac or PC computer.	🔋	The battery level and charging status of your iPad.

Navigate Within an App

There are differences in the ways that various apps work, but the majority of apps use one or more of the following techniques to navigate within the app:

- **Drag your finger** up or down or left or right to slowly *scroll*, or move to other areas of the app.
- **Flick or swipe your finger** up or down or left or right to quickly scroll or move to other areas of the app.
- **Tap a link**, such as a title, an item in a list, a picture, or a highlighted phrase, to display the page associated with that link.
- **Tap a control**, such as left-pointing and right-pointing arrows and Next and Prev buttons, to go to the previous or next page in an app, or buttons that say things like "Buy Now," "Add To Cart," and "Sign Up" to go to a page indicated.

Leave an App

When you are done using an app, you can leave it in four ways:

- Press the **Home** button to redisplay the Home screen.
- Bring all five fingers together in a pinching movement in the center of the screen to redisplay the Home screen.
- Quickly press the **Sleep/Wake – On/Off** button to turn off the screen, lock the iPad, and put it in sleep mode.
- Press and hold the **Sleep/Wake – On/Off** button to fully power down the iPad.

 TIP You can think of the Home button as a "return," "go back," or "escape" key or command.

Switch to Other Apps

When you are in one app and want to switch to another, there are four techniques:

- Press the **Home** button to redisplay the Home screen, and tap the app you want to switch to.
- Press the **Home** button twice in rapid succession to open the Multitasking view, and then tap the app you want to switch to.
- Swipe up with four or five fingers to open the Multitasking view and then tap the app you want to switch to.
- Swipe left or right with four or five fingers to scroll through the various apps that are open in the order of the most recently used.

 TIP If you don't see the recently used app you want on the multitasking view, scroll the bar by dragging one finger from right to left.

Go Beyond the Home Screen

As you download new apps you will see that they do not appear on your Home screen; rather, the iPad puts them on their own screen, a second Home screen if you will, as shown in Figure 2-2. Later in this chapter you will see how you can rearrange the app icons so they appear on whatever screen you want. In any case, the iPad has multiple screens on which you can have apps. Just above the set of apps at the bottom of the screen there are one white and one gray dot, as you can see in Figure 2-2. These dots represent alternatives you have for the Home screen. The

Searching with Spotlight

Spotlight is the iPad's general-purpose search engine. With it you can search the information you have stored on the iPad, such as Contacts, Music, and Notes, and the apps you have downloaded. It will search for apps, names, authors, artists, titles, and words, as well as email messages, appointments, and websites.

Open Spotlight

- From any of the Home screens, swipe down beginning at or below the first row of apps (if you swipe down from the top of the screen, you will get the Notification area).

- From any app, press the **Home** button and then do the "midway" swipe down.

Use Search

In the Search box at the top of the screen, begin to type what you want to search for. As you type, items matching what you typed appear in a list below, as you can see in Figure 2-3.

- If it is an app you want, tap the app name to open the app.

- If it is a contact, tap the name to open Contacts.

- If it is a song, a movie, or other media, tap the item to begin playing it.

Figure 2-2: Apps you add to your iPad are not initially placed on the Home page, but you can move them there.

Figure 2-3: The iPad's Spotlight lets you search practically anything that can be reached through the iPad.

white dot signifies the page you are on. You can navigate among these screens by swiping to the left or right.

- Dragging or swiping the screen from right to left to move to screens on the right, or from left to right to move to screens on the left.
- From any of the alternate Home screens, pressing the **Home** button will return to the Home screen.
- From any app not on the Home screen, pressing the Home button or doing the five-finger pinch will return you to the Home screen.

ENTER INFORMATION INTO YOUR IPAD

So far we've looked at what is on the iPad's screen and how to manipulate it. In addition to getting information out of the iPad, you need to put information back into it, to tell it where to go, as in typing an address in Safari, or what to do, such as typing a piece of music to play. You also will probably want to add text into Mail, Messages, Notes, Reminders, Contacts, and Calendar. To do this you can use the onscreen keyboard, as briefly described in Chapter 1, or voice dictation, which the iPad has available, or even connect an external or Bluetooth keyboard.

▷▷ Expand Your Use of the Onscreen Keyboard

Chapter 1 has a brief QuickFacts to get you started using the onscreen keyboard and facilitate setting up your iPad. Here we will review what was said in Chapter 1, look at a number of additional features used in entering text, and look at the international onscreen keyboards that are available.

Review Chapter 1

The primary techniques used with the onscreen keyboard are as follows:

- **Tap a text box** to open the onscreen keyboard.
- **Tap the SHIFT key**, the upward-pointing arrow, to capitalize a letter or use the top character in a two-character key.
- **Double-tap the SHIFT key** to lock it and type all capital letters until you turn it off by tapping the SHIFT key again.
- **Tap the RETURN key** to complete a line and go to the next one. You can also tap a new line on the screen.
- **Tap the .?123 key** to open the first alternate keyboard for typing numbers and some special characters.

- **Tap the #+ key** to open the second alternate keyboard for typing additional special characters.

- **Tap the BACKSPACE key** to erase the previous key and replace it.

- **Tap the Close key** to put the onscreen keyboard away.

Benefit from Typing Shortcuts and Aids

The iPad has a number of shortcuts and aids to help you quickly type and correct text. Many of these, which are on by default, can be turned off in Settings, as you will see later in this chapter.

- **Automatic capitalization** is added to the first character in a text box or after a period.

- **Automatic spelling** correction is attempted with a dictionary-based spelling checker as you type. When what the iPad thinks is an incorrect word is found as you type, a suggested correction is displayed beneath the supposedly incorrect word. Tap a space to accept the correction. Tap the correction to reject it.

- **Manual spelling correction** can be done in several ways:
  - **Undo** and **Redo** in the second and third onscreen keyboards. Tap **Undo** in the numbers keyboard to

remove and retype the incorrect word. Tap **Redo** in the special characters keyboard to restore the original word.

- **Suggested corrections** are provided when you tap a word suspected of being misspelled, identified with a dotted red underline.

- **Automatic periods** and a space are added at the end of a sentence when you tap a space twice.

- **Automatic apostrophes** are added to many contractions, such as "don't," "won't" and "shouldn't," when you type the word without it. Press a space to accept the apostrophe or touch the suggestion to reject it.

- **Slide to the correct letter** when you see you are pointing at a wrong letter. Don't lift your finger off the keyboard, but slide it to the letter you want. The letter isn't selected until you lift your finger.

- **Alternative letters** are available to add accent marks to a character, like è, é, and ë, when you hold your finger on the letter. Vowels are the most common characters with alternatives, but "s" and "c" have alternatives, and some special characters, like the dollar sign, which shows other currency symbols, also have alternatives.

- **Keyboard shortcuts** can be created so that you can type "btw" or "syl" and get "By the way" or "See you later" on the screen. From the Home screen, tap **Settings | General | Keyboard | Add New Shortcut**. In the Phrase text box, type the expanded phrase you want—for example, <u>By the way</u>—tap **Return**, type the shortcut—for example, <u>btw</u>—and tap RETURN again. The next time you type "btw" you will get "By the way."

SHORTCUTS	
btw	By the way, >
omw	On my way! >
qsb	QuickStepsBooks.com >
syl	See you later >
Add New Shortcut...	>

NOTE In this book, the "|" or "pipe" character is used to replace repetitions of the leading verb. For example, instead of saying "tap **Settings**, tap **General**, tap **Keyboard**…," we use "tap **Settings | General | Keyboard**," making it less verbose and easier to read and follow.

Edit Text

The iPad gives you a number of ways to assist in editing text, including using a magnifying glass to place an insertion point; selecting the text you want to change; and cutting, copying, and pasting text as needed:

- **A magnifying glass** is displayed when you hold your finger on a piece of text. You can then drag your finger to exactly place the insertion point.

- **Select text**, after placing the insertion point and lifting your finger you get the options to select the current word, select all text, and, if you have recently cut or copied something, to paste it. Tap the option you want, or you can type a character to insert it at the insertion point, or use BACKSPACE.

- **Change the selection** by dragging the blue icons at the ends of the selection.

- **Cut, copy, and paste text** options are available if you have chosen Select or Select All. Like all such computer options, Cut removes the selected text and makes it available to be pasted elsewhere; Copy leaves the selected text and makes it available to be pasted elsewhere; Paste places the text that was most recently cut or copied at a new insertion point. There may be additional options such as Suggest, which suggests alternatives to a word, and Define, which provides a definition of a word.

- **Shake to undo** cuts, pastes, and typing. You saw earlier how on the numeric keyboard you can tap Undo to restore something you have just changed. You can also shake your iPad (not too vigorously) and get a menu of undo and redo options pertinent to what you have just done. Tap the option you want.

Undo Typing
Undo
Cancel

▷▷ Consider Other Keyboards

In addition to the standard onscreen keyboard you have seen earlier in this chapter, the iPad offers several others on screen and the alternative to connect an external keyboard. On screen, you have the option to use a split keyboard for thumb texting, a specialized keyboard for use in Safari, an Emoji keyboard that gives you a wide range of emoticons, and a number of international keyboards.

Use a Split Keyboard

If you hold the iPad in your hands, it is pretty difficult to use the standard onscreen keyboard. For that reason the iPad offers a split keyboard with which you can type with your thumbs. To open the split keyboard, open the standard onscreen keyboard as you normally would. Then you can

- Place your two thumbs in the middle of the standard keyboard and drag them to the edges. The keyboard will

split, as you can see in Figure 2-4. You can also do this one-handed, if your hand is big enough, by spreading apart two fingers in the middle of the keyboard.

- Hold your finger on the Close key in the lower-right corner of the keyboard. The Undock and Split menu will appear. Tap **Undock** to let the keyboard move to the center of the screen. Tap **Split** to split the keyboard in two and move it to the vertical center of the screen.

- Join a split keyboard together by pinching two fingers together. Start out by touching the two halves, or hold your

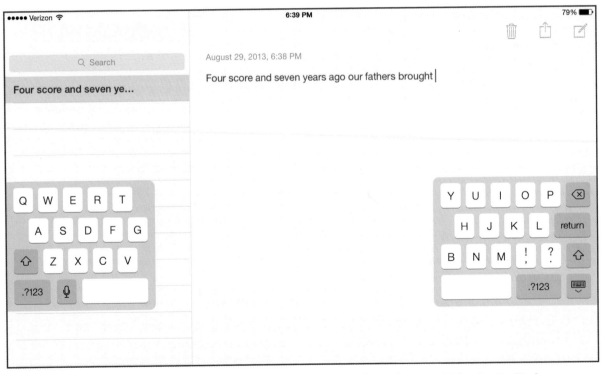

*Figure 2-4: **The split keyboard can be very useful when you don't have a flat surface on which to lay the iPad.***

finger on the Close key in the lower-right corner to display the menu, and then tap either **Merge** or **Dock And Merge**.

 TIP If your split keyboard is stuck on the bottom of the screen, merge the two halves. Undock the keyboard by holding your finger on the Close key and tapping **Undock** and then splitting the keyboard again, either with your fingers or by selecting the menu option.

Use an International Keyboard

The standard iPad keyboard is designed for use with U.S. English and, as you have seen, has a number of alternative characters with accents, umlauts, and so on. The iPad, though, goes a major step further by offering a number of international keyboards that you can choose from and, for many languages, multiple layouts and regional formats. To select an alternative keyboard and its related settings:

1. From the Home screen, tap **Settings | General | International | Keyboards | Add New Keyboard**. A list of new keyboards you can add is presented.

2. Scroll through the list of languages by dragging it up until you find the one you want. Tap it. A list of the languages you have chosen is displayed.

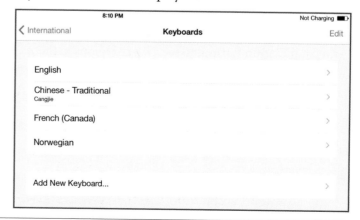

3. Tap the new keyboard you have just added to see a list of layouts you can also choose from.

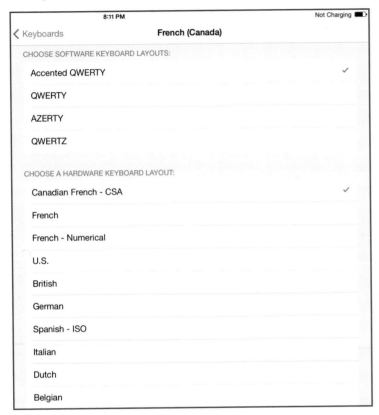

4. Tap **Keyboards | International** in the upper margin, and then tap **Region Format** to see a list of regions in the world with different language formats.

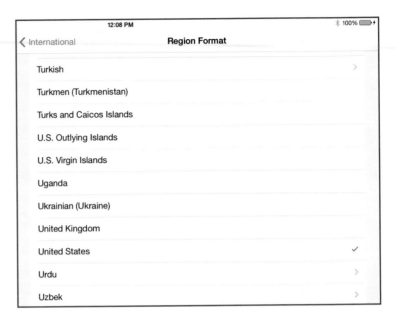

5. Scroll through the list of regions and tap the one you want to use. Press the **Home** button to return to the Home screen.

To switch to another keyboard:

1. Display your standard keyboard as you normally would. Notice that there is a new globe key to the left of the SPACEBAR.

2. Tap the globe key once to display the keyboard you have most recently used. Keep tapping it to display the other keyboards you have chosen.

–Or–

Touch and hold on the globe key to see a list of the keyboards you have selected. Move your finger to the keyboard that you want to use.

To rearrange and remove a keyboard:

1. From the Home screen, tap **Settings | General | International | Keyboards | Edit** (the latter in the upper right) to display the list of your keyboards.

2. Touch and hold the three bars on the right of a keyboard (the "grip strip") and drag the keyboard up or down to reposition it in the list.

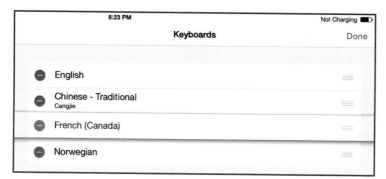

3. Tap the delete icon next to the keyboard that you want to remove and then tap **Delete** to confirm it.

4. When you are done deleting and/or rearranging your keyboards, tap **Done**.

Add an External Keyboard

Apple and many other manufacturers make wireless external, Bluetooth keyboards for the iPad. At the end of Chapter 1, two of these keyboards were discussed. To connect and use an external Bluetooth keyboard:

1. Open and read the instructions for your keyboard. Each manufacturer is a little different.

2. From the iPad's Home screen, tap **Settings | Bluetooth | On** to turn on Bluetooth. Your iPad begins searching for the keyboard.

QuickFacts

Using an Emoji Keyboard

The iPad also provides an alternative Emoji keyboard that allows you to add smiley faces and other icons to your text. You can select and use the Emoji keyboard in the same way you do any international keyboard.

1. From the Home screen, tap **Settings | General | International | Keyboards | Add New Keyboard**.

2. Scroll down until you see Emoji and then tap it.

3. In a text document, open a keyboard, touch and hold the globe key, and then tap **Emoji**. The Emoji keyboard will be displayed.

4. Drag or swipe the characters from right to left and tap the options in the bottom of the keyboard to display the many available characters.

5. Tap a character to add it to your document.

3. Follow your keyboard's instructions. You may need to turn on the keyboard and then press a button that sends a signal to your iPad, which then, after a moment, tells you it has connected with the keyboard.

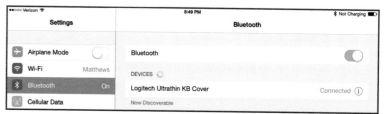

After being connected, the onscreen keyboard will no longer pop up so long as the external keyboard is within range of the iPad. You can do your typing on the new keyboard.

 TIP When you have paired the iPad with a Bluetooth device such as a keyboard, the Bluetooth icon appears in the status bar as you saw earlier in this chapter. This icon is white on a dark background or black on a light background when the paired device is currently active, but the icon becomes gray when the device is out of range, sleeping, or turned off. With a keyboard, it may go to sleep if it isn't used for a while, and you will have to press a key several times to awaken it.

Set Up Siri and Use Dictation

Siri is the iPad's voice assistant. It allows you to speak to the iPad and have it respond. It can use information in your computer, as well as what it can find on the Internet. You can say, "What time is my appointment with John?" and Siri will look it up in the Calendar and give you the answer. You can also say, "Where is the movie *Lincoln* playing?" and Siri will search the Internet for the answer and tell you what it found. Siri is discussed further in Chapter 6.

Turn On and Use Siri

To use Siri, it must be turned on (if you don't see a microphone key on the onscreen keyboard, Siri is not turned on), and you must be connected to the Internet by either Wi-Fi or a cellular service. If you use Siri, some information about you will be sent to Apple to facilitate this use—for example, your contacts, which might allow you to say to Siri "call Home" and Siri will look at your contacts for "Home" to carry out your request. If you don't want to do that, then you should not use Siri.

1. From the Home screen, tap **Settings | General | Siri | On**.

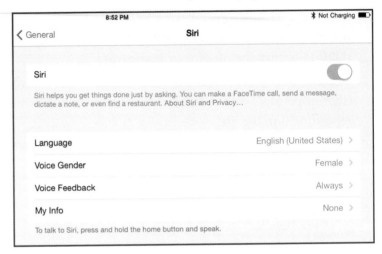

2. To use Siri, press and hold the **Home** button until a wavy line appears. When that happens, Siri will ask what it can help you with. Speak in a normal voice to respond.

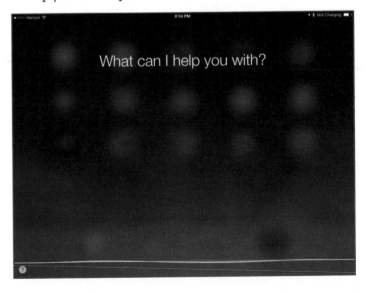

Use Dictation

The iPad's dictation, which runs under Siri, allows you to verbally add text anywhere the onscreen keyboard would normally appear, such as Mail, Messages, Calendar,  Contacts, Safari, Notes, and Reminders, as well as the apps you have downloaded. You can tell if Siri is available by whether there is a microphone key on your keyboard. If there isn't, use the previous steps to turn on Siri.

To use dictation, tap the microphone key and begin talking. You should see the modulated voice wave while you are talking. When you have finished, tap **Done**. After a bit, the text you dictated will appear. It is not fast. Pause often to let it catch up. You can verbally indicate punctuation by saying the words like "period," "comma," and "new paragraph." When you are done with dictation, tap **Done** to turn it off.

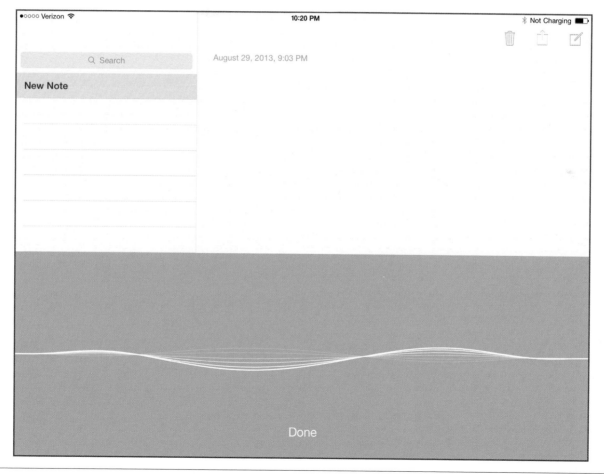

NOTE The reason that you must be connected to the Internet to use Siri and do dictation is that your voice is sent over the Internet to servers at Apple where it is converted to text and then sent back to you. To facilitate the conversion, Apple also collects a lot of information about you like your name, address, the names in your contacts list, your current location, and so on. If you are not comfortable with this, turn off dictation by reversing the previous steps to set up Siri.

▷▷ Print from Your iPad

Several standard apps let you wirelessly print using Apple's AirPrint technology, which is standard in the iPad, to printers using the same technology. The standard apps that can use AirPrint include Notes, Mail, Photos, Camera, and Safari, as well as a number of apps you can download from the App Store. The printers that use AirPrint or compatible technology (most say "wireless printing") include recent (since 2010) models from Brother, Canon, Dell, Epson, Hewlett-Packard, Lexmark, and Samsung, among others. In addition to the need for AirPrint, both the iPad and the printer must be connected to the same Wi-Fi network.

To use AirPrint:

1. Open one of the supported apps and display what you want to print.

2. Tap the share icon and then tap **Print**.

3. In the Printer Options dialog box, if the printer you want to use isn't displayed, tap **Select Printer**.

4. Tap the printer you want to use. If you don't see the printer you want listed, make sure the printer is turned on, that it is connected to a Wi-Fi network, and that it is the same Wi-Fi network that the iPad is connected to (go to **Settings | Wi-Fi** and notice the name of the network; most printers also have a way of telling you the name of the network it is connected to; these must be the same).

5. Tap **Print**. The item you wanted should be printed.

Many printing apps are available in the App Store. A number are free, especially those from printer manufacturers like Canon, Epson, and Hewlett-Packard. Some of these apps say they will print everything on your iPad, but I have not verified that. For the most part, the standard AirPrint technology in your iPad does everything that most people need and may well satisfy you.

CUSTOMIZE YOUR IPAD

Your iPad should look and operate the way you want it to. The apps on the Home screen should be in the locations and possibly folders that make the most sense to you. The wallpaper on your Home screen should be pleasing to you, and the settings for your iPad in general and for your apps should reflect your wishes.

▷▷ Organize Your Home Screen

Organizing your Home screen includes putting the apps where you want them, deleting the ones you no longer want, and using folders to organize and store others.

Rearrange Apps

You can put the apps on your Home screen or on any of the additional Home screens in any location you want, including on the dock at the bottom of the screen.

1. Place and hold a finger on one of the apps on the Home screen until all the app icons begin to wiggle.

2. Drag an app you want to move to a new location. That can be

- Anywhere on the current screen.

- The area at the bottom of the screen, where there can be six apps, as you can see in Figure 2-5 (you need to use your imagination for the wiggling), by simply dragging the app to that location, or if needed or desired, dragging an app off the dock.

- On a different screen by dragging the app to the adjoining edge of its current screen, holding there for a moment until the new screen opens, and then continuing to drag the app onto the new screen and its final location.

Figure 2-5: Once you loosen up the app icons and get them wiggling, they can be moved wherever you want them.

3. When you are done rearranging your Home and other screens, press the **Home** button to stop the icons from wiggling.

> **TIP** The principal reason for the dock at the bottom of the screen is that it remains on screen when you move to the ancillary Home screens.

Delete Apps

You can delete apps you have downloaded, but not the original apps that came with the iPad. However, the latter can be hidden from the Home screen by tapping **Settings | General | Restrictions**, entering your Passcode, tapping **Enable Restrictions**, and tapping Off for the app you don't want to be used.

> **NOTE** Deleting an app on the iPad does not delete it from your iTunes account; it still shows that you have purchased the app. You can only totally delete an app in iTunes on your computer.

1. Start the app icons wiggling as you read in the last section.

2. Delete the apps you no longer want by tapping the **x** in the upper-left corner of the app.

3. When you are done, press the **Home** button to end the wiggling.

Organize with Folders

Adding folders in which to contain your apps gives you two benefits: they can save space on the screen with multiple apps in a folder taking only the space of one app, and they can gather and therefore organize common apps. The negative, of course, is that to open an app you now have to first tap the folder and then tap the app. For whatever reason, if you want to add folders:

1. Start the app icons wiggling as you did in the earlier section.

2. Drag an app you want in the folder on top of another app you want in the folder. Do this slowly, because the bottom app will tend to jump out of the way. As you hold one app over the other you will see a box larger than the app forming with the bottom app in it and the top app moving in, as you can see in Figure 2-6. You can also change the name of the folder from what it defaults to if you choose.

3. Remove your finger to see the dock and folder fully formed. Drag as many more apps into the folder as you want. You then can drag the folder anywhere you can drag an app.

4. When you are done, press the **Home** button to end the wiggling.

If you want to put an app back on the Home screen, restart the wiggling, drag the app out of the folder, and stop the wiggling. If you drag all but one of the apps out of the folder, the last app will automatically appear on the Home screen and the folder will disappear.

Change the Screen Wallpaper

The background or wallpaper behind the apps on the Home screen starts out with a default image. You can change that to anything you may want, perhaps a picture of your new grandchild, a favorite sunset, or a beautiful flower. If you have the picture on your computer or iPad or can get it, it can be your wallpaper. If it is in your photos, you can choose to use it as wallpaper by tapping the picture and then the share icon at the bottom-left area. This opens the share menu, as shown in Figure 2-7.

Figure 2-6: *Folders are easy to create, use, and get rid of.*

Get Photos from Your Computer to Your iPad

Start with one or more pictures on your computer and look at how to get them through iTunes to your iPad.

1. On your computer, in My Pictures in Windows or iPhoto on a Mac, create a folder named "For iPad." Place in this folder the photo or photos that you want on your iPad.

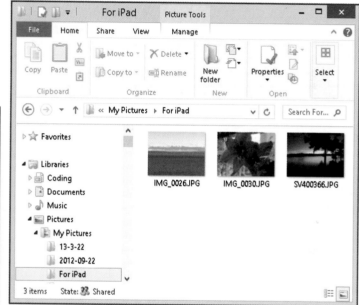

2. Still on your computer, start iTunes. Under Devices on the left, click your iPad and then click **Photos** in the upper-right corner.

3. If it is not already checked, click **Sync Photos From** and select **My Pictures** in Windows or **iPhoto** on a Mac.

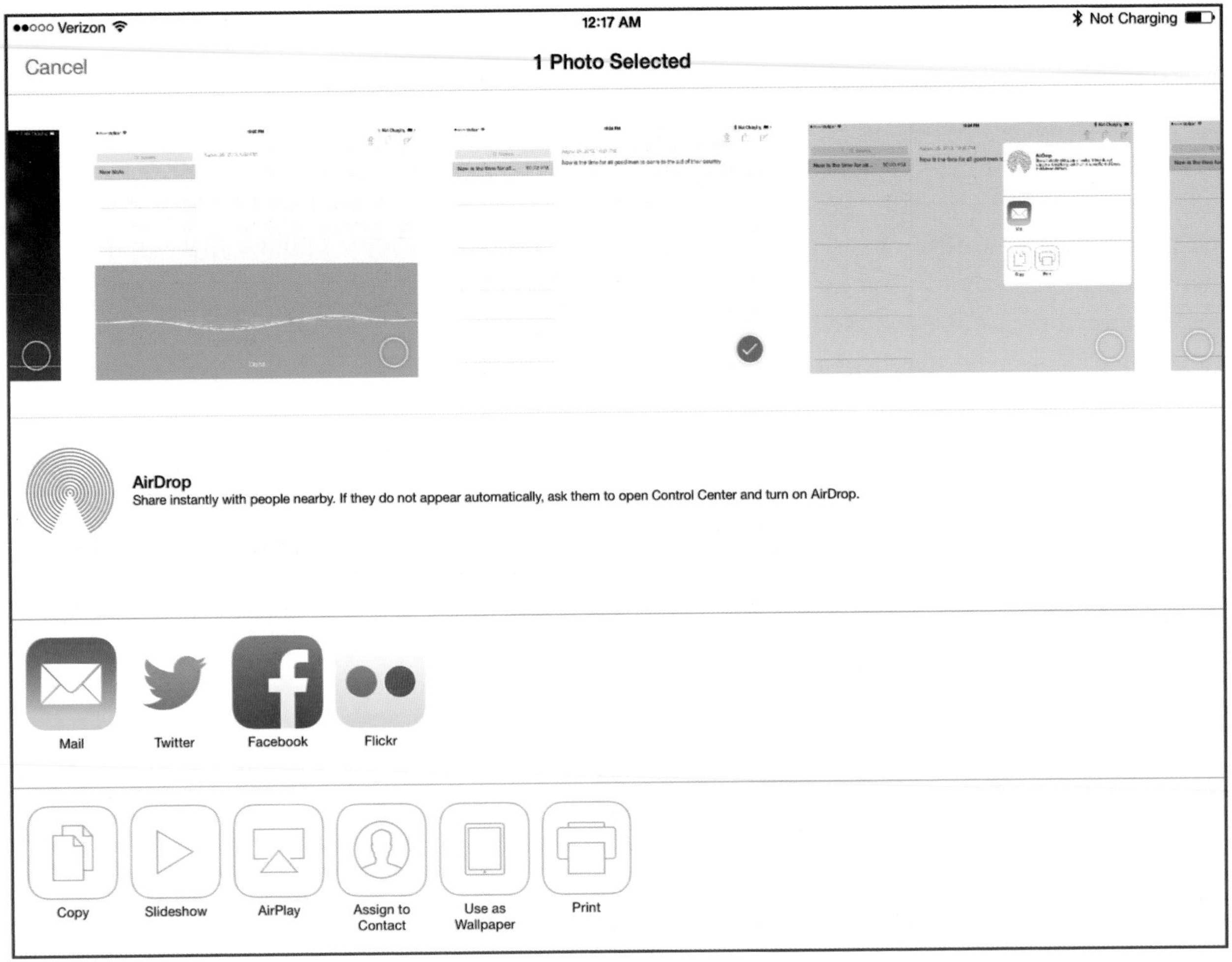

Figure 2-7: The share menu gives you a number of actions you can take with a selected object—a photo in this case.

4. Click **Selected Folders** and, under Folders, click **For iPad**, as you can see in Figure 2-8.

5. In iTunes on your computer, click **Apply** to sync the photos in the For iPad folder with a similar folder on your iPad. You should see a message at the top of iTunes on your computer that synching is taking place.

Get a Photo to Wallpaper

Once you have the photo you want on your iPad, the final step is to turn it into wallpaper on your screen.

Figure 2-8: Syncing photos between iTunes on your computer and your iPad will move photos both ways.

1. On your iPad's Home screen, tap **Photos**. You should see an album labeled "For iPad."

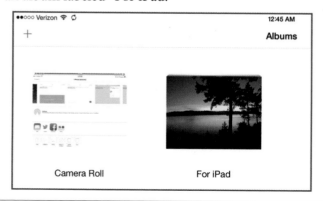

2. Tap the **For iPad** album to open it, and you should see the photos you transferred in the album.

3. Press the **Home** button to return to the Home screen.

4. Tap **Settings | Wallpapers & Brightness** to open those settings, and then tap **Wallpaper**.

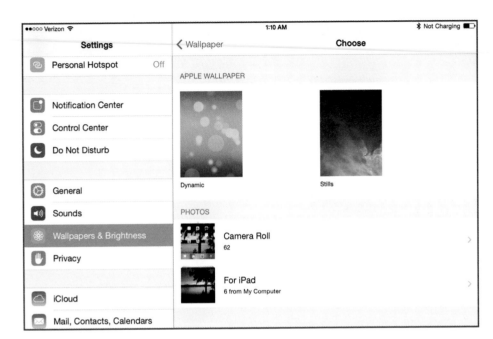

Figure 2-9: *Apple provides a number of choices for wallpaper on the iPad, but you may prefer your own photo.*

10. Press the **Home** button to see if you like your new Home screen (see Figure 2-10). If not, repeat Steps 4 through 6 to try other Apple-supplied wallpaper, or Steps 7 through 9 to try other photos of yours.

Change Settings

Settings are where you can customize how your iPad operates; where you can review and change the options that are available to you both for the iPad itself and for many of the apps. All settings work similarly: You can turn options on or off by tapping them, or you can select an option from within a list by tapping the option you want. Often, you will tap an option to be presented with other options.

5. Tap **Wallpaper** again. This displays the current choices that Apple provides, as well as your photo albums (see Figure 2-9).

6. Tap one of the wallpaper alternatives to see it full screen. Tap **Set Lock Screen** to use it there, tap **Set Home Screen** to use it for that purpose, or tap **Set Both** to use it in both the Lock and Home screens. Press the **Home** button to see your new wallpaper.

7. To use one of your photos for your wallpaper, repeat Step 4 and then tap the **For iPad** folder. You should see the photos you placed there.

8. Tap the photo you want for your wallpaper to see it full screen.

9. If you like it, tap **Set Lock Screen**, **Set Home Screen**, or **Set Both**, as you choose.

Figure 2-10: *If you have a photo that you really like, use it for your Home screen.*

You have seen in the previous section, and in other places in this chapter, demonstrations of using the iPad's settings. Here we will take a look at Settings in general and how to use several of them. Throughout the rest of the book you'll see how to use other settings. Many of the settings are self-explanatory, and I encourage you to explore them on your own.

Explore General Settings

General settings are the catch-all for settings not in a particular app or contained elsewhere.

From the Home screen, tap **Settings | General**. The General Settings are displayed, as you see in Figure 2-11. Some of the settings you have already configured or will shortly read about. Some of the more important settings include the following:

- **About** allows you to change the name of your iPad and see information about it, such as the serial number that Apple asks you for when you contact them.

- **Lock Rotation** lets you use the side slide switch to lock the rotation of the screen so it doesn't change when you rotate your iPad. The default is to use the side switch to mute sound.

- **Usage** displays the amount of internal memory and iCloud memory that is being used, as well as how long your iPad has gone since it was charged and what your cellular data usage has been.

- **Auto-Lock** lets you set the number of minutes the iPad goes before it automatically shuts down the screen and locks itself. This can be set from 2 to 15 minutes or Never.

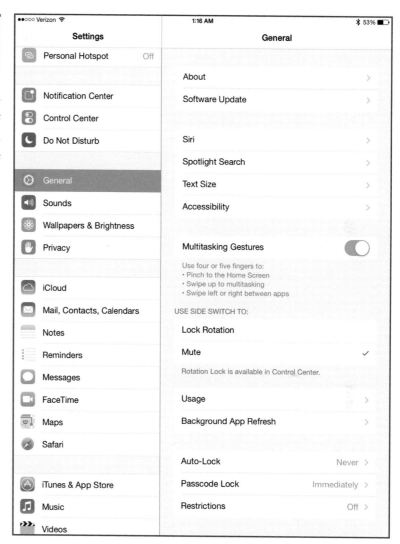

Figure 2-11: *Through Settings you have the ability to control how your iPad operates.*

- **Passcode Lock** lets you require a four-digit passcode be entered each time you unlock your iPad.

- **Restrictions** lets you set limits on the usage and type of apps and content you want to allow on your iPad.

Use Accessibility Settings

Accessibility settings enable iPad features that try to compensate for physical disabilities, such as hearing, vision, learning, and motor abilities.

From the Settings General screen, tap Accessibility to open the accessibility settings shown in Figure 2-12. It is best to try each of these, one option at a time, to see if they are helpful. Chapter 10 provides a more detailed description of them. Here are some hints for the less obvious ones:

- **Voice Over** lets you select items on the Home screen and have iPad speak the name of the item. This provides speech with a single tap of an item and selects the item with a double-tap.

- **Typing Feedback**, which is part of Voice Over, announces the character and words that you type.

- **Zoom** magnifies the entire screen when you double-tap with three fingers and scroll by dragging with three fingers.

- **Guided Access** lets you keep the iPad in a chosen app with only certain features available by starting an app and then pressing the Home button three times.

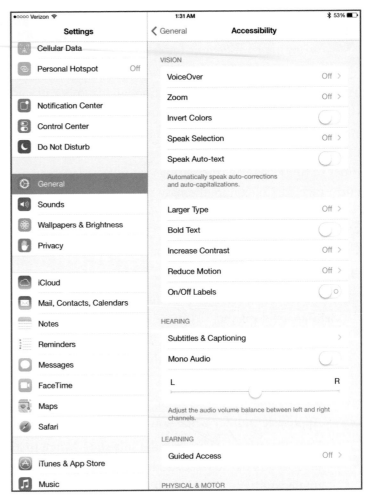

Figure 2-12: **Accessibility options can make using an iPad easier in certain circumstances.**

- **Assistive Touch** provides assistance in using the touch screen with both fingers and with touch accessories like a stylus.

- **Accessibility Shortcut** lets you select the accessibility you want to turn on by pressing the Home button three times.

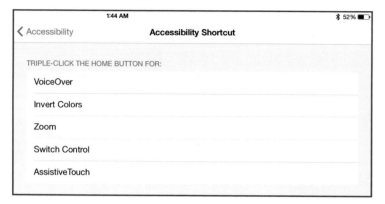

- **Wi-Fi** allows you to turn on Wi-Fi and select a network with which to connect.
- **Cellular Data** allows you to turn it off and force all data to use Wi-Fi, or to choose the apps that can use cellular data.
- **Notification Center** lets you choose which apps can send you notifications and alerts and the method of the notification.
- **Sounds** lets you choose the volume of the ringer and alert sounds and what sounds are made in various events.

Review Other Non-App Settings

The majority of other settings are related to particular apps and are discussed elsewhere in this book with the relevant app. Here we'll look at several of the less obvious non-app-related settings:

- **Airplane Mode** allows you to turn off the cellular, Wi-Fi, and Bluetooth transmissions by your iPad if you are requested to do so on an airplane (or when traveling to a different country to prevent incurring data charges).

- **Privacy** lets you choose what services and which apps can use potentially invasive features of the iPad, such as Location Services, shown in Figure 2-13.

▷▷ Use the Control Center

One of the best new features of iOS7 is the Control Center, which takes the most heavily used settings and gives you immediate access to them. You can open the Control Center by swiping up from the bottom of the Home screen and most app screens, as you can see in Figure 2-14.

The controls that are on the Control Center include:

- **Media player controls** allow you to start and pause playing the currently selected playlist, to go to the beginning of the song (single tap) and the previous song (double-tap), to the next song, and to any point within a song on the bar at the top.

- **Volume control** allows you to adjust the current volume.

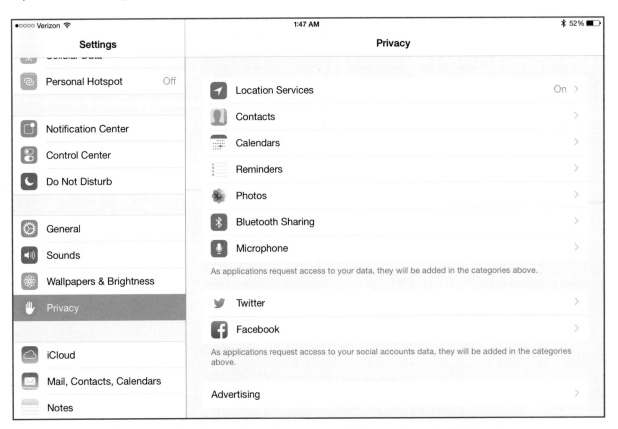

Figure 2-13: The iPad gives you a lot of control over what apps can do that may be potentially invasive.

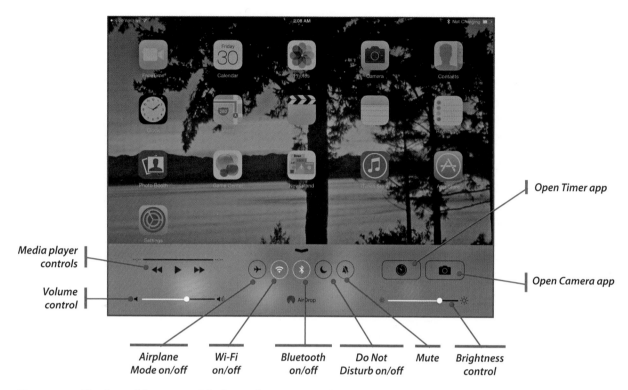

Media player controls

Volume control

Open Timer app

Open Camera app

Airplane Mode on/off *Wi-Fi on/off* *Bluetooth on/off* *Do Not Disturb on/off* *Mute* *Brightness control*

*Figure 2-14: **The Control Center provides immediate access to the most heavily used settings.***

- **Airplane Mode on/off** allows you to turn on or off cellular, Wi-Fi, and Bluetooth transmissions, which you might be required to do on an airplane.

- **Wi-Fi on/off** allows you to turn on or off Wi-Fi.

- **Bluetooth on/off** allows you to turn on or off Bluetooth that is used to communicate with accessories such as headphones and keyboards.

- **Do Not Disturb on/off** allows you to turn on or off the silencing of alerts and incoming FaceTime calls.

- **Mute** allows you to turn on or off the silencing of alerts.

- **Brightness control** allows you to adjust the brightness of the screen.

- **Open Timer app** allows you to open the Timer app, which includes the clock, alarm, and stopwatch.

- **Open Camera app** allows you to open the Camera app and take still and video images as described in Chapter 8.

- **AirDrop** allows you to turn off or make your iPad discoverable by nearby compatible computers and devices. You can limit discoverability to just people in your Contacts list or with everybody. Using AirDrop, you can directly

Using AirDrop

Using AirDrop is very simple:

1. Have two compatible devices (a Mac with OS X Lion or later or an iPhone, iPod, or iPad with iOS7) "nearby," which I interpret as "in the same room," but as Apple has said, "There is no need for them to touch," referring to non-Apple devices that must touch to accomplish similar communication.

2. In one of the devices, display and select something you want to send to the other device, such as a photo, a document, or a webpage.

3. Tap the share icon to open the share menu. The discoverable devices near you should appear at the top of the menu.

4. Tap the device to which you want to send the file or link.

5. On the receiving device, you should see a notice that the other device would like to share a file. If you want to accept it, tap **Accept**.

share files without the need for Wi-Fi. See the "Using AirDrop" QuickSteps in this chapter.

 TIP AirDrop is an example of near-field communication (NFC), which allows two devices to communicate without the use of Wi-Fi or Bluetooth.

Grant Heiken

The original reason for purchasing an iPad was to download books to read while traveling. It is perfect, especially while reading in the low-light situations that you find on airplanes and in hotel rooms. We still buy books, but find the iPad to be perfect for use during trips. We also use the iPad for storing and viewing photos (wonderful resolution), for email and the Internet, games, the world atlas, and so on. I found that my wife was frequently borrowing my iPad, so we purchased a second one, which has so many more options, including the excellent camera, Siri, streaming movies, better screen resolution, and a better speaker.

Grant's Favorite Apps

Netflix   Movies and television series.

iBird Pro   Everything, including bird calls, for birding in North America.

QuakeWatch   Real-time monitoring of the earthquakes of the world, including Google Earth maps with the epicenters marked.

Living Language   Easy learning of languages visually and with pronunciation. The best language programs I have encountered anywhere.

WeatherLive   Clear, easy, real-time weather coverage of anywhere in the world.

National Geographic World Atlas   Phenomenal.

Moon HD   Everything for the moon buff.

Chapter 3

Exploring the Internet

The Internet provides a major means for worldwide communication between both individuals and organizations, as well as a major means for locating and sharing information. The Internet is at the foundation of the iPad; the iPad wouldn't exist without it because most of what you do with the iPad is done with the Internet. To use the Internet, you must have a connection to it using either a cellular or Wi-Fi connection. With this connection you then can send and receive email; access the World Wide Web; shop; use social networking sites such as Facebook; listen to music; watch movies and TV; and participate in blogs, forums, and newsgroups, among many other things.

In this chapter we'll review how to get connected to the Internet, take a good look at Safari and its settings, and then see how you can use Safari to explore the Internet by both navigation and searching. Next, we'll go over how to customize Safari with your opening screen, your tabs, your bookmarks, and how to use your history. Then we'll review how to get and use information on the Internet, including audio and video files, and finally how to control Internet security.

CONNECT TO THE INTERNET

With a cellular service, you sign up with AT&T, Sprint, or Verizon (in the United States), start your iPad, tap the Safari icon, and you are on the Internet. With Wi-Fi, you can use someone else's connection, such as in a coffee shop, library, hotel, or airport, often for free (we'll talk about how to connect there in a moment). If you want Wi-Fi in your home or office and don't already have a connection, you can get one from a telephone company, a cable TV company, a satellite link, or an independent Internet service provider (ISP). If you already have Wi-Fi available in your home or office and just need to connect your iPad to it, skip to "Establish an iPad Wi-Fi Connection" a little later in this chapter.

Across the various types of connections there are a number of speeds, degrees of reliability, and costs. The most important factor is what is available to you at the location where you want to use it. In urban and most suburban areas, you probably have several alternatives among phone and cable TV companies, all with several service options. As you move away from the urban area, your alternatives will decrease to a slow-speed telephone connection and/or a satellite link. With both higher-speed telephone and cable TV, you will probably have several speed options, as was shown in Chapter 1 with my phone company. Your task is to choose the service and speed that best suits your situation.

QuickFacts

Reviewing Types of Internet Connections

Table 3-1 provides a summary of Internet connection types to give you a starting place for determining the type you want, if it is available to you. The speeds and costs in the table are representative averages and may not be correct for the ISP you are considering or for your location. You must get the correct numbers from your local providers. Dial-up service cannot be used with your iPad, and some satellite services may be problematic.

Table 3-1: Comparison of Internet Connection Types

Connection Type	Down/Up Speed	Availability	Reliability	Average Cost/Mo
Telephone dial-up	48 Kbps/34 Kbps	Most places	Fair	$10 to over $20
Telephone DSL	6 Mbps/2 Mbps	Urban/suburban	Good	$30 to over $60
Telephone fiber	20 Mbps/8 Mbps	Urban	Very good	$50 to over $120
Cable TV	10 Mbps/6 Mbps	Urban/suburban	Good	$40 to over $100
Satellite	2 Mbps/250 Kbps	Most places	Fair	$60 to over $300

▷▷ Establish a Wi-Fi Internet Connection

With most forms of Wi-Fi Internet connections, you have a choice of not only speed, but also ancillary services, such as the number of free email accounts and possibly a personal website. Also, depending on the type of connection, you may need dedicated equipment, such as a digital subscriber line (DSL) router, or satellite receiving equipment, which may or may not be included in the monthly price. Talk to your neighbors, friends, and associates about their experience using Internet service providers. Then contact a couple of ISPs, if you have that option, and ask them about the services and costs they offer.

 TIP Often, setup, installation, and equipment charges for an Internet connection are waived if you sign a one- or two-year contract and/or prepay for a year or two of service.

Set Up Wi-Fi Communications

To set up a Wi-Fi communications link between your iPad and the Internet, you must first choose and enter into a contract for a type of connection. The ISP that provides this service normally will help you set it up.

NOTE To connect to the Internet, you need to have an account with an ISP who will help you establish a user name and password for your account and give you an email address, the type of mail server (POP3, IMAP, or HTTP), and the names of the incoming and outgoing mail servers (such as mail.anisp.net).

A broadband connection—made with a DSL phone line, a TV cable, or a satellite connection—is normally made with a device called a *router* that provides the Wi-Fi wireless connection to your iPad and to your computer, if you have

one. This broadband connection is always on and connected to the Internet.

Establish an iPad Wi-Fi Connection

To use your iPad in a Wi-Fi area, called a "hotspot," you must tell the iPad about it and probably give the iPad the password for the hotspot. When you first enter a Wi-Fi hotspot that you want to use with your iPad, after turning on your iPad:

1. Tap **Settings | Wi-Fi** and turn Wi-Fi on if it isn't already. Review the list of Wi-Fi networks that are available at your location, as shown in Figure 3-1.

*Figure 3-1: **Many commercial locations have a number of Wi-Fi networks, necessitating knowing which one you should use.***

2. Tap the wireless network you want to use. This may open the Password dialog box.

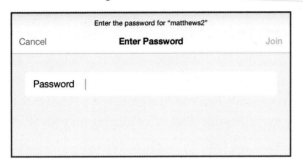

3. If needed, enter the network password and tap **Join**. You will be connected to the Wi-Fi network and, in most cases, to the Internet.

USE THE WORLD WIDE WEB

The *World Wide Web* (or just the *Web*) is the sum of all the websites in the world—examples of which are CNN, Amazon, and the BBC (which is shown in Figure 3-2). The World Wide Web is what you can access with a *web browser,* such as Safari.

Get Familiar with Safari

Safari comes standard with the iPad and provides an excellent means to access the Internet and do anything it is possible to do with a web browser. Several other browsers, including Google Chrome, are available as apps you can download from

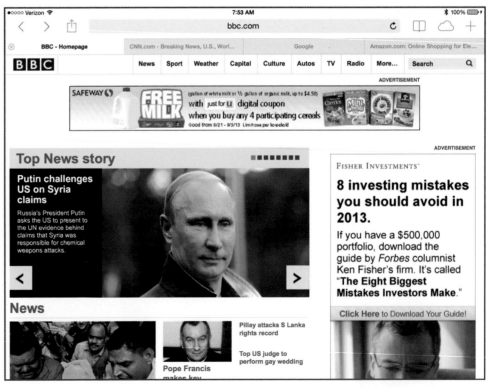

Figure 3-2: The easiest way to see if you have an Internet connection is to try to connect to the Internet.

the App Store, but this book assumes you are using Safari to access the Internet.

Review Safari's Controls

Start Safari and review its controls.

From the iPad's Home screen, tap **Safari**.

At the top of the Safari screen is a series of icons and features that let you control it. From left to right these are

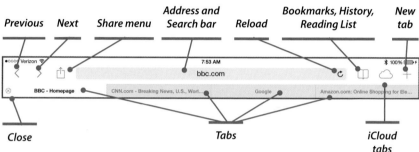

Previous   Next   Share menu   Address and Search bar   Reload   Bookmarks, History, Reading List   New tab

Close   Tabs   iCloud tabs

- **Previous** and **Next** let you return to the pages you have visited previous to or following the present page.

- **Share menu** allows you to tap various actions you can take to share the current website address, including AirDropping, text-messaging, or emailing it to a friend; putting it on Twitter or Facebook; adding it to your Home screen; printing or copying it; or adding it to either your Bookmarks or Reading List.

- **Address and Search bar** allows you to type in a web address or URL to open the website in Safari in the currently selected tab or in a new tab you have just opened (see the "New Tab" bullet). For example, if you wanted to open CNN, you would type cnn.com in the address bar. This same bar also allows you to enter keywords to use in searching the Internet, as you might do directly in Google. As you will see in the next section, you can select the search engine that is used to do the searching for this field. Google is the default, but Yahoo! and Bing are also options.

- **Tabs** identify separate website pages that you have opened; simply tap a tab to see its page.

- **Reload** lets you re-download the selected webpage from its server to see any changes in the page, such as late-breaking news or latest prices on an auction site. If a webpage is not behaving the way it should, reloading it can often fix the problem. While a webpage is being loaded, the Reload icon is replaced with a Stop icon (an X) that, if you click it, will stop the loading of the webpage.

- **Bookmarks, History, and Reading List** opens a set of three lists: one for the bookmarks (website pages) that you tap to keep, one for the history of the webpages you have visited, and one for webpages with articles you want to come back and read.

- **iCloud tabs** opens a list of webpages that have been

opened on other Apple devices (Macs, iPhones, and iPods) that you have synced with through iCloud.

- **Close** closes the currently selected webpage and removes the tab.
- **New Tab** creates a new tab in which you can open a new webpage without replacing one of the webpages that are currently open. You can open up to ten separate tabs that are displayed. As you open additional tabs, the tab on the far left disappears and an ellipsis (…) appears on the right. When you tap the ellipsis, you will see the tabs that have disappeared and you can tap them to go to those sites.

 TIP When you see a web address like http://www.amazon.com, all you have to type is amazon.com; the "http://www." is assumed. If you have been to the site recently, you only have to type enough of the name to be unique; as you see in the illustration, typing am got me Amazon.com.

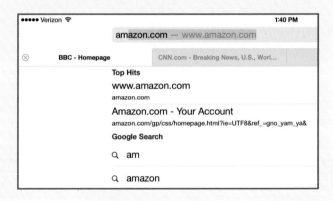

Look at Safari's Settings

In iPad's settings there is a full set for Safari, as shown in Figure 3-3.

From the Home screen, tap **Settings | Safari**.

Safari's settings include the following:

- **Search Engine** allows you to choose the search engine that is used currently from Google (the default), Yahoo!, and Bing.
- **Passwords & AutoFill** allows you to turn on or off the automatic filling out of web forms with your contact information, including names, passwords, and other information that you have previously given to a website.

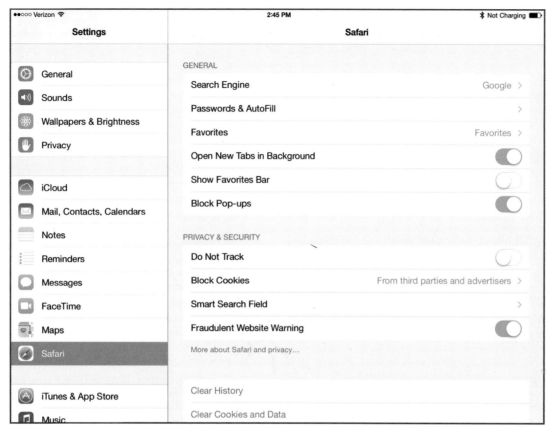

Figure 3-3: Since you will probably be using Safari a lot, it is worthwhile exploring its settings.

This is turned off by default and it is a good idea to leave it that way. While it is handy, it can lead to giving out information when you don't want to do so.

- **Favorites** allows you to establish the defaults that are suggested when you enter an address or search term.

- **Open New Tabs In Background** allows you to control whether clicking a link or opening a new page replaces the current page in the current tab, or opens a new tab displaying the new page.

- **Show Favorites Bar** allows you to turn the Bookmarks bar (between the Address bar and the tabs—see more later in this chapter) permanently on or off. When the Bookmarks bar is not permanently on, you can open and use it by tapping the address bar.

- **Block Pop-ups** allows you to prevent a website from opening a second little window for whatever purpose. Here again, history has colored the prevailing view of pop-ups. They can be a pain if they are giving you information you don't want, but if they open a web form you need to fill out, they can be useful. The default is **On**, blocking pop-ups. Depending on what you are doing, you might want to turn this off.

- **Do Not Track** allows you to turn on or off the prevention (if it is on) of collecting information, such as websites you visit and your name, address, and other information you have entered into web forms. With Do Not Track on, AutoFill does not collect information and it doesn't fill in forms. Also, the history of the websites you have visited is not maintained.

- **Block Cookies** allows you to choose whether you want to always, never, or, only from sites you visit, accept cookies that are stored on your iPad. (Cookies are small snippets of information that identify you to the website based on information you gave them.)

- **Smart Field Search** allows you to accept search engine suggestions and loads the website of the top search result based on your browsing history (if you have visited any of the suggested sites in the past) and your bookmarks.

- **Fraudulent Website Warning** tells the iPad to warn you when you are visiting a website that is not what it seems to be and is suspected of phishing. Phishing sites masquerade as a real site, like your bank, and fraudulently ask you to enter your personal information, such as user names and passwords. If you get such a warning, you want to immediately leave the site and not enter any information.

- **Clear History** and **Clear Cookies And Data** allow you to remove the information on your iPad from or about the websites you have visited.

- **Use Cellular Data** tells the iPad that it can use your cellular network to save Reading List information to iCloud for offline reading.

- **Advanced** provides three more options:
  - **Website Data** allows you to look at which websites are storing how much information on your iPad. The Web Inspector option is for use by app developers to debug (remove problems from) their apps.

Website Data	157 KB
www.yahoo.com	13.2 KB
seattletimes.com	13.1 KB
www.nytimes.com	12.9 KB
www.cnn.com	12.7 KB
reviews.cnet.com	12.7 KB
online.wsj.com	12.3 KB
www.cnet.com	12.2 KB
www.amazon.com	12.1 KB
www.apple.com	12.0 KB
www.bbc.co.uk	12.0 KB

Show All Sites

Remove All Website Data

- **JavaScript** allows you to turn off accepting programs or apps that use JavaScript, a programming language. Generally, you want to leave JavaScript turned on. Many apps legitimately use it, and if you want to use the app, you have to accept the use of JavaScript. Historically, bad things were done with JavaScript, and, of course they still

can be, but if you are running apps from the App Store, they are reasonably safe. Apple has vetted these apps.

- **Web Inspector** allows you to open Safari on your computer, connect the computer to your iPad with a cable, and look at what a website is doing on the iPad using Safari's Advanced Preferences option on your computer.

Browse the Internet

Browsing the Internet refers to using a browser, like Safari, to go from one website to another. You can browse to a site by directly entering a site address, navigating to a site from another site, or using the browser controls. First, of course, you have to open the browser as you saw earlier.

Enter a Site Directly

To go directly to a site:

1. Open your browser, tap in the address bar, and tap the **X** on the right of the bar to erase the current contents.
2. Type the address of the site you want to open (see Figure 3-4), and tap **Go** to open that webpage.

 TIP The onscreen keyboards that appear when the address bar is tapped changes the label of the **RETURN** key to **GO**.

Use Site Navigation

Site navigation uses a combination of links and menus on one webpage to locate and open another webpage, either in the same site or in another site.

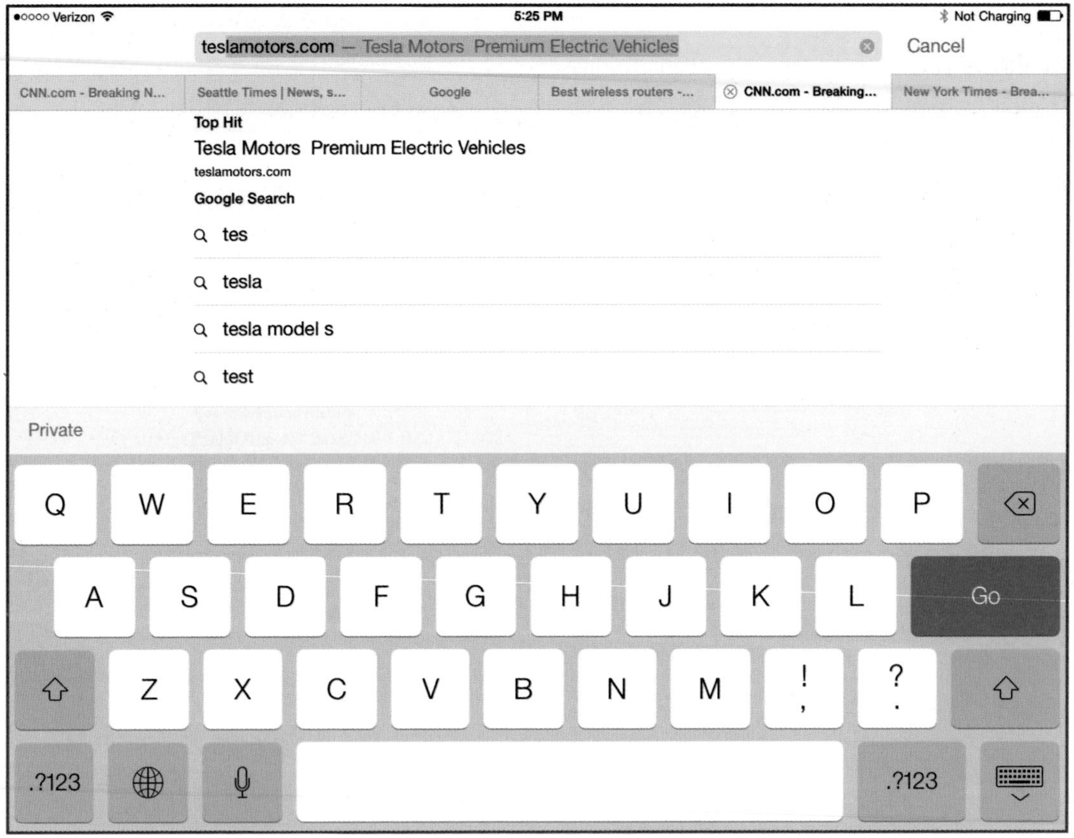

Figure 3-4: ***The iPad will give you suggestions on filling in the address bar. I got these after typing only "tes" and needed to only tap the suggestions to go there.***

- **Links** are words, phrases, sentences, or graphics that, when tapped, take you to another location. They are often a different color or underlined when you tap them.

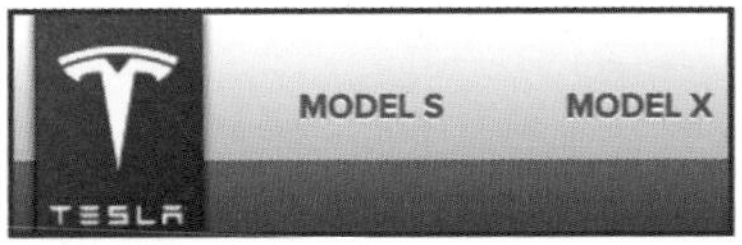

- **Menus** contain one or a few words in a horizontal list, vertical list, or both that, when tapped, take you to another location.

If you hold your finger on a link or a menu option, which is really a link within a menu, a pop-up menu will be displayed, allowing you to open the link in the same tab, open it in a new tab, add it to your Reading List, or copy it, allowing you to paste it in an email, text message, or elsewhere.

Use Browser Navigation

Browser navigation uses the controls on your browser at the top of Safari, as described in "Review Safari's Controls" earlier in this chapter, to go to another location.

Search the Internet

You can search the Internet in two ways: by using the search facility built into Safari and by using an independent search facility on the Web.

Search from Safari

There are two parts of Safari's search facility: search for sites you have recently visited, and search for sites that contain keywords.

- To search for recently visited sites, tap or delete the current contents of the address bar and begin typing what you want to search for. As you are typing, Safari looks at sites you have recently visited and, if a possible match is found, a site is suggested and others are listed, as you saw earlier in Figure 3-4 and elsewhere.

- To search for sites based on keywords, also type those words in the address bar, for example, spicy shrimp.

The search engine—Google is the default—will display several suggested webpages while you are typing, as well as whether there are any matches on the current webpage. You can tap any of the suggestions to open those pages, or you can tap **Go** on the keyboard and open the search engine's (Google's) page, displaying its search results, as you can see in Figure 3-5.

Search from an Internet Site

There are several other, directly accessed Internet search sites. Among these are Google, Bing, and Yahoo!.

1. In Safari, tap and delete the current address in the address bar, type bing.com, and tap **Go**.

2. In the site's text box (Bing's in this case), type what you want to search for, and tap **Search**. The resulting website is shown in a full webpage, shown in Figure 3-6.

3. Tap the link of your choice to go to that site.

 TIP When you enter search criteria, place quotation marks around certain keywords or phrases to get only results that match those words exactly.

Save a Bookmark

Sometimes, you visit a site that you would like to return to quickly or often. As you have seen, Safari has the ability to save sites as bookmarks for easy retrieval.

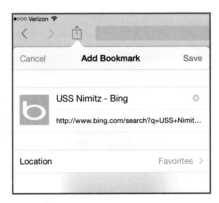

●○○○○ Verizon 🔋 11:53 AM ⚡ Not Charging ▬▬

🔒 spicy shrimp

| Political News, Analysis... | Microsoft news and fea... | Google | Product reviews - Elect... | Model S \| Tesla Motors | ⊗ spicy shrimp - Googl... |

+You **Search** Images More ▾   Sign in ⚙

Google   spicy shrimp   ✕   🔍

Web   Images   Maps   Shopping   Recipes   More ▾   Search tools

Spicy Shrimp Recipes - Food Network
www.foodnetwork.com/recipe-collections/**spicy-shrimp**/
Try new ways of preparing shrimp with **spicy shrimp** recipes and more from the expert
chefs at Food Network.

4 Minute **Spicy** Garlic **Shrimp** Recipe : Rachael Ray : Recipes : Food ...
www.foodnetwork.com › Recipes › Seafood
★★★★★ Rating: 5 - 94 reviews - 17 mins
Get this all-star, easy-to-follow Food Network 4 Minute **Spicy** Garlic **Shrimp**
recipe from Rachael Ray.

Moroccan **Spicy Shrimp** Recipe - A Recipe for Spicy Sauteed Shrimp
fishcooking.about.com › ... › Shrimp Recipes
★★★★★ Rating: 5 - 1 review - 20 mins
A recipe for **spicy** sauteed **shrimp** cooked in a Moroccan style, with cumin,
paprika, coriander and a little ginger. This **shrimp** recipe is very quick, and easy
to ...
More by Hank Shaw - in 87 Google+ circles

Spicy Shrimp | The Pioneer Woman Cooks | Ree Drummond

Related searches

spicy **garlic** shrimp

spicy shrimp **appetizer**

spicy shrimp **recipe**

spicy shrimp **stir fry**

spicy **grilled** shrimp

spicy shrimp **pasta**

cajun shrimp

spicy shrimp **scampi**

*Figure 3-5: **The results of a search using Safari's search, which defaults to Google.***

Add a Bookmark

To save a site to the Bookmarks list:

1. Open the webpage you want to add to your Bookmarks list, and make sure its correct address (URL) is in the address bar.

2. Tap the **Share menu** icon next to the address box, and tap **Bookmark**. The Add Bookmark dialog box will open.

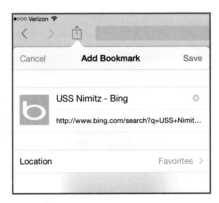

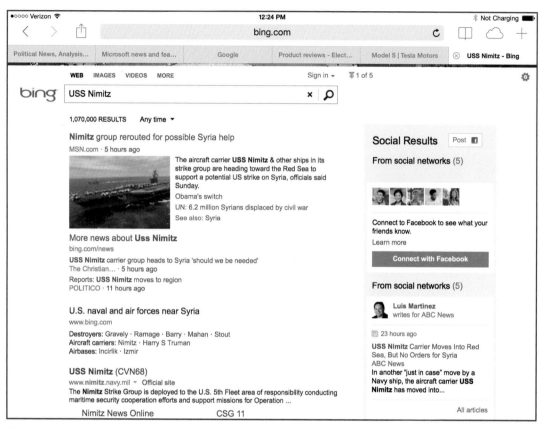

< 〉 ⬆️ 　　　　　　　　bing.com　　　　　　　　↻ 📖 ☁️ ＋

Political News, Analysis...　Microsoft news and fea...　　Google　　Product reviews - Elect...　Model S | Tesla Motors　⊗　USS Nimitz - Bing

WEB　IMAGES　VIDEOS　MORE　　　　　　　　　Sign in ▾　　☗ 1 of 5　　　　　　　⚙️

bing　USS Nimitz　　　　　　　　　　　× 🔍

1,070,000 RESULTS　　Any time ▾

Nimitz group rerouted for possible Syria help
MSN.com · 5 hours ago

The aircraft carrier **USS Nimitz** & other ships in its strike group are heading toward the Red Sea to support a potential US strike on Syria, officials said Sunday.
Obama's switch
UN: 6.2 million Syrians displaced by civil war
See also: Syria

More news about **Uss Nimitz**
bing.com/news

USS Nimitz carrier group heads to Syria 'should we be needed'
The Christian... · 5 hours ago
Reports: **USS Nimitz** moves to region
POLITICO · 11 hours ago

U.S. naval and air forces near Syria
www.bing.com

Destroyers: Gravely · Ramage · Barry · Mahan · Stout
Aircraft carriers: Nimitz · Harry S Truman
Airbases: Incirlik · Izmir

USS Nimitz (CVN68)
www.nimitz.navy.mil ▾ · Official site
The **Nimitz** Strike Group is deployed to the U.S. 5th Fleet area of responsibility conducting maritime security cooperation efforts and support missions for Operation ...
Nimitz News Online　　　　　CSG 11

Social Results　　Post ▣

From social networks (5)

Connect to Facebook to see what your friends know.
Learn more

Connect with Facebook

From social networks (5)

Luis Martinez
writes for ABC News

📅 23 hours ago

USS Nimitz Carrier Moves Into Red Sea, But No Orders for Syria
ABC News
In another "just in case" move by a Navy ship, the aircraft carrier **USS Nimitz** has moved into...

All articles

Figure 3-6: The results of a search using Bing

3. Adjust the name as needed in the text box (you may want to type a new name you will readily associate with the site).

4. Initially, the Location option is "Favorites," meaning that the link will be saved to the Favorites bar. If you tap that option, though, you can choose to save the link to the Bookmarks list.

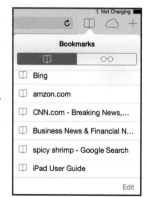

✴ Not Charging
↻ 📖 ☁️ ＋
Bookmarks
📖 ◯◯
📖 Bing
📖 amazon.com
📖 CNN.com - Breaking News,...
📖 Business News & Financial N...
📖 spicy shrimp - Google Search
📖 iPad User Guide
Edit

5. Choose where you want to save the link and tap **Save**.

Save to the Home Screen

You can choose to have a link to a website added to the Home screen as you would an app.

1. Open the webpage you want to add to your Home screen, and make sure its correct address (URL) is in the address bar.

2. Tap the **Share menu** icon and tap **Add To Home Screen**. The Add To Home dialog box will open.

3. Adjust the name as needed in the text box and tap **Add**. You'll see the icon for the page appear on the Home screen.

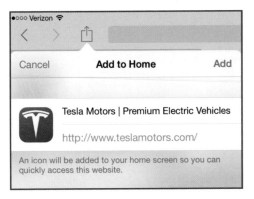

⏭ Organize Bookmarks

You will probably find over time that you have accumulated a number of bookmarks and it is becoming hard to find the one you want. Safari provides two places to store your Bookmarks: a Bookmarks list, which is presented to you in the form of a menu you can open, and a Favorites bar, which can be displayed at all times. There are several ways to organize your bookmarks.

> **TIP** The webpages that you have pinned to the Home screen from Safari can also be organized in any way you want, as described in Chapter 2.

Rearrange, Edit, and Delete Bookmarks

The items on your Bookmarks list are displayed in the order you added them, with the name you left them with, but you can move them to a new location, edit their names, and delete them.

1. In Safari, tap the **Bookmarks** icon. Tap **Edit** on the bottom right. The Bookmarks editing features are displayed.

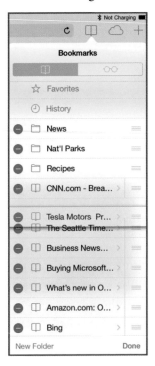

2. Locate the site you want to reposition. Touch and hold the three bars (grip strip) on the right of the bookmark, and drag it up or down to where you want it.

3. To edit a bookmark's name, tap the greater-than sign on the mid-right of the bookmark to open the Edit Bookmark dialog box.

4. In the top text box, edit the name as you would edit other text on the iPad (see Chapter 2).

5. In the bottom text box opposite Location, tap the greater-than sign and tap where you want to store the bookmark (see the following section).

6. To delete a bookmark, tap the delete icon to the left of it and then tap **Delete**. When you are done editing bookmarks, tap **Done**.

Create New Folders

You can add your own folders within Bookmarks.

1. In Safari, tap the **Bookmarks** icon and tap **Edit** on the bottom right. The Bookmarks editing features are displayed, as you saw earlier.

2. Tap **New Folder** in the lower left, type the name for the folder, tap where you want to store the folder, and tap **Done** on the keyboard.

3. Use the steps in the "Rearrange, Edit, and Delete Bookmarks" section earlier to move the desired bookmarks to the new folder.

Put Bookmarks in Folders

You can put a site in either your own folders (see "Create New Folders") or the default Bookmarks list or Favorites bar, which operate like folders.

1. Open the webpage you want in your Bookmarks, and make sure its correct address or URL is in the address bar.

2. Tap the **Share menu** icon, tap **Bookmark**, adjust the name as needed in the text box, tap **Location** at the bottom, tap the folder to use, and tap **Save**.

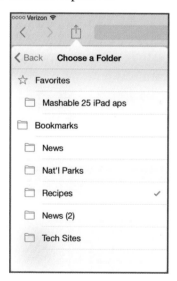

USE INTERNET INFORMATION

Of course, the reason for accessing the Internet is to use the information that you find there, to read it, save it, play its media, or send it to a friend.

Work with a Webpage

An iPad screen displaying a webpage in Safari works just like any other iPad screen and gives you the same tools you've used elsewhere on the iPad. In Safari, you can

- **Select pages**, links, items, and options by tapping them
- **Move a page** being displayed up or down, left or right, by dragging it with your finger
- **Change a page** by swiping from right to left or bottom to top of a page
- **Enlarge a page** by spreading two fingers apart
- **Reduce a page** by pinching two fingers together
- **Enlarge just an article** if it is in a separate frame by double-tapping the article
- **Scroll just an article** if it is in a separate frame by dragging with two fingers
- **See a link's destination** by tapping and holding the link, which also allows you to open the link in a new tab and add it to the Reading List

- **Fill out a form** by tapping the first field, typing what is requested, and then tapping **Next** or **Previous**
- **Return to a closed page** by tapping and holding on the New Tab plus sign

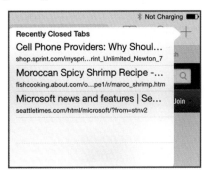

> **TIP** Webpages from different publishers can behave very differently. One publication can present itself one screen wide and have you scroll down by dragging or swiping up to go through a lengthy section. Another publication can present itself one screen high and have you scroll right by dragging or swiping from right to left.

Read Webpages

The iPad with a Retina display is a particularly good device from which to read, and Safari has a reader with which you can separate out an article from advertisements and make reading an excellent experience.

1. Navigate in Safari to an article you want to read and tap it. On the left end of the address bar you should see the Reader icon, a stack of lines.

2. Tap the Reader icon. The article will appear in its own window, filling the screen, as you see in Figure 3-7.

3. Scroll by swiping up (from bottom to top) as you would any other page.

4. To close the Reader, tap the Reader icon again in the address bar.

 NOTE The Reader is a good way to forward an article since it removes the ads and transfers just the article. Use the Share menu to do this, which works with the Reader as well.

Figure 3-7: ***The Safari Reader provides a great way to read webpage articles.***

Play Internet Audio and Video Files

You can play audio and *some* video files on the Internet with Safari directly from a link on a webpage. The exception is that the iPad cannot play video files that use the Adobe Flash technology (there are several apps in the App Store, such as the Rover browser, that will allow you to play Flash content). Many webpages have links to audio and video files, such as

the one shown in Figure 3-8. To play these files, simply tap the play button. The player will open to play the requested piece.

> **TIP** To search for information within an open webpage in Safari, type the keywords you want to search for in the Address/Search bar at the top of the screen, and then tap the entry or entries under **On This Page**.

Figure 3-8: Play an audio or video file on a webpage by tapping the play button.

Control Internet Security

As you saw earlier in this chapter, Safari Settings allow you to control several aspects of Internet security. You can determine how you want to handle cookies placed on your computer by websites and use Do Not Track to prevent the website from bothering you in the future, among several other settings (see Figure 3-3 earlier in this chapter). These controls are found in Settings.

Handle Cookies

Cookies are small pieces of data that websites store on your iPad so that they can remind themselves of who you are. These can save you from having to constantly enter your name and ID. Cookies can also be dangerous, however, letting people into your computer where they can potentially do damage. Safari lets you determine when you will block cookies.

1. In the Home screen, tap **Settings | Safari**.
2. In Safari Settings, tap **Block Cookies**.
3. Consider the three choices you have:

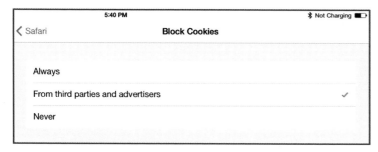

- **Always** means that every time you visit a site, you must sign in and there is no memory of your last visit that might take you back to what you were doing the last time you were on the site.

- **Never** means that any site you come across can add whatever information they want.

- **From Third Parties And Advertisers** means that you will only block cookies from these sites.

The default, and my recommendation, is **From Third Parties And Advertisers**. In my mind, cookies can be more of a benefit than a problem. You can see who has stored information on your iPad by tapping **Advanced** at the bottom of Safari Settings and then tapping **Website Data**, as discussed earlier in this chapter.

Use Do Not Track

Safari's Do Not Track option in Safari Settings gives you a way to visit a website and not leave any information about your visit on either your iPad or the visited website. This allows you to take a peek at a website and not leave any trace so as to more safely browse and view websites. While you have Do Not Track turned on, your browsing history, temporary Internet files, and cookies are not stored on your iPad, preventing anyone looking at your iPad from seeing where you have browsed. In addition, information about you is not passed on to Internet content providers.

NOTE If you are using your iPad in a school or business that has security controls, they may be able to see where you have browsed, even with Do Not Track, and it is not perfect at preventing a website from knowing who you are.

99 **QuickQuotes**

Joann Anderson

My iPad has become an extension of my life. I carry it with me all the time as a constant resource. I use it for email (synced with my desktop computer), Internet searches, the Dictionary app, weather tracking for my family (Intellicast), navigation on trips (Maps), searching hotels and restaurants when traveling (Yelp), Calendar, Netflix, Calculator, and Quicken 2013's new iPad app, which will sync with my desktop computer. Another great app is Spider Oak for secure storage of such things as passwords. This is helpful when you are getting a lot of requests for password entries.

An important tip when buying apps is to check ratings and reviews before buying—both positive and negative. I've saved myself a lot of headaches by doing this.

I recommend buying extended service, a small stylus with a padded end, and a separate keyboard built into a case. At any rate, an iPad enhances life in many ways, no matter what our age! (I am nearly 80 and love it!)

QuickSteps to...

Chapter 4

Using Email and Messages

For many people, email and messaging have become their primary means of communicating and are, therefore, major reasons for them to have an iPad. The iPad comes with the Mail, Messages, and Contacts apps already installed. In addition, the App Store has many alternatives for emailing and messaging. To use any apps for emailing and messaging, however, you must have a connection to the Internet and an email account, as described in the previous chapter. If you do not yet have an Internet connection, go back to Chapter 3 and do that now.

This chapter will discuss getting an email account; setting up the Mail and Messages apps; creating and using the Contacts app; sending, receiving, and managing email; and sending and receiving text messages. In addition, we'll look at web mail with Safari.

USE MAIL

The iPad's Mail app allows you to send, receive, and manage email over the Internet. This book primarily focuses on the use of the Mail app because it is a modern email program that works well and comes with and is designed for Apple's iOS. You can also send and receive email through other email apps, as well as web mail accounts using Safari, but this section will be devoted to using Mail. See "Use Web Mail" later in this chapter for a discussion of that subject.

⏩ Set Up Mail

To begin the use of Mail, you must establish an email account with an email provider recognized by Mail and then convey that information to Mail.

Establish an Email Account

For an email account, you need:

- An email address—for example, mike@anisp.com.
- The password for your mail account.
- You may also need to know the type of mail server you are using, either IMAP or POP (if you have a choice, choose IMAP; it is newer and provides more flexibility). Internet Message Access Protocol (IMAP) keeps a copy of your mail on the server and does not delete it until you do or until some set time, like three months. This allows you to read your mail on several devices until you delete it on one of them. Post Office Protocol (POP) allows you to download your messages once and then deletes it, unless you choose otherwise, making it hard to use with both an iPad and a computer.

At the time this was written, Mail recognizes accounts with iCloud, Microsoft Exchange, Gmail, Yahoo!, AOL, Microsoft Hotmail, Microsoft Outlook, and a number of smaller email services. Since you had to have an email account to get an Apple ID to use your iPad, you can generally use that for your Mail account. It is also likely that when you set up an Internet connection, you were given an email account that you can use. Finally, you can open Safari and

go to Google.com, Yahoo.com, Outlook.com (not the Office product, but the replacement for Hotmail), and others to create a new account. Here are the steps with Google:

1. On the Home screen, tap **Safari**. Tap the address bar, tap the delete icon, and type the site from which you want an email account—in this case, type google.com.

2. Tap **More | Gmail | Create an Account**. Enter your name, choose a user name, create and confirm a password, and complete filling out the registration form, as you see in Figure 4-1.

3. When you are done, tap **Next Step**. You are asked if you want to create a public Google+ profile. If you do, tap **Create Profile**. If you don't, tap the **Google May Use My Account** check box to uncheck it. Tap in the address bar, type gmail.com, and tap **Go**.

4. You are asked if you want the Gmail app. Since you already have the native iPad Mail app, for the moment I suggest you ignore that and tap **Go To The Mobile Site**. This shows you your Google mail in Safari. For now, close Safari.

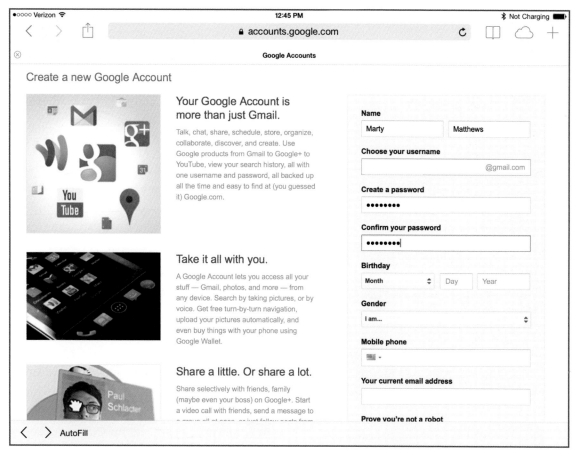

*Figure 4-1: **It is very easy to create a number of free email accounts on the Internet.***

After creating an email account, put aside looking at your mail and return to the Home screen to set up Mail. We'll come back later in the chapter to look at web mail accounts.

Set Up Gmail in Mail

With a Gmail account, you can not only view your mail in a web mail account on Safari, but also set it up in Mail.

1. In the Home screen, tap **Mail**. Mail will display a number of mail servers, as shown in Figure 4-2. Tap Google.

2. Enter your name, email address, password, and a description of the account, and tap **Next**. If you want, choose to link

Figure 4-2: Besides the six mail servers listed, the iPad can connect to many other, less prominent mail servers.

Contacts, Calendars, and Notes to Gmail, and tap **Save**. Your Gmail account will open in Mail (see Figure 4-3).

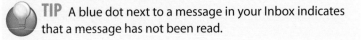
TIP A blue dot next to a message in your Inbox indicates that a message has not been read.

Set Up Outlook.com in Mail

Outlook.com (which used to be Hotmail, the Microsoft mail service) is set up in Mail in a similar way to Gmail, but once you have any account configured in Mail, you start in a different way. If Outlook.com is your first account, start with Step 1; otherwise, start with Step 2.

1. In the Home screen, tap **Mail**. Mail will display a number of mail servers, as shown in Figure 4-2. Tap Outlook.com and skip to Step 3.

2. If you have other Mail accounts, from the Home screen, tap **Settings | Mail, Contacts, Calendars | Add Account | Outlook.com**, as shown in Figure 4-4.

3. Enter your email address, password, and a description of the account. Do that and tap **Next**. Choose if you want to link Mail, Contacts, Calendars, and Reminders to Hotmail and tap **Save**. You are returned to Settings.

NOTE Hotmail accounts are being changed to Outlook (the mail service, not the Office app) and so you may use the steps in "Set Up Outlook.com in Mail" for Hotmail mail accounts.

Set Up Other Accounts in Mail

Besides the major six email servers, there are a great number of other mail servers you can access on your iPad, including smaller email servers and email on a personal website. To set up an account for these types of mail servers:

1. From the Home screen, tap **Settings | Mail, Contacts, Calendars | Add Account | Other | Add Mail Account**.

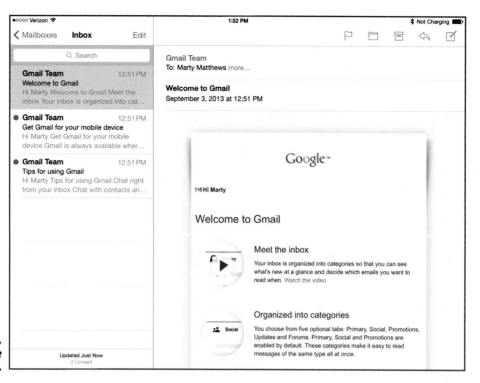

Figure 4-3: **Within Mail, Gmail looks the same as other accounts.**

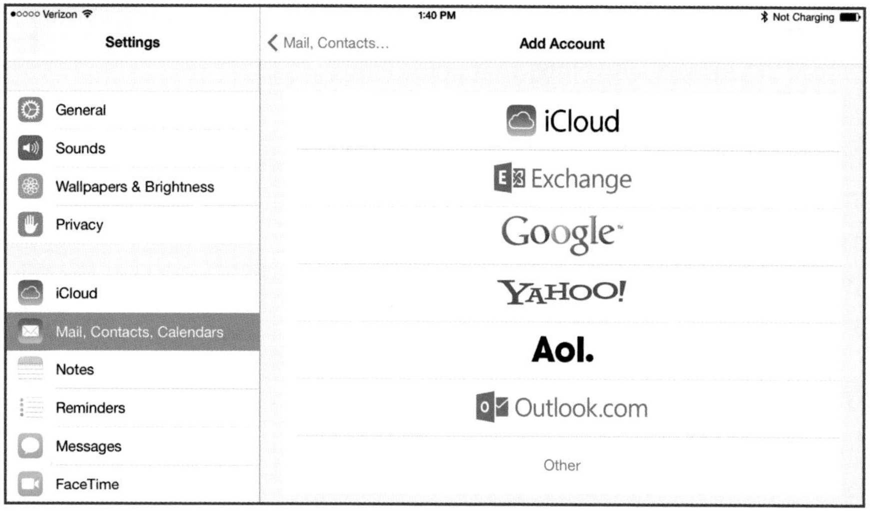

Figure 4-4: **After you have one account, you need to go into Settings to set up another.**

2. Enter your name, email address, password, and a description of the account, and tap **Next**.

3. Tap the host name of your incoming mail server and enter it along with your outgoing mail server, and the user name for your incoming server. You may need to ask your email provider what entries you need to use for these fields.

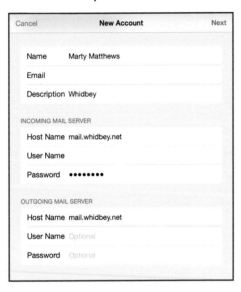

4. If you want, choose to link Mail and Notes to this account, and tap **Save**. You are returned to Settings.

5. Press **Home** and tap **Mail** to look at your new account(s). If you open an account and want to look at others, tap the name of the account—for example, **Gmail** in the upper-left corner—to open the list of inboxes and accounts, as you can see in Figure 4-5.

▷▷ Change Mail Settings

Mail settings include settings for each account, as well as for Mail itself.

Change Account Settings

The accounts settings vary by account and can go into a fair amount of technical depth, most of which, if you have been able to complete the setup, you don't need. The general Mail settings are discussed under "Change General Mail Settings" later in this chapter. To view the settings for a particular account:

 TIP If you are having trouble setting up a mail account, the quickest solution is to contact the mail provider (or Internet service provider—ISP), or IT help desk and have them lead you through the setup. They will help you with the detail settings within their account.

1. Tap **Settings | Mail, Contacts, Calendars |** *account name* (for example "Gmail"), as you can see in Figure 4-6.

2. The account's top-level settings will open. Here you can turn on or off portions of the mail service, delete the account, and, by tapping **Account**, go into the account's detail settings.

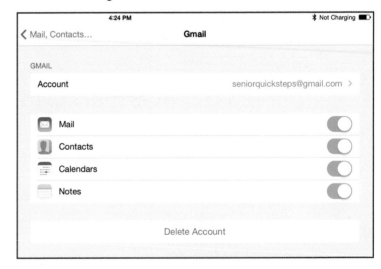

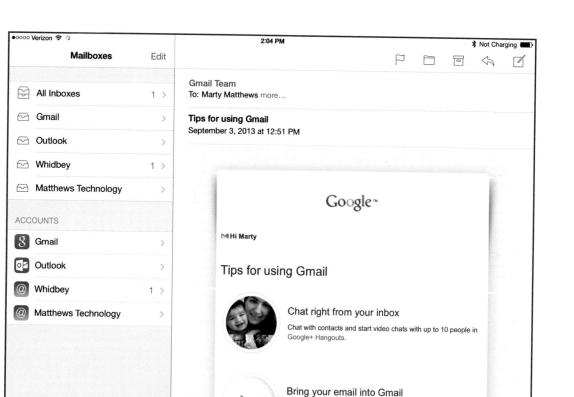

Figure 4-5: *You can have and manage several email accounts on the iPad. (Whidbey is a local ISP I use, and Matthews Technology is our own domain with email services.)*

3. In the detail settings, you can change your basic logon information and open the advanced settings for your mail provider. For the latter, I'd recommend that you make any changes with the help of the mail provider.

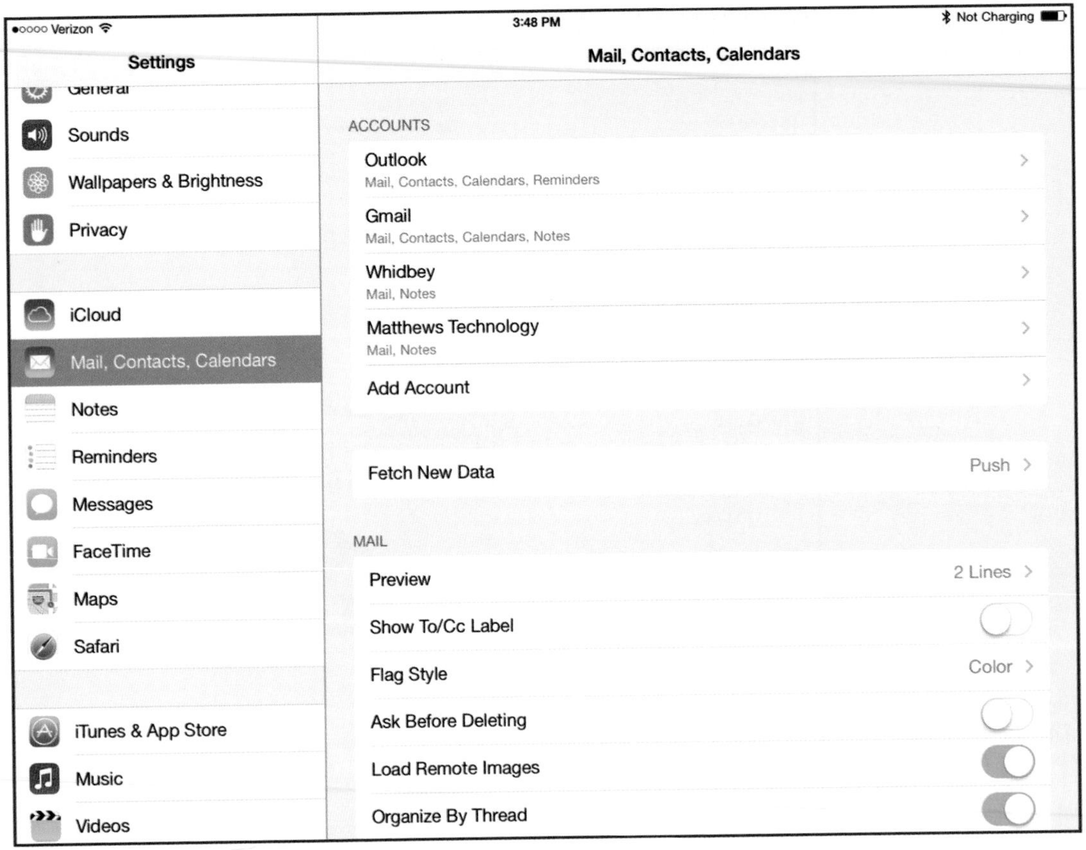

Figure 4-6: After setting up a mail account, there often isn't a need to use the account settings.

NOTE Some mail providers, Gmail in particular, provide the ability to archive messages that you might want, but might not want them to take up room on your iPad. See the discussion under "Archive, Delete, and Recover Messages" later in this chapter.

Change General Mail Settings

The general settings that apply to all mail accounts are below the account-specific settings discussed earlier. As mentioned there, tap **Settings | Mail, Contacts, Calendars** and scroll down a bit. The general settings include:

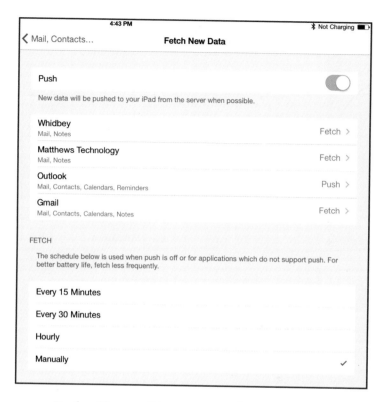

- **Fetch New Data** allows you to choose how you receive your email from your mail provider. You essentially have three choices, with some subchoices. From the Mail, Contacts, Calendars settings, tap **Fetch New Data**. On the screen that opens, you have these choices that affect all services:

- **Push** Your mail is automatically pushed to you by the server whenever the mail is available, causing the iPad to be more active and, therefore, using more of the battery. Only some mail services provide the Push option (in the examples here, it is only Outlook), and you can turn that off by tapping the **On/Off** button.

- **Fetch** The iPad's Mail app requests the server to send you your mail. This can be done automatically every 15 minutes, 30 minutes, hourly, or manually where you determine when to download your mail. Manually puts the least drain on the battery. Tap the option you would like.

Individual mail services' settings can be changed by tapping the service you want to change, and then tapping the selection you want.

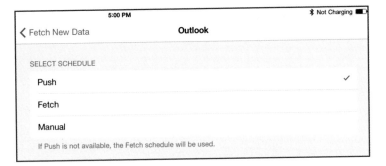

NOTE With Push email, the email is received whenever it is available, provided the iPad is not powered off, even when it is sleeping and whether or not the Mail app is active. With Fetch set to a time interval (15 minutes to hourly), mail is received only when Mail is first opened and then periodically on the time interval, so long as Mail remains open. With Fetch set to manual, email is only received when you manually drag down the top of the Inbox with your finger.

- **Preview** allows you to determine the number of message lines you want displayed in the Inbox.
- **Show To/Cc Label** adds a label to received emails telling you if you are an addressee or a Cc. If no label appears, the email probably came from a mass mailing and may be spam.

- **Flag Style** allows you to select the style of the flags that can be attached to mail messages.

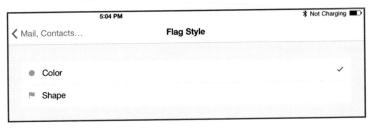

- **Ask Before Deleting** gives you a warning and a second chance when you delete a message.
- **Load Remote Images** allows photos to be received with email when they are attached.
- **Organize By Thread** organizes your email by subject instead of time and date.
- **Always Bcc Myself** sends a copy of an email to you so you can get it on another computer, such as your desktop or laptop computer, if you share an email account with that computer.

- **Increase Quote Level** increases the indentation of replies and replies to replies in the list of messages in your Inbox. This works particularly well when you organize your messages by their thread (subject).

- **Signature** allows you to enter a block of text that is added at the end of your email messages. If you want to have different signatures for each of your email accounts, tap **Signature**, tap **Per Account**, and add to or replace the default "Sent from my iPad" text with the signature block you want to use.

- **Default Account** allows you to specify the email account to use when you send email from apps other than Mail, like Notes or Photos, when you tap the **Share** icon and tap **Mail**.

⫸ Send, Receive, and Respond to Email

The purpose, of course, of email is to send messages to others, receive messages from them, and respond to the messages you receive. Mail does this with a simple elegance.

Create and Send Email

To create and send an email message:

1. Tap **Mail** on the Home screen and in the page that opens, tap the **New** icon ☑ in the upper-right corner. The New Message pane will open, similar to the one in Figure 4-7.

2. Start to enter a name in the To text box. If the name is in your Contacts (see "Use Contacts" later in this chapter), it will be suggested in a list and you can tap to accept that name. If the name is not automatically completed, finish typing a full email address (such as tim@apple.com) and then tap **Return**.

3. If you want more than one addressee, after accepting a suggested name or tapping Return after typing one, as directed in Step 2, where a space is automatically added, simply begin typing a second address.

Figure 4-7: Email messages are an easy and fast way to communicate.

TIP To look up a name in Contacts, tap the plus sign icon on the right of the To address box to open the All Contacts list, where you can scroll down to find a name and then tap it.

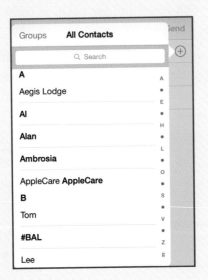

4. If you want to differentiate the addressees to whom the message is principally being sent from those for whom it is just information, tap **Cc/Bcc** to open text boxes for those items, and enter the desired addressees there as you did in the To text box.

5. If you want to send the message to a recipient and not have other recipients see to whom it is sent, tap the **Bcc** text box, and type the address(es) to be hidden. (Bcc stands for "blind carbon copy.")

6. Tap in the **Subject** text box and type a subject for the message.

7. Tap the area beneath the line under Subject and type your message.

8. When you have completed your message, tap **Send** [Send] in the upper-right corner of the message. For a brief time, you may see a message in your Outbox and then, if you look, you will see the message in your Sent Items folder. If you are done, close Mail.

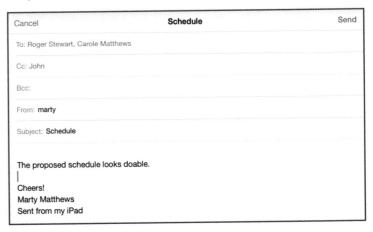

NOTE If you want to delete or move an email addressee, touch and hold on the name. While you are holding it, it will pop away from the text box and you can drag it where you want. If you just tap it to select it, you can then tap **Delete**.

Receive Email

Mail can be received automatically if the account is pushing messages to the iPad or if you have the account set on automatic fetch. Otherwise, you need to manually download your mail by dragging down the Inbox in the left pane. Once you have unread mail in your Inbox:

1. Open **Mail** and tap **Inbox**, which contains all of the messages you have received and haven't deleted. (The number beside the word "Inbox" is the number of unviewed messages, as is the number beside the Mail icon on the Home screen.)

 TIP Have a friend send you an email message so you know whether you are receiving messages. Then send the friend a message back and ask them to let you know when they get it so you know you are sending messages.

2. Tap a message in the Inbox message list on the left to have it displayed, and then read it in the reading pane on the right of the Mail window, as you saw earlier in Figure 4-3.

3. If you wish, you can delete a message while it is selected by tapping the **Delete** icon (a trashcan) on the top-right corner.

 NOTE You can also delete an email message you haven't opened by swiping across it and tapping **Delete**, or if it is available, archive it by taping **Archive.**

Respond to Email

You can respond to messages you receive.

Tap the message in the message list and then tap the **Reply** icon on the right of the screen.

From the menu that appears, tap:

- **Reply** to return a message to just the person who sent the original message.

- **Reply All** to return a message to all the people who were addressees (both To and Cc) in the original message.

- **Forward** to relay a message to people not shown as addressees on the original message.

- **Save Image** to save on your iPad an attached image or an embedded image that you received in the original message.

- **Print** to print the original message.

In the first three cases, a window similar to the New Message window (see Figure 4-8) opens and allows you to add or change addressees and the subject and to add a new message.

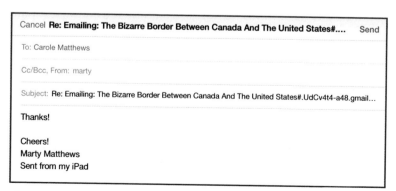

Figure 4-8: With email, you can quickly respond to a message you receive by simply tapping Reply.

⮀ Apply Formatting

In iPad Mail, you can add **bold**, *italic*, and underline formatting to the words, phrases, and paragraphs in an email message. You can also indent paragraphs.

1. Open an email message you want to create or that is in response to a message you received, as described in the previous sections of this chapter.

2. Type the text you want in the message, and then tap the text you want specially formatted. The Select bar will appear; tap **Select**.

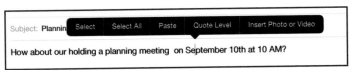

3. When the text is selected, drag the ends of the selection box as needed to select the words you want to format.

4. If it isn't already displayed, tap the selected text to open the Cut, Copy, Paste bar.

5. Tap **B***I*U in the middle to open the Bold, Italics, Underline bar.

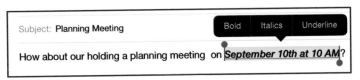

6. Tap the style(s) you want to use (you can use more than one). When you are done, tap outside of the selection.

7. To indent a paragraph, select it and open the Select bar, as in Step 2.

8. Tap **Quote Level**, and then tap either **Decrease** or **Increase** to either outdent (move to the left) or indent (move to the right), respectively. You can do this several times if you choose. When you are done, as you can see in Figure 4-9, tap outside the selection.

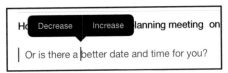

⮀ Handle Attachments

When you send email, you may want to include a photo, a video, a note, an iWorks (Pages, Numbers, and Keynote) document, a Safari webpage, or many other items on your on iPad. You can do that either while you are working on a message or while you are looking at the item.

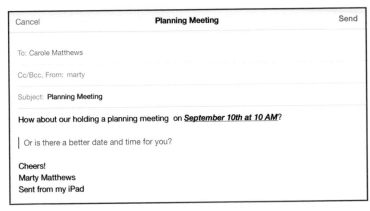

Figure 4-9: Formatting can add both levity and emphasis to a message.

Add a Photo to a Message

From within an email message, you can attach a number of documents. Look at attaching a photo as an example:

1. Open an email message you want to create or that is in response to a message you received, as described in the previous sections of this chapter.

2. Type the message you want to start with. When you are at the spot where you want to insert the photo, press RETURN to leave a blank line.

3. Press and hold for a moment on the blank line to open the Select bar, and then tap **Insert Photo Or Video**.

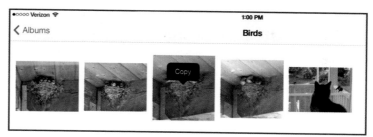

4. A list of your photo folders will appear. Tap the folder, tap the photo, and then tap **Use**. The picture will appear in your message, as you can see in Figure 4-10.

   –Or–

   When you are at the point described at the end of Step 2, you can also press Home and tap Photos to open the Photos app.

5. Open the album needed to locate the photo you want. Then press and hold for a moment on that photo to have "Copy" pop up.

6. Tap **Copy**. Press the **Home** button and tap **Mail**. The email message that you have been working on will appear.

7. Press and hold for a moment on the blank line to open the Select bar, and then tap **Paste**. The photo will appear in your message

8. When you are ready, send the message as you would normally.

| Cancel | **Cat & Birds** | Send |

To: Carole Matthews

Cc/Bcc, From: marty@whidbey.com

Subject: **Cat & Birds**

Here is a great photo of our cat watching through the window at some baby birds learning to fly.

Figure 4-10: You can attach a photo or video without leaving an email message.

Email Items Directly

In the preceding section, you have seen how to insert, and cut and paste items into an open email message. You can also send photos and other items directly from their respective apps.

1. Open the app with the item you want to email. In that app, open the folders or otherwise navigate to where you can see the item.

2. Select the item, tap the **Share** icon, and tap **Mail**, as shown in Figure 4-11. A new email message pops up containing the item you selected.

3. Add the addressees, a subject, and any message you want to include. When you are ready, tap **Send**.

 NOTE Email that is sent directly from an app other than Mail is sent using your default mail provider, as described earlier in "Change General Mail Settings."

Handle Received Attachments

You also may need to handle attachments you receive in email on your iPad. You can tell if a message has an attachment by the paperclip icon in the message header. The attachment can be a photo, video, or other document, including Microsoft Word, Excel, and PowerPoint files, as well as Adobe PDF files and webpages. To process an attachment:

1. Open a message with an attachment as you would any message. The body of the message will open, and at the bottom you will see the attachment, as shown in Figure 4-12.

2. Tap the attachment to open it. If the attachment is a document that the iPad can open, it will do so and you can read or view it. If you want to save it, tap the **Share** icon and then tap the app that you want to save it in. In the case of the Word document shown in Figure 4-12, choose **Open In Pages**, where it is automatically saved (see Figure 4-13).

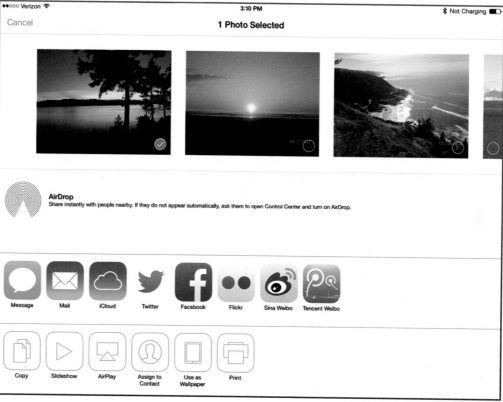

Figure 4-11: A number of apps allow you to send their media or documents directly.

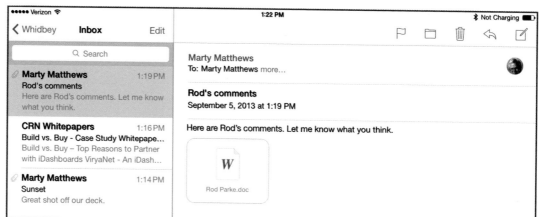

Figure 4-12: The iPad will tell you the app that it thinks created the document, Microsoft Word here, if it can open the document.

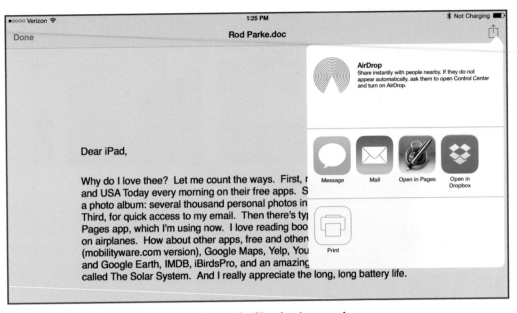

Manage Email

Mail allows you to organize your mail in both existing and new folders; to archive, delete, and recover messages; and to flag, mark, and search your messages.

Understand Email Folders

Email that you receive and send is stored in folders, both in the Mail app on the iPad and the mail server you are using. The folders that you have available depend to some degree on the mail service and, if you have previously used it on another computer, how you set it up there. In

Figure 4-13: *The iPad can only open and save the files that it recognizes.*

3. If the attachment is a photo, it will automatically open in Mail and you can save it by pressing and holding on the photo to open the Share menu shown in Figure 4-14. Tap **Save Image** to place it in your Camera Roll.

4. If the attachment is not recognized by Mail, you can normally resend it in another email, or possibly do something with it using apps you have gotten from the App Store. Tap the attachment to see what options are available. Here you can see that a file created with a program called Xara, a graphics program I use with my website, can be resent in email, and stored in Dropbox, which is an app I downloaded from the App Store.

Figure 4-14: Photos are easy to send and receive via email, but they also take up a lot of storage space as well as a lot of your data plan.

the latter case, the iPad will mimic the folder structure on your computer. Figure 4-15 compares Gmail's folder structure with that of Whidbey (my local ISP), Matthews Technology (my website), and Outlook.com.

To work with folders:

1. From an Inbox, shown in Figure 4-14, the most common working area of Mail, tap the mail provider's name in the upper-left corner. This may take you to the set of folders

for that particular mail provider, four of which were shown in Figure 4-15, or to Mailboxes, depending on where you originally started. If you are showing Mailboxes, tap an account in the lower-left column to see the folders for that account.

2. If your left column is displaying the folders for a provider, tap **Mailboxes** in the upper-left corner. This shows you your mail accounts, both in terms of their Inboxes, where tapping any of the accounts takes you to their Inbox, and

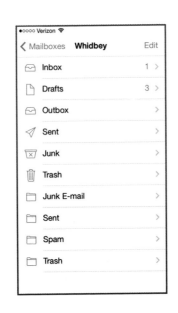

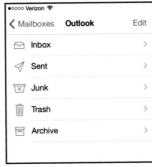

Figure 4-15: Not only do different email providers have different sets of folders, but common folders are in a different order.

the accounts themselves in the lower part of the left column, where tapping takes you to the set of folders for that account.

3. Tap an account at the top of the Mailboxes pane and observe the respective Inbox. Then return to Mailboxes by tapping the provider's name in the upper-left corner.

4. Tap an account under Accounts to open and observe the set of folders for this account. Tap **Inbox** to open and observe the Inbox arrived at in this manner. You can see there is no difference in the Inboxes.

5. Return to Mailboxes by tapping first the provider's name in the upper-left corner and then tapping **Mailboxes** in the same location.

Understanding this navigation from Mailboxes to account folders to Inboxes and back is important to easily getting around Mail.

Add and Delete Folders

If you find that you would really like to have additional folders to better organize your mail, you can do that easily.

1. From the Mailboxes pane shown in the previous section, tap in the Accounts area the mail provider where you want the extra folder. The list of existing folders for that provider will appear.

2. Tap **Edit** at the top-right corner of the pane and then tap **New Mailbox** in the bottom-right corner.

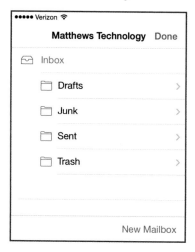

>  **NOTE** NOTE Some folders in Mail can be moved, have their name changed (which might satisfy the need for a new folder), and deleted, while others can't. You can tell which can be edited after you tap **Edit**, because they are darker.

3. Type the name for the new folder and then tap the account field beneath **Mailbox Location** to choose where in the current folder hierarchy you want the new folder.

4. Tap where you want the new folder, and then tap **Save** in the upper-right corner.

5. If you want to change the position or name of the new folder, or any other folder, tap **Edit** in the upper-right area, and tap the folder you want to change.

6. In the Edit Mailbox pane, make any desired changes to the name, tap **Mailbox Location**, tap the new parent folder, and tap **Save**.

7. If you want to delete a folder, perform Step 5, and then in Edit Mailbox, tap **Delete Mailbox**. Confirm that by tapping **Delete** again and then tapping **Done**.

Organize Messages with Folders

Use the various folders that you have by moving your mail among them:

1. From Mailboxes in the left column, tap an account in the upper part of the column to open the Inbox for that account, or tap an account in the lower part of the left column to open another folder for a given mail provider to display the message(s) you want to move to other folders.

2. Tap the message you want to move so it is displayed on the right of the screen.

3. Tap the folder icon ⊡ at the top of the screen. The message will shrink as you can see in Figure 4-16.

4. Tap the folder in which you want to store the message. The message will disappear from its current folder and appear in its new one.

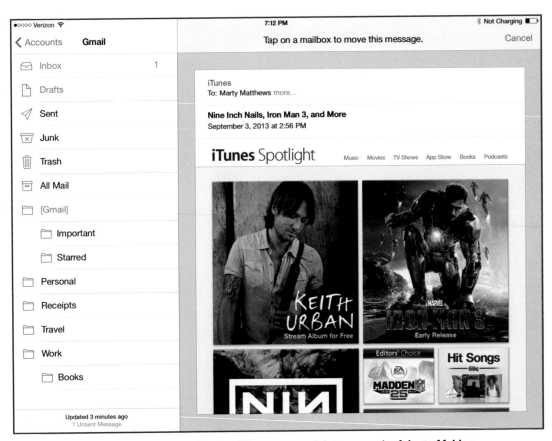

Figure 4-16: The basic tenet of organizing mail is to separate it into a meaningful set of folders.

Archive, Delete, and Recover Messages

You may have noticed that in Gmail in the icons on the top-right area there is an archive box , while in other mail providers there is a trashcan ⎕. This is because Gmail allows you to "archive" a message as well as to delete it. Archiving is an intermediate step between placing an item in a normal folder and deleting it.

- To delete or archive a message, open the message and tap either the delete or archive icon.

- To delete a message when Archive is activated, open the message, and press and hold the archive icon until the pop-up menu opens.

- To recover a message, move it to a new folder using the technique described in "Organize Messages with Folders," earlier in this chapter. (Go to Mailboxes and tap the account in the lower part of the left column to display that column's folders.) Deleted messages are in either the Trash or Deleted Messages folder; archived messages are in the All Mail folder.

- Determine whether or not to use archiving, if it is available, from the Home screen. Tap **Settings | Mail, Contacts, Calendar | *account name* | Account | Advanced | Archive Mailbox** or **Deleted Mailbox**.

✓ QuickFacts

Delete, Move, and Mark Several Messages at Once

Mail has the means to delete, move, and mark a number of messages at one time.

1. Open the Inbox containing the messages you want to delete, move, or mark.

2. Tap **Edit** in the upper-right corner of the left pane.

3. Tap the messages you want to work on. A white checkmark will appear in a blue dot on the messages headers on the left that are selected, and a copy of the message itself will appear in a stack in the center of the reading pane on the right, as shown in Figure 4-17.

4. Tap the command button at the bottom of the left pane for the action you want to carry out:

   - If you tap **Trash**, the selected items go into the Trash folder for that account.

   - If you tap **Move**, the list of folders for that Mail account will open and you can tap where you want the messages to move to.

   - If you tap **Mark**, a menu pops up giving you the choice to flag the message, mark it as unread, or move it to the Junk folder, if such a folder exists.

NOTE If the Mail account in which you want to delete, move, or mark messages has the archive ability and it is activated, then the Trash button will be replaced with an Archive button. When you use that button, the messages will be moved to the All Mail folder. If you tap **Edit** in an All Mail folder and tap **Delete**, the messages will go into the Trash folder.

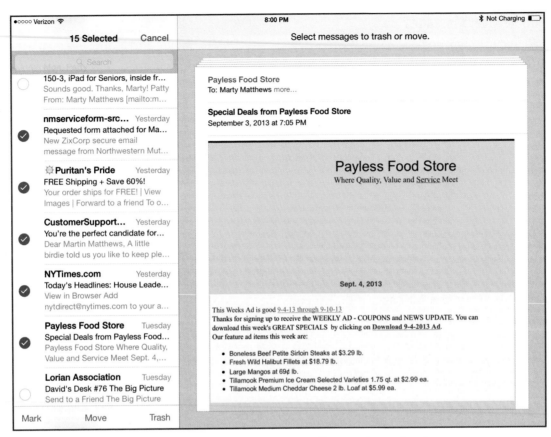

Figure 4-17: If you get a lot of spam, Mail's ability to delete it all at once is very handy.

Flag and Mark Individual Messages

You can also flag and mark as unread individual messages, which you saw how to do for a number of messages in the preceding QuickFacts.

From an account's Inbox, tap the message you want to flag or mark, tap the **Flag** icon in the

upper-right area of the right pane, and tap **Flag**, **Mark As Unread**, **Move To Junk** as you desire.

Search Messages

As the number of messages you have in various mailboxes begins to stack up, it may become difficult to find a message that you want to look at. You can use Mail's Search feature for that purpose.

1. Open the Mail account and folder that you want to search.

2. Tap in the search text box near the top of the left pane. The search text box will move to the very top of the panes.

3. Type the keywords to search on. As you type, Mail will begin to select messages that match what you're typing and display their headers in the left pane.

4. Tap **Edit**, now in the bottom-right area, to select and then, en masse, delete, move, or mark the messages.

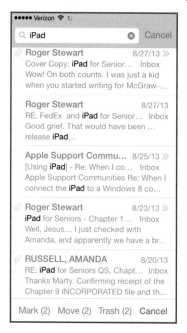

 TIP You can search the Inboxes of all of your mail accounts at one time by going to the list of all of your mailboxes, tapping **All Inboxes**, and beginning the search.

Use Web Mail

Web mail enables you to send and receive email over the Internet using a browser, such as Safari, instead of an email program, such as Mail. There are a number of web mail programs, such as Outlook (outlook.com), Yahoo! Mail (mail.yahoo.com), and Google's Gmail (gmail.com). So long as you have access to the Internet, you can sign up for, or may already be signed up for, one or more of these services. The basic features (simple sending and receiving of email) are generally free. For example, to use Outlook.com:

 NOTE Many web mail accounts, including Gmail, Yahoo!, and Outlook, can be used in Mail as well as with a browser. The benefit of web mail is that if you are somewhere without your iPad, you can borrow any computer connected to the Internet and check your mail.

1. Open Safari. In the address box, type <u>outlook.com</u> and press **Go**. Outlook's Sign In page will open. If you already have an account, enter your email address and password, tap **Sign In**, and skip to Step 3. Otherwise, tap **Sign Up Now**.

 NOTE If you already have a Microsoft, Hotmail, Windows Live, or SkyDrive account, you can use your ID and password for that with Outlook.

2. Fill out the sign-up form that is presented to you. When you have completed it, you will be automatically signed in.

3. The Outlook.com page will open and display your mail, as shown in Figure 4-18.

4. Tap a message to open and read it.

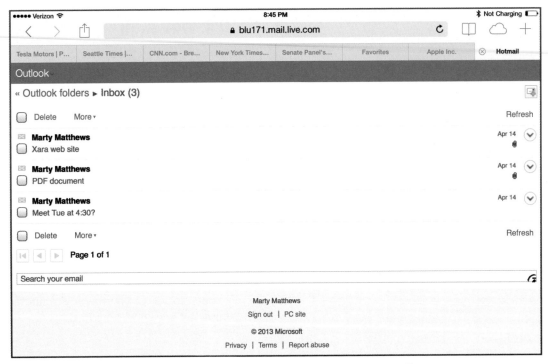

●●●●● Verizon 🛜   8:45 PM   ❊ Not Charging ▭

< > ⬆️   🔒 blu171.mail.live.com   ↻ ▯ ☁ +

| Tesla Motors | P... | Seattle Times |... | CNN.com - Bre... | New York Times... | Senate Panel's... | Favorites | Apple Inc. | ⊗ | **Hotmail** |

Outlook

« Outlook folders ► Inbox (3)   ⬚

☐ Delete   More ▾   Refresh

✉ **Marty Matthews**   Apr 14 ⌄
☐ Xara web site   📎

✉ **Marty Matthews**   Apr 14 ⌄
☐ PDF document   📎

✉ **Marty Matthews**   Apr 14 ⌄
☐ Meet Tue at 4:30?

☐ Delete   More ▾   Refresh

⏮ ◀ ▶   **Page 1 of 1**

| Search your email   🔄 |

Marty Matthews

Sign out | PC site

© 2013 Microsoft

Privacy | Terms | Report abuse

Figure 4-18: Web mail accounts are a quick and free way to get one or more email accounts.

5. Tap the **New** icon on the top-right corner to write an email message. Enter the To address, a subject, and the message. When you are done, tap **Send**.

6. When you are finished with Outlook.com, close Safari.

 TIP A way to quickly open Outlook.com is to add it to your Bookmarks or Bookmarks bar. See the discussion in Chapter 3 to do this.

USE CONTACTS

Contacts, shown in Figure 4-19, allows you to collect email addresses, phone numbers, and other information about the people and organizations with whom you correspond or otherwise interact.

▷▷ Add New Contacts

You can add contacts or, in some cases, have contacts automatically added to iPad's Contacts directly by typing them in (see "Add Contacts Directly" later in this chapter) or in several other ways, including from:

- **iCloud** Transferred from other iOS devices (iPhone, iPod, and iPad) automatically using Wi-Fi if they are synched with iCloud and you have chosen to use iCloud as described in Chapter 1. On your iPad, tap **Settings | iCloud | Contacts | On**.

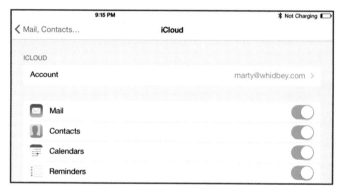

- **iTunes** Transferred from a Windows or Mac computer if iTunes is installed on the computer and synched with the iPad, as described in Chapter 1. In iTunes on the computer with the iPad connected to it, select your iPad in the left pane, select **Info** in the top command bar, and click **Sync Contacts**. You will be told your contacts are being synced, as you see in Figure 4-20.

> **NOTE** It is possible to get duplicate contacts when using both iTunes and iCloud, but it is possible to use both, with iTunes getting contacts from your computer, while iCloud is getting them from other iOS devices.

- **Facebook** Transferred from Facebook creating a Contacts group of your Facebook friends. On your iPad, tap **Settings | Facebook | Contacts | On**.

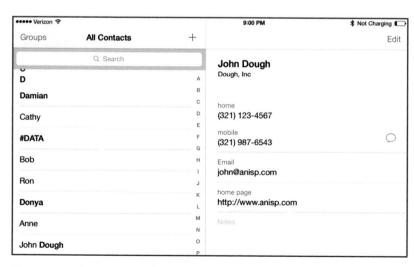

Figure 4-19: Contacts provides a way to collect the people or organizations you correspond with across various accounts.

Figure 4-20: iTunes is a good conduit between email apps on your computer and iPad, most of which are not in iCloud.

- **Exchange** Transferred from a Microsoft Exchange Global Address List. On your iPad, tap **Settings | Mail, Contacts, Calendars | Exchange** account **| Contacts | On**.
- **Mail** and **Safari** Picked up from incoming email or from a website as described in the next section.

Pick Up Contacts from Mail and Webpages

When you get a piece of email with a phone number, email address, or snail-mail address, all you need to do is touch and

hold for a moment on the number or address and a menu will pop up, allowing you to add it to Contacts, among other options.

Similarly, when you are browsing through websites and find an email address, phone number, or mailing address, touch and

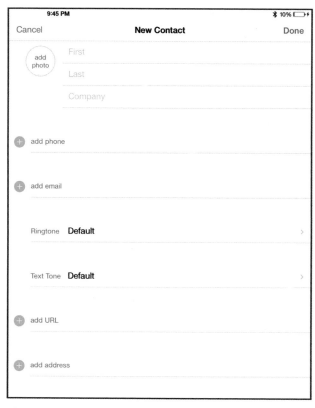

Figure 4-21: Contacts allows you to store a lot of information about an individual.

hold on it for a moment to get a pop-up menu you can use to save it to Contacts.

Add Contacts Directly

You can, of course, directly add individuals to Contacts one at a time.

1. Open **Contacts** and tap the **Add** symbol at the top right of the All Contacts on the left. The New Contact page opens as shown in Figure 4-21.

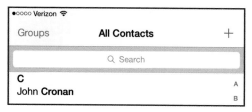

2. Enter as much of the information as you have or want. For email, you need at least an email address and a name. If you have additional information, such as another email address, a phone number, or a home address for the contact, tap the text boxes for those items and fill in the desired information.

3. When you are done, tap **Done** in the upper-right corner to close the New Contact page.

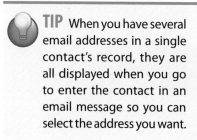
TIP When you have several email addresses in a single contact's record, they are all displayed when you go to enter the contact in an email message so you can select the address you want.

⊳⊳ Use Contacts

Contacts is an electronic address book that you can easily carry with you and reference often. It is very intuitive and easy to use.

Enter Contacts

1. Open a new email message page as described earlier in this chapter. In the To text field, begin to type a name. A Contacts list will pop up suggesting possible contacts for you to use.

2. Tap the contact you want to use. To get more information about the contact, double-tap on it to have an information box pop up.

Change and Link Contacts

1. Open Contacts, locate the contact you want to change, and tap **Edit** [Edit] in the upper-right corner of the contact page. A page similar to the one for a new contact will open filled in with the contact's existing information.

2. Make changes to any of the fields or add information to fields not already used.

3. If you want to link a contact with another contact, meaning that if you email one, you will also email the other, scroll down to the bottom and tap **Link Contacts** 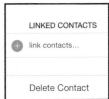. Go through the All Contacts list to locate the other party. When you find her or him, tap the name and tap **Link**.

4. When you are done with editing and linking, tap **Done** [Done] in the upper-right area.

Delete Contacts

To delete an entire contact entry, edit the contact as just discussed, then scroll to the bottom of the page, and tap **Delete Contact.**

⊳⊳ Review Contacts Settings

The settings relating to Contacts are rather modest. Tap **Settings | Mail, Contacts, Calendars** and scroll down to Contacts. You have these settings available:

- **Sort Order**   Specifies the order in which the entries in your contact list are displayed.
- **Display Order**   Specifies how entries are shown in the list.
- **Short Name**   Specifies whether a short name is used and how it is constructed.

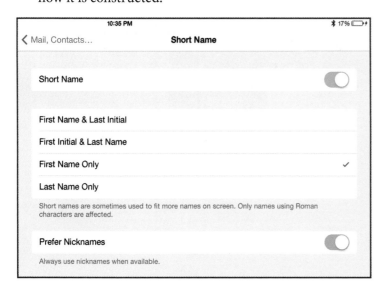

- **My Info**   Specifies the owner of or the one responsible for the list.
- **Default Account**   Specifies the mail account that will be associated with contacts that aren't associated with any other mail account.

USE MESSAGES

Messages allows you to send and receive text messages using email address or cellular service with any device, phone, or tablet that will receive them. It will also send and receive messages using Apple's iMessage instant messaging (IM or *chat*) with other iPhone, iPod, iPad, and Mac (Mountain Lion

and later) users who are online at the same time as you. You can include photos and videos.

▷▷ Start and Use Messages

Messages, by default, is installed on the Home screen. The use of iMessage requires your Apple ID, which you must have to use your iPad. As a result of that, you will automatically be signed in when you open Messages.

1. From the Home screen, tap **Messages**. Messages will open.
2. If you see a To text box, tap in it and begin to type a name. If you don't see the To box, tap the **New Message** icon ✐ in the upper-right area of the left pane. If you want to search for a name, tap the **Add A Contact** icon ⊕ on the far right to open the list of your contacts. Scroll down and tap the contact you want to chat with.
3. Tap the text tray at the bottom of the right pane, type your message, and tap **Send**.

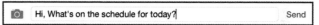

4. If you have a photo that you want in the message, you can attach it by tapping the **Photo** icon and tapping either **Take Photo Or Video** or **Choose Existing**. In the latter case, select the photo, tap **Use**, and tap **Send**. In the former case, select the front or back camera, tap the shutter release, and then, if you are happy with the photo or video, tap **Use**.

5. Continue the conversation as your correspondent replies, as shown in Figure 4-22.

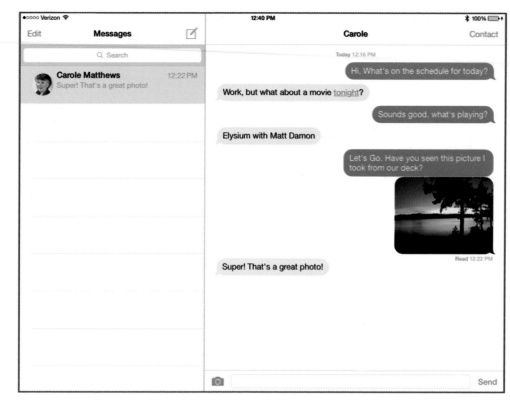

Figure 4-22: Messages provides a trail of a conversation that can be useful.

▷▷ Review Messages Settings

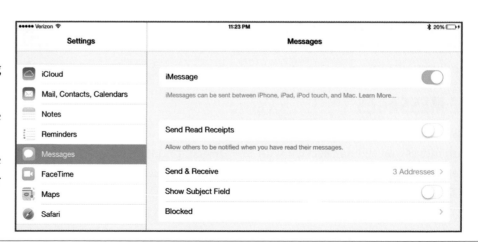

The Messages settings, opened by tapping **Settings | Messages**, provide these options:

- **iMessage** Allows you to turn iMessage on and off.

- **Send Read Receipts** Provides a notice to the sender when you have read their message.

- **Send & Receive**   Lets you set the addresses and phone number where you can be sent messages and from which you can send messages.

- **Show Subject Field**   Allows you to display the Subject field or not.

- **Blocked**   Allows you to open your Contacts and select people who you do not want to receive messages or FaceTime calls from.

Chapter 5

Scheduling with Calendar, Reminders, and Notifications

Unfortunately, our lives are too often controlled by the events that surround us, from meetings and special occasions, to appointments and invitations. The best we can do is to try and keep track of what is going on. The iPad provides three apps, Calendar, Reminders, and Notifications, to help you do that. This chapter provides a review of all three, showing you how to set them up, handle their settings, and use them in several circumstances.

SET UP AND USE CALENDAR

The primary purpose of a calendar, of course, is to keep track of upcoming events, such as weddings, birthdays, meetings, and appointments. You can also note date-related objectives, such as projects to be completed (book deadlines in my case), and goals to be accomplished, such as weight loss by a certain date. Whatever the purpose, Calendar has tools to work with it and several views to look at it.

▷ Get Familiar with Calendar

The iPad Calendar has implemented on the screen four views of calendar entries and given you easy ways to navigate among them. Open Calendar by tapping its icon on the Home screen. One of Calendar's four views will appear. Tap **Day** at the top of the screen if the Day view isn't already selected. This will give

us a common starting point to talk from, as you see in Figure 5-1.

Review Calendar Controls

Calendar has controls across the top and bottom of its screen, as shown in Figure 5-1. These include:

- **Views** provides four views of the calendar, as described in the next section.

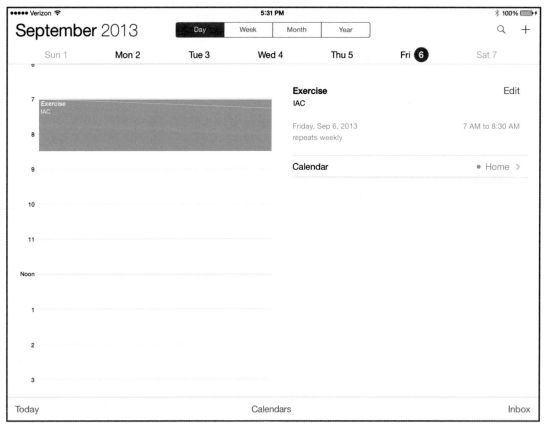

Figure 5-1: Day view gives you the most detailed view of your schedule.

- **Search** opens a summary of near-term events and a search text box where you can enter keywords on which to search Calendar.

- **Add Event** [+] opens the Add Event dialog box, with which you enter the information about events into the calendar.
- **Date Selector**, which can be scrolled in either direction, allows you to select a date to view. See "Select a Date" later in this chapter.

- **Today** displays the current day.
- **Calendars** opens a list of the various calendars that you have available. From this list, you can choose which you want to display, if not all of them. Also, by tapping one of the calendars, you can choose which color you want to represent that calendar.

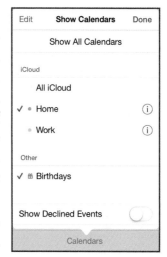

- **Inbox** displays the invitations you have received and lets you reply by accepting, declining, or returning "Maybe."

Explore Calendar Views

Take a look at each of the four views:

- **Day** view provides a time-of-day display on the left and the detail for a selected event on the right, as you saw earlier in Figure 5-1. The time-of-day view is similar to the day books that were popular before computers.
- **Week** view provides the same information as you saw on the left side of the Day view, but for seven days at one time, as shown in Figure 5-2.
- **Month** view provides the typical paper-based wall calendar view with 35 days on it (see Figure 5-3). Each event in this case gets only a single short line.

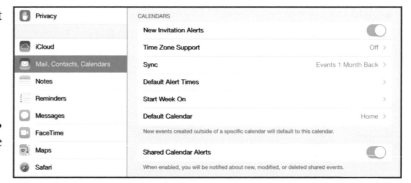

Figure 5-2: *Week view is a good way to plan for a new week.*

Year view displays 12 months on one screen with the current day marked with a red dot, as you can see in Figure 5-4.

All of the views have value to varying degrees. Try them all.

Change Calendar Settings

The calendar settings, opened by tapping **Settings | Mail, Contacts, Calendars** and scrolling down to the bottom of the right-hand pane, include:

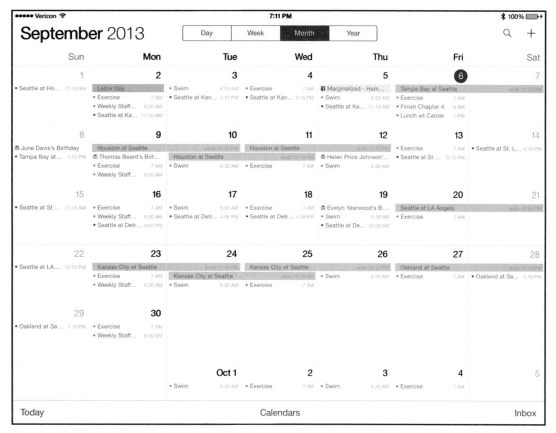

Figure 5-3: Month view consolidates a lot of information in a small space.

- **New Invitation Alerts**, if on, triggers an alert when an invitation is received.

- **Time Zone Support** allows you to associate a time zone with a calendar and thereby display events in that calendar in the event's time zone. This is useful when you travel so you can keep in mind the local time. You can turn time zone support on or off and select the default time zone to use.

- **Sync** lets you automatically sync historical as well as future events. Tapping this option allows you to select among several time periods.

- **Default Alert Times** determines when alerts are created for birthdays, events, and all-day events. For each you have a choice of when the alert is posted and sounded, from the time of the event to one week before the event.

- **Start Week On** lets you specify which day of the week is on the left of a weekly calendar.

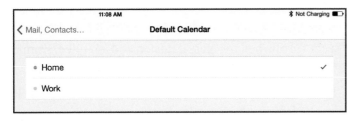

Figure 5-4: Year view primarily allows you to select the month in which you want to work.

- **Default Calendar** lets you specify which calendar to use with events that are created outside of Calendar.

- **Shared Calendar Alerts**, if on, notifies you when changes are made to events that are shared with others.

▷▷ Use Calendar

The iPad's Calendar app is made for active use as you are on the go. It will sync the entries you have from your desktop or laptop computer or such online calendar resources as Facebook and Google Calendar. It is also a good resource for directly entering and managing events as you go along.

Choose Your Calendar

Depending on your email accounts and what you have on desktop and/or laptop computers, you may have a number of calendars, as you can see from my calendar list shown earlier. To start, I'd recommend that you work with only one. Later in this chapter we'll come back and look at how to handle multiple calendars.

If you have multiple calendars, begin by turning off all but one and make sure it is set as your default. You can then use it for the next several sections until we get to the discussion of multiple calendars.

1. From the Home screen, tap **Calendar** and then tap **Calendars** in the bottom-middle area. You will see the list of your calendars.

2. Choose which calendar will be your primary one. By default, the iPad uses your "Home" calendar for this purpose.

3. If you have other calendars turned on (they have a checkmark beside them), tap all but your primary calendar to turn them off.

4. Make sure your chosen calendar is set as the default by pressing the **Home** button and tapping **Settings | Mail, Contacts, Calendars**.

5. Scroll down until you see the Calendar settings and then tap **Default Calendar** to open the list of your calendars.

6. Tap the calendar you want to be the default, where all events will be placed that are entered outside of Calendar.

Select a Date

Calendar events, of course, are on a certain date or series of dates, and so the first task in using Calendar is to select a date. You have several options, depending on where you start from.

- If you are seeking a date within a few days of the date currently displayed, swipe the Date Selector from right to left to select a future date, or from left to right to select a date prior to the current date.

- When in Day view, select a day by tapping that date in the Date Selector displayed in the upper part of the page.

- To select the current date, tap **Today** on the bottom-left area of the screen.

NOTE In Month view you can select an event within a day, but not the day itself. In Year view you can select a month, but not a day or week.

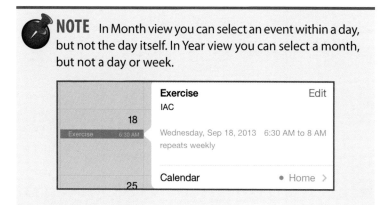

Add Calendar Events

To add events and their specifics:

1. If the Home screen is not already displayed, press the **Home** button to display it.

2. Tap **Calendar** and select the date of the event as described in the previous section.

3. Tap **Add Event** in the top-right corner of the screen to open the Add Event dialog box.

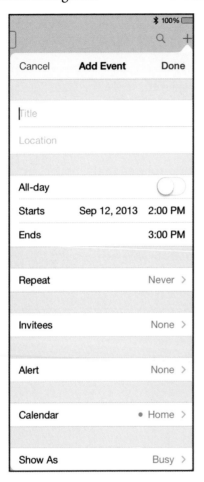

4. Type the title of the event, tap in the **Location** text box, and type the location.

5. If it is an all-day event (or close enough to call it that), tap the **On/Off** button for that.

6. Tap the time block to open the Start & End dialog box. Move your finger up and down on the date to select it and then do the same thing with the hour, minutes, and AM/PM to select the start time.

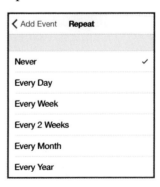

7. Tap the **Ends** time and select the appropriate time.

8. If you have Time Zone Support turned on in the Calendars settings (see "Change Calendar Settings" earlier in this chapter), change the Time Zone selection, if needed, and tap **Done**.

9. If the event will happen periodically, tap **Repeat**, and tap the period of repetition.

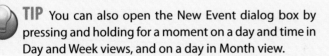

TIP You can also open the New Event dialog box by pressing and holding for a moment on a day and time in Day and Week views, and on a day in Month view.

10. If you want to invite people to the event, tap **Invitees**.

    a. Begin typing a name in your Contacts list. When the name that you want is displayed, tap that name.

b. To add more invitees, tap the **Add** icon (the plus sign) to open your All Contacts list, and tap the person you want to invite. Repeat this for as many people as you want to invite.

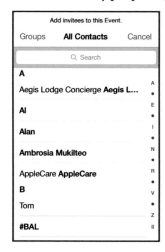

c. When you are finished adding invitees, tap **Add Event** to return there.

11. Tap **Alert** and tap when you want the alert. Repeat this for the second alert if desired.

12. Tap **Calendar** if you want this event listed on a calendar other than the default, tap the calendar (see "Work with Multiple Calendars" later in this chapter), and tap **Add Event** to return there, if necessary.

13. The default is to show your time as being "Busy" when you have an event. This is for shared calendars so others will not schedule events for you. If you want to change from "Busy" to "Free," tap **Show As** and tap **Free**.

14. If desired, you may type in a uniform resource locator, or URL (a web address), and notes for the event. When you are ready, tap **Done**.

TIP For the URL and notes sections of a new event, you can copy and paste information from a website that might be of interest to the people you are inviting to an event.

Change Calendar Events

Changing an event is very easy.

1. With Calendar open on the screen, select the date of the event, as described earlier in this chapter.

2. In Day, Week, or Month view, tap the event and tap **Edit** to open the Edit dialog box as shown in Figure 5-5.

3. In the Edit dialog box, tap the field you want to change and make the desired changes. See "Add Calendar Events" earlier in this chapter for field-by-field considerations.

4. When you have made the changes that you want, tap **Done**.

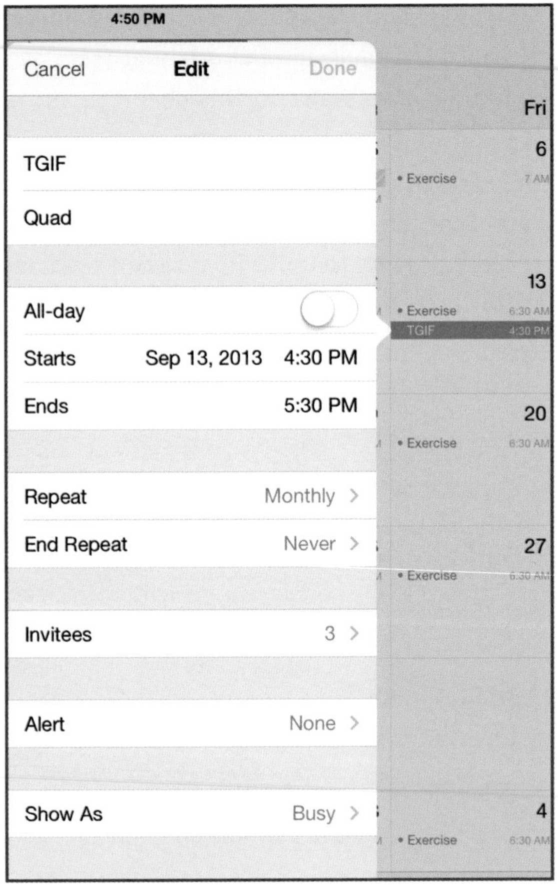

Figure 5-5: *The Edit dialog box is almost identical to the Add Event dialog box.*

Delete Calendar Events

Deleting events is even easier.

1. Follow Steps 1 and 2 in "Change Calendar Events" immediately preceding this section.

2. In the Edit dialog box, scroll to the bottom and tap **Delete Event**. Tap **Delete Event** a second time to confirm it.

If the event is repeated, you will have a choice of deleting the current event only or this and all future repetitions of the event.

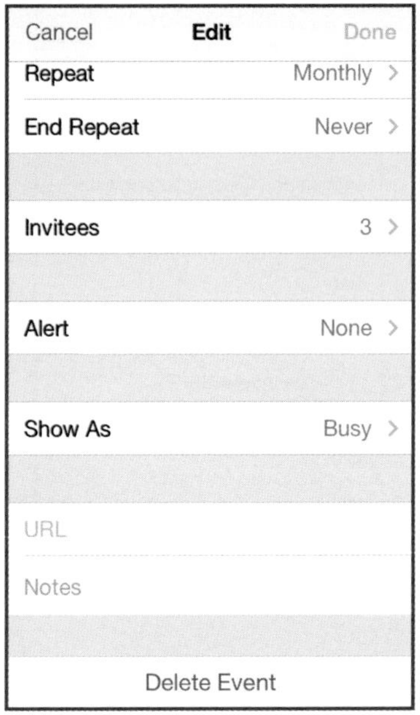

⊳⊳ Work with Multiple Calendars

As you begin to use Calendar, you may find that you are getting events from several sources that you would like to keep on different calendars so you can manage them as a group. Also, you probably want to look at all your calendar events together periodically on one calendar display. The iPad provides ways to do both of those.

When you start up your iPad for the first time after setting it up and syncing to iCloud, you will see that, by default, Calendar with iCloud starts out with three independent calendars labeled "Home," "Work," and "Birthdays." You can, therefore, immediately place events on more than one calendar.

Add Events to a Different Calendar

To add events to one of several calendars, you can use one of three techniques:

- While entering a new event in the Add Event dialog box, tap **Calendar**, and then tap the calendar you want to use.

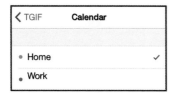

- To add a number of events to a single calendar—for example, your Work calendar—turn off all other calendars so that when you open the Add Event dialog box, the default is your Work calendar.

- If you are going to be working primarily with one calendar, but don't want to turn off other calendars, you can change the default calendar in Settings. From the Home screen, tap **Settings | Mail, Contacts, Calendars | Default Calendar** and then tap the calendar you want to be the default.

Figure 5-6: The colors of different calendars help you distinguish which one an event belongs to.

Show Several Calendars Together

With just one calendar, there is no problem finding an event you want to look at, but as soon as you add another calendar, you have to ask the question, "Which calendar do I look at?" The answer, of course, is to superimpose one calendar on the other so you can see them both at the same time. Calendar allows you to do this by simply turning on the calendars that you want to display.

1. With Calendar open on your iPad, tap **Calendars**.

2. Tap the calendars in the Show Calendars dialog box that you want to be displayed, as you can see in Figure 5-6.

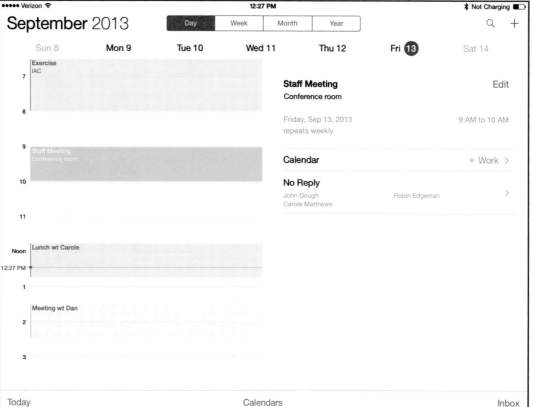

Add Another Calendar

The Calendar app has two types of calendars: those tied to mail accounts, like Gmail, Outlook, and iCloud, and those created within Calendar. You can, therefore, add calendars from either source. To add a calendar within Calendar and not connected with a mail account:

1. From within Calendar, tap **Calendars** to open the Show Calendars dialog box.

2. Tap **Edit** in the upper-right corner, and then tap **Add Calendar**.

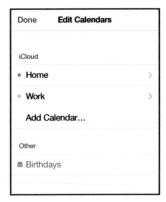

3. In the Add Calendar dialog box that opens, type the name of the new calendar and tap the color that you want to associate with that calendar.

4. When you are ready, tap **Done**.

To add a calendar from a mail account:

1. Press **Home** to return to the Home screen.

2. Tap **Settings | Mail, Contacts, Calendars** and tap the mail account whose calendar you want to add. The mail accounts settings will open. Tap the Calendars' **On/Off** button on the right to turn it on (not all mail servers have calendar services).

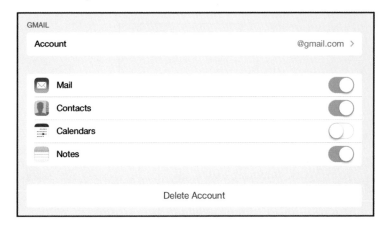

3. Press **Home** and tap **Calendar** to return there and eventually see your mail calendar(s).

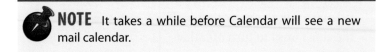

NOTE It takes a while before Calendar will see a new mail calendar.

Delete a Calendar

As in adding calendars, you can delete them from either mail accounts or from Calendar itself. You can delete a mail account–related calendar by, in essence, turning it off.

1. From the Home screen, tap **Settings | Mail, Contacts, Calendars**.

2. Under Accounts on the right, tap the account with an associated calendar that you want to turn off (those with a calendar will say "Calendars").

3. In the mail account details, tap the **On/Off** button to turn it off.

4. Tap **Delete** to confirm that is what you want to do, and tap **Done**.

To delete a calendar created within Calendar:

1. From the Home screen, tap **Calendar | Calendars** in the bottom middle.

2. Tap the right end (the "i" in a circle) of the calendar that you want to delete to open the Edit Calendar dialog box. You can alternatively tap **Edit** and tap the calendar that you want to delete.

3. Scroll to the bottom of the dialog box, tap **Delete Calendar**, and then tap **Delete Calendar** again to confirm the deletion.

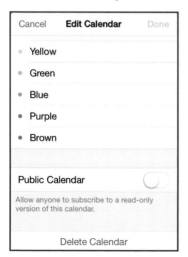

 TIP Facebook's calendar is deleted like a mail account's calendar. Tap **Settings | Facebook | Calendar** to turn a Facebook calendar off if it is on, and tap **Contacts** off to remove Facebook Birthdays.

Add an Online Calendar

There are a number of calendars on the Internet that you can add to and display in your Calendar app on your iPad. Here is an example of how this works. I am a fan of the Seattle Mariners baseball team (yes, very long suffering!) and I want to keep track of their schedule on my iPad in Calendar. The schedules that can be used with Calendar on the iPad must conform to Apple's iCalendar (files with an .ics extension) standards and can be used with the Mac's iCal calendar, the Google and Yahoo! calendars, and the iPad's calendar. To add the Mariners' calendar:

 NOTE In addition to iCal calendars, you can add calendars from Microsoft Outlook and Microsoft Exchange, as well as Google and Yahoo! Calendars.

1. From the Home screen, tap **Safari**. In the address box, type the URL for the organization whose calendar you want. In my case, I type seattle.mariners.mlb.com, tap **Go,** and tap **Schedule** in the top menu bar (I could also have done a Google search on "Seattle Mariners schedule").

2. One of the choices on the Mariners' website is "Downloadable Schedule," which I tap. This opens the page shown in Figure 5-7.

Figure 5-7: Most schedules on the Internet give you some means to download the schedule in the form that can generate an iPad calendar.

3. There is a link to "Download iCal" and instructions for the iPhone, which also work for the iPad. The easy solution is to tap **Download iCal**. A list of calendar entries appears.

4. Tap **Add All** Add All . When you do that, iPad's Calendar opens the Choose Calendar dialog box.

NOTE If you are adding a calendar that was created in Google (you must have a Gmail account), you click the plus sign at the bottom right to add the calendar to your calendars. This brings up a dialog box that asks if you want to add this calendar and, if you do, adds it to your Gmail calendar, but not immediately to your iPad calendars. In the iPad Calendar you must have Gmail turned on as one of the calendars you can view, and then, after a bit, you will see the entries from the new calendar.

5. Choose the calendar you want to use. Because of the quantity of calendar entries in the Mariners' calendar, I tap **New Calendar** to create a separate calendar for the Mariners.

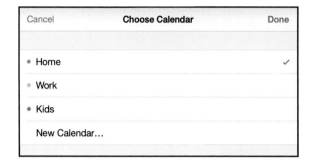

6. Type the name for the calendar; choose its color, tap **Done**, and then tap **Done** twice more. Close Safari and open Calendar.

7. Close all other calendars, leaving only your new one you just added to Calendar, as you can see in Figure 5-8.

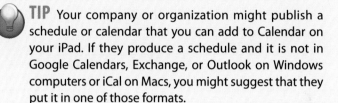

TIP Your company or organization might publish a schedule or calendar that you can add to Calendar on your iPad. If they produce a schedule and it is not in Google Calendars, Exchange, or Outlook on Windows computers or iCal on Macs, you might suggest that they put it in one of those formats.

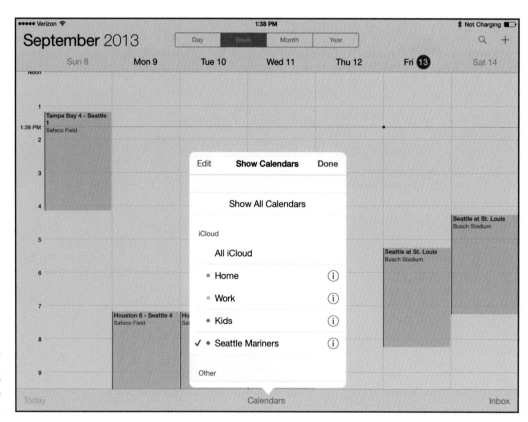

Figure 5-8: For organizations that are important to you, getting their complete schedule can be a real benefit.

Subscribe to iCalShare Calendars

One site that has a number of public calendars that you can subscribe to is iCalShare. To look at iCalShare and subscribe to a calendar:

1. From the Home screen, tap **Safari**. In the address box, type icalshare.com and tap **Go**. The iCalShare home page is displayed as shown in Figure 5-9.

2. Review the calendars on the Home page, then tap the options across the top (Categories, Calendars, Popular, and so on) and review the calendars. I find it useful to have the U.S. holidays on my calendar, so I can either tap **US Holidays** in the bottom center of the home page or tap **Popular** and review several alternatives.

3. When you find a calendar that you want to subscribe to, tap the calendar and then tap **Subscribe To Calendar**. Finally, tap **Subscribe**.

4. When you do that, your new calendar's events are added to Calendar on your iPad. Tap **View Events** to see them.

5. Tap Calendars in the bottom-center area to see how your subscribed-to calendar is listed.

Handle Invitations

Earlier in this chapter you saw how you can add invitations to a new calendar event. When you do that, an email invitation is sent to the invitee. The mailed invitation has three links the recipient can click or tap to accept, decline, or maybe accept the invitation.

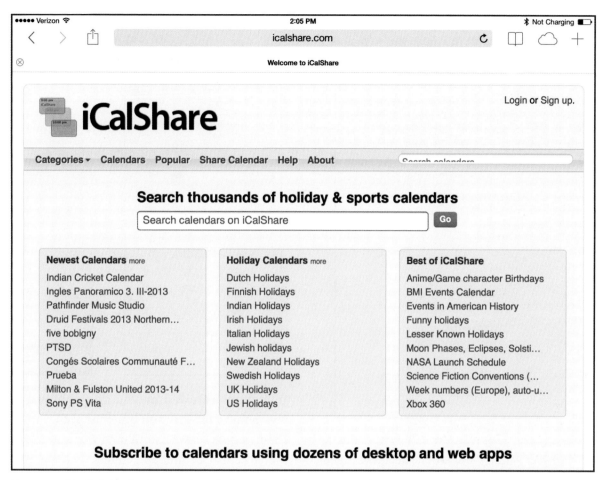

Figure 5-9: iPad's Calendar does not have holidays listed on it, as some other calendars do, but they are available on iCalShare.

In the email (on top in Windows) there is an attachment that you can drag or double-click to add the date either Outlook's Calendar in Windows (shown next) or iCal's Calendar in a Mac.

When the invitation is accepted or rejected, iCloud opens in the recipient's default browser acknowledging the decision. Again there is a link that, if you click or tap it, will add the event to your calendar app.

On the iPhone in Mail, tap an invitation in the Inbox, tap its detail date in blue, and tap **Show In Calendar** to open Calendar and display the event.

Invitations received by you on your iPad work and look very similar to what you have just seen. In Mail you will see an invitation that is similar to the one shown earlier with the Accept, Decline, and Maybe buttons you can tap. The attachment at the bottom generates a calendar event that you can see both by tapping the attachment (see Figure 5-10) and on the calendar.

⟫ Share a Calendar

If several people are working together, sharing a project, have a family in common, or are in an organization together, it can be worthwhile sharing a calendar to better coordinate what they are doing. iPad's Calendar provides two tools to facilitate this:

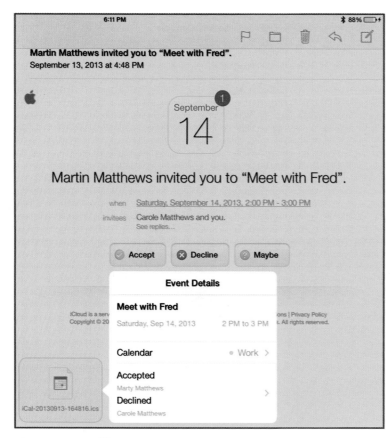

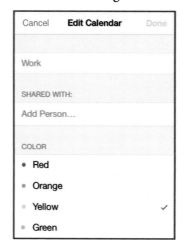

Figure 5-10: *Email invitations you receive on your iPad contain an attachment that generates a calendar event.*

fully sharing with one, or a couple of other people, a calendar that all can change; and publishing a public calendar that others can subscribe to, but only you can change.

Share a Common Calendar

To create a common calendar that two or more people can share with equal ability to add and change events:

1. From the Home screen, tap **Calendar**. Tap **Calendars** and tap the right arrow on the calendar you want to share. This opens the Edit Calendar dialog box.

2. Under Shared With, tap **Add Person** and begin typing the name of the person in your address book with whom you want to share this calendar. The person and their email address should pop up. Tap the person to select them.

3. If you want to share with another person, either begin typing a name or tap the plus sign on the right and repeat Step 2.

4. When you have added all the people you want, tap **Add** to be shown the Edit Calendar dialog box. Here you can tap **View & Edit** to disallow the other person from editing the calendar or making and changing events.

5. Tap **Edit Calendar | Done** when you are ready. Upon returning to the Show Calendars dialog box, you will see that the calendar you chose to share will now have "Shared With…" under the name of the calendar.

The recipient gets an email notification that you want to share a calendar with them. They need to tap **Join Calendar** and sign in to iCloud. You are then told that they have joined the offered Calendar.

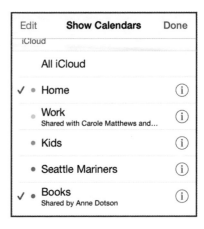

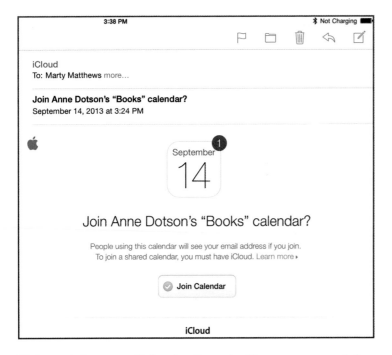

The originator will get a notice that the recipient has accepted the invitation.

If the recipient taps **Calendar** from the Home screen and then taps **Calendars** they should see the newly shared calendar in the list of calendars.

On a PC, the recipient gets an invitation that looks like other invitations and is able to access the calendar through a link in the invitation to an iCloud PC web app, shown in Figure 5-11. On a Mac, the recipient gets an invitation and then can look at the calendar in iCal.

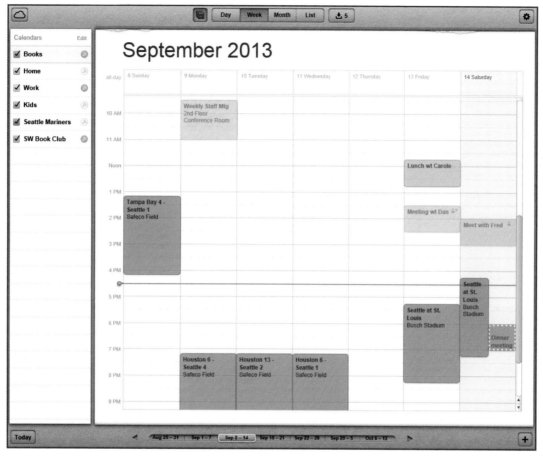

Figure 5-11: A person on a PC can share a calendar created on an iPad using an iCloud app.

Publish a Public Calendar

If you are responsible for a larger public group, such as a Boy or Girl Scout troop, a Little League team, or a book club, and you want to make available a calendar for that organization, you can make a calendar a public calendar that allows anyone to subscribe to it and peruse it. They will not be able to change or write to that calendar. To publicly share a calendar:

1. In Calendar, tap **Calendars** and tap on the right (the "i" in a circle) of the calendar that you want to make public.

2. In Edit Calendar, tap the **On/Off** button opposite Public Calendar to turn it on. This will allow anyone to subscribe to a read-only version of the calendar.

3. After turning on the public calendar, a new option appears: Share Link. Tap this.

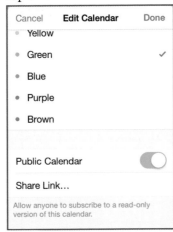

4. You are allowed to send the Internet link (URL) for your public calendar to anyone you want using AirDrop, email, text messaging, or copying it to a document, website, or blog. Tap the option you want to use. For example, tap **Mail**, fill in the addressees, as you see in Figure 5-12, and tap **Send**.

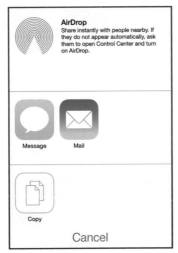

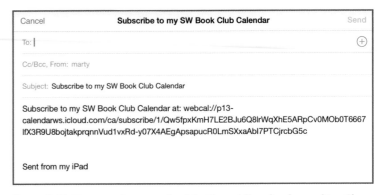

Figure 5-12: **You can always go back to the public calendar and tap Share Link to send it to additional people.**

5. When you are done, tap **Cancel**.

The recipient initially gets an email invitation, which, when they open it, gives them a very long Internet link. When they tap or click that link, they are asked if they want to subscribe to the public calendar. If they tap or click **Subscribe**, they are told that the calendar has been added, and they can tap or click **View Events** to see it.

WORK WITH REMINDERS

Reminders is for making lists, such as to-do lists, shopping lists, and lists of steps to complete a project, as shown in Figure 5-13. Reminders may be date- and time-sensitive and can be marked as completed. They can also remind you that an item has not been completed and can be assigned a priority. Lists can be by date or by list, several of which have been created for you, but you can create as many more as you like. You can sync lists with iCloud and several other products, such as Hotmail's Calendar. If you add a date and time to an item on a list, the item will appear on both the Scheduled and Reminders lists as well as the original list on which you added it.

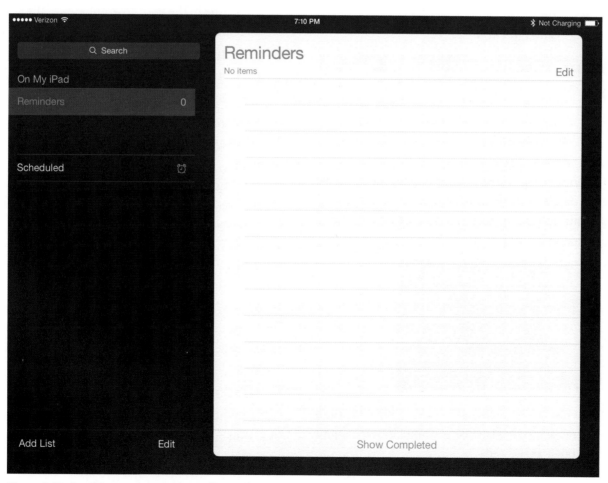

Figure 5-13: Anything you can put into a list can be entered into Reminders.

▷▷ Set Up Reminders

Reminders is very simple. The only setup necessary is the adding, deleting, renaming, and rearranging of lists, and there is only one setting to consider. To set up Reminders:

1. From the Home screen, tap **Reminders**, which should open a page similar to what you saw in Figure 5-13.

2. Tap **Add List** in the lower-left corner, type a name for the list, pick a color, and tap **Done**.

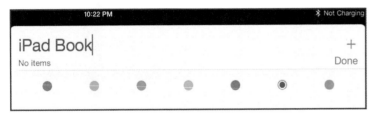

3. Tap **Edit** in bottom-right area of the left column, tap the list you want to delete, note the line changes from horizontal to vertical, and tap **Delete** twice, once on the word "Delete" and once again to confirm.

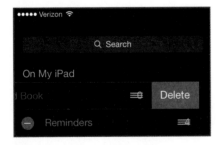

4. While in Edit mode (see Step 3), press and hold on the right end lines ("grab strips") of the list you want to move up or down, and drag it as desired.

5. Tap **Done** in the bottom-right area of the left column when you have made the changes you want.

6. Tap **Edit** in the upper-right corner. Press and hold on the list name to place the insertion point to change the list name.

7. Tap **Color** and, if desired, select a different color.

8. Tap **Done** in the upper-right corner when you have made the changes you want.

9. Review Reminders settings by pressing the **Home** button, and taping **Settings | Reminders**. Tap **Default List**, tap the list you want other apps outside of Reminders to automatically add to, and tap **Reminders**.

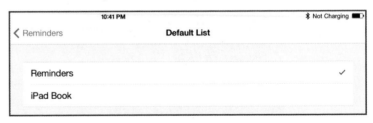

▷▷ Use Reminders

Using Reminders involves little more than entering something you want to be reminded about or that you want to be in a particular list. The first step is to make sure you have the list available in which you want to place the item. If not, go to the preceding section to create the list.

Enter Items

To enter an item once you have the list:

1. In Reminders, tap the list in which you want to enter one or more items.

2. Tap a line on the list and type the item you want on the list.

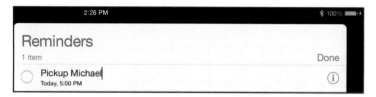

3. Tap **Done** or tap **Return** to complete the entry.

Add Details

The items you enter go in without a date or time. Other than the brief line that you typed, there is no other detail. To add detail to an item:

1. If you haven't tapped Done or Return, tap the information icon ⓘ on the right of the line. If you have tapped Done or Return, tap the item to display its information icon.

2. Tap the information icon to open the Details pane.

3. Tap the item name in the Details pane to edit or change it. Use the standard iPad editing techniques of pressing and holding on a piece of text to place the insertion point there.

4. If you don't want to be reminded, tap the **On/Off** button to change that feature.

5. If you want to change the item's date and time, tap that entry in the Details pane to open the Date/Time selector. Drag the selector's elements to select what you want.

6. If you want to have this item repeat on a periodic basis, tap **Repeat**, tap the period, and tap **Done**.

7. If you have a cellular-model iPad and want to be reminded based on your location, tap the **On/Off** button to change that feature. You will be asked if Reminders can use your current location. If you tap **OK**, you are asked if you want to be reminded when you leave or when you arrive at that location. Tap your choice.

 TIP If you want to be reminded upon leaving or arriving at a location that is different from your current location, tap the current location shown, tap the location delete icon, and either type an address or tap the plus sign and select an address from Contacts.

8. Tap a priority for the item, change the list it is on, or add notes to the item at the bottom of the Details pane.

9. When you have completed adding details to an item, tap **Done** at the top-right area of the Details pane.

Complete and/or Delete Items

To complete an item and indicate that you have finished it, tap the circle on the left of the item.

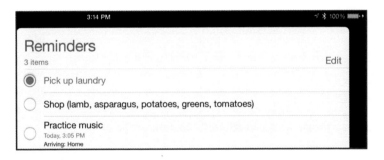

To remove an item from the list, tap **Edit** in the upper-right corner, tap the red circle on the left, and tap **Delete**. Tap **Done** when you are ready.

HANDLE NOTIFICATIONS AND ALERTS

If you have used your iPad for any time, you have probably seen alerts pop up and notify you about something. They can come from your mail, from your calendar, or from apps you have installed, especially news, sports, and investment publications, as you have seen in the previous discussion of Reminders, as well as earlier in this and previous chapters. Alerts generally have self-explanatory buttons, such as "OK," "View," "Close," and "Options," that you can tap to carry out that command.

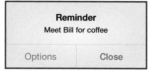

Notifications are another form of alerts, repeating their message. Not all notifications have a related alert, but all alerts have a notification. Notifications are in the form of a banner that can be pulled down from the top of the screen by swiping down, usually with a number of other notifications, as you can see in Figure 5-14. Tap a banner notification to open the related app and display the item in the notification.

⯈⯈ Set Up and Use Notifications

The most important aspect of notifications and alerts is the need to control what you get so you get what is important for you, and don't get so much it overwhelms you. Notifications and alerts are controlled in Settings.

1. From the Home screen, tap **Settings | Notification Center** to open the list of apps in the Notification Center and other settings, as shown in Figure 5-15.

2. Many, if not most, apps, when they are downloaded and set up, put themselves in the Notification Center and you get

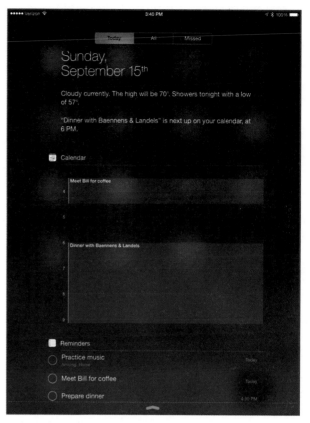

Figure 5-14: You only see notifications when you want to and swipe down from the top, but many notifications also pop up as alerts.

a haphazard list of your apps. The default is the sorting of apps manually, but that means you must do it.

a. Tap **Edit** in the upper-right corner.

b. Press and hold on the grip strip (lines) on the right of an app you want to move.

c. Drag the app where you want it in the list.

d. Repeat Steps b. and c. for all the apps you want to move.

e. Tap **Done** when you are ready.

3. Each app has several settings within the Notification Center. As an example, tap **Messages**.

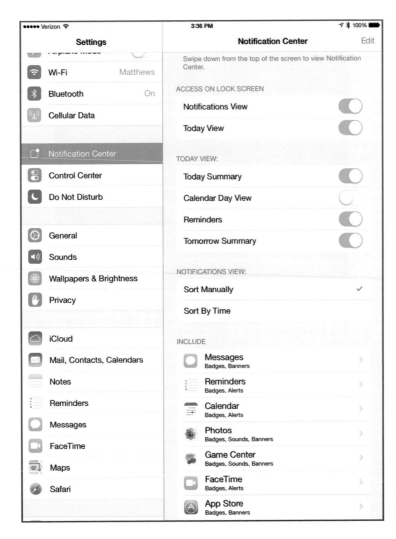

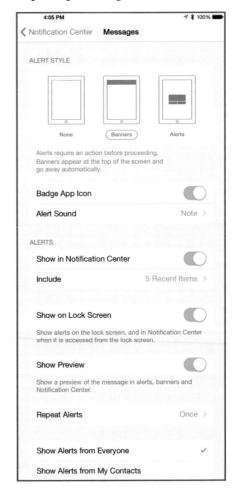

Figure 5-15: Depending on the apps you have downloaded, you may have more or fewer apps than shown here.

a. You have a choice of three styles of alerts:

- None
- A banner in the Notification Center pulled down from the top of the screen
- Alerts that pop up in the middle of the screen in addition to the banner

b. If you want to see on the Home screen that an app has notifications or alerts in the form of a number in a red circle, turn on **Badge App Icon**.

c. Set the tone that is played when a notification or alert happens by tapping **Alert Sound** to open a list of tones. You can hear what each of these sounds like by tapping it.

d. You can remove the app from the Notification Center by tapping the **On/Off** button to turn it off.

e. Determine the number of alerts/notifications you want to show by tapping **Include** and selecting the number of items you want.

f. If you want alerts to appear even when the screen is locked, which is the default for many apps, tap the **On/Off** button on the right of Show On Lock Screen.

4. Repeat Step 3 for all the apps whose notification settings you want to change. Some apps have one or more special settings, such as whether to repeat the alert and who to allow alerts from.

5. When you are ready, return to the Home screen.

 NOTE At the bottom of the list of apps in the Notification Center is an equally important list of apps not in the Notification Center. For each of these, ask yourself if they are properly categorized.

Using Do Not Disturb

Do Not Disturb, which you can turn on or off from the Control Center (the crescent moon icon) and from Settings | Do Not Disturb, allows you to silence alerts and incoming FaceTime calls by tapping the crescent moon icon in the Control Center or tapping the **On/Off** button opposite Manual in settings. If you tap **Do Not Disturb** in Settings, you can:

- Override the prohibition of alerts for scheduled events by tapping the **On/Off** button opposite Scheduled
- Allow FaceTime calls from certain individuals by tapping **Favorites** opposite Allow Calls From and tapping who to allow
- Allow FaceTime calls when the call is repeated from the same person within three minutes.
- When Do Not Disturb is turned on, do you want FaceTime calls and notifications silenced always or only while the iPad is locked?

When Do Not Disturb is turned on, a crescent moon icon ☾ ⌖ ✳ 93% ■■▸ appears to the left of the group of icons on the right at the top of the screen.

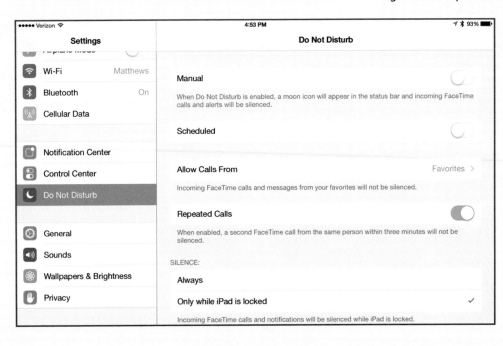

Sherryl Christie Bierschenk

There are so many options for the iPad—I both love that and find it overwhelming! I think it's important to decide what you really want to do with it and focus on that.

I want to get to the point where the iPad is the only computer I travel with, instead of the combination of a laptop and the iPad that I carry now. I need the ability to access a number of electronic documents, and that concerned me with the limited memory in the iPad. I solved it by putting my documents in Dropbox in the cloud (on the Internet) and have them available on my iPad as needed. I also write a lot and give presentations and have found that both the Apple Pages and Keynote apps work well for my needs, even though I have used Microsoft Office applications for most of my life. I have a case for my iPad that includes a removable Bluetooth keyboard in it that I find works well for writing.

Much of my writing involves taking notes, and I am exploring two approaches for that other than typing them out. One is handwritten notes using a stylus and apps like Notability and Note Anytime. I'm not far enough along with either of these to recommend them, but I can say that both are looking promising!

The second approach is dictating. I started working on this before Siri was available, so I have used Dragon Dictation. I am now also using Siri to send quick text messages to people and to send notes to myself.

I use a mail service shared with my iPad, my laptop, and my desktop computers, and, in spite of some earlier confusion, they are all now synced. The trick was to get my mail service fully engaged in helping me solve the problem, which they did, along with a warning not to use iCloud to sync my Contacts list. I also use Google Calendar by itself instead of as a part of iPad's Calendar so I can keep it synced online with an assistant, colleagues, and family members, as well as with my other computers.

Other things I do with my iPad include purchasing and reading books from iBooks, doing a daily Bible and devotional reading, listening to music, using Skype to talk with my family, and using Instagram to share photos. I use CamCard on both my iPhone and my iPad to photograph and enter business cards into my address book and I'm exploring RTM (Remember the Milk) as a to-do list maker and tracker.

I continue to be amazed at what I can do with my iPad—it's a great tool for so many things in my life—both for business and personally.

Chapter 6

Talking to Siri and Dictating

One of the most exciting features in recent iPads is Siri, a voice-activated personal assistant that allows you to verbally ask questions and often get the answer you are looking for, or tell her or him to do a task and see it done. In this chapter you'll see how to set up and use Siri to do many helpful things for you. After you're done talking to Siri, you'll see how to use dictation in general and for Notes in particular.

SET UP AND USE SIRI

Using Siri is quite easy once it is turned on, and there is little in the way of settings.

Set Up Siri

Open Siri's settings and consider how you want them to be configured.

1. From the Home screen, tap **Settings | General | Siri** to open the Siri settings.

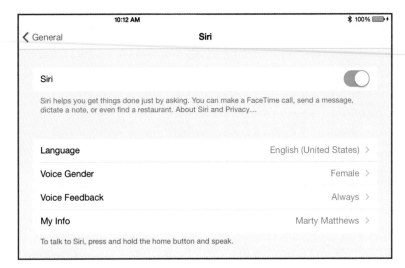

To talk to Siri, press and hold the home button and speak.

2. If Siri is not turned on, tap the **On/Off** button to do this.

3. If the default language, English in the U.S., is not what you want, tap the current language, tap the language you want to use, and then tap **Siri** at the top-left corner of the Language screen.

4. For some languages, U.S. English in particular, you can choose whether Siri has a female (the default) or male voice by tapping **Voice Gender**, tapping your choice, and tapping **Siri** at the top-left corner.

5. The default is for Siri to always provide voice feedback to your requests, including repeating your requests. If you do not want that—for example, in a noise-sensitive

environment—tap **Always** and tap the alternative, **Handsfree Only**, which will not provide voice feedback when you are holding your iPad. Tap **Siri** at the top of the screen.

6. Tap **My Info** and tap your name in the All Contacts list, which should contain the information about you to which you want Siri to have access. Siri uses this when you refer to yourself, such as the request "call my home phone." Of course, your name, address, phone number, and other information must be in Contacts to start with.

7. When you have made the changes to Siri's settings that you want, press **Home** to return to the Home screen.

CAUTION! To operate and be responsive to your requests, Siri needs to know a lot of information about you, your contacts, your location, and much more. Siri does not reside in your iPad, but in Apple servers at some location. This means that your information is transmitted to Apple and stored on their computers. Apple, of course, does what it can to protect your data and not misuse it (see the Apple Privacy statements both in the Siri iPad settings and on the Apple website at Apple.com/privacy).

⟫ Use Siri

Using Siri has few limits. Most of the default Apple apps that came with your iPad can be used verbally with Siri, and you can

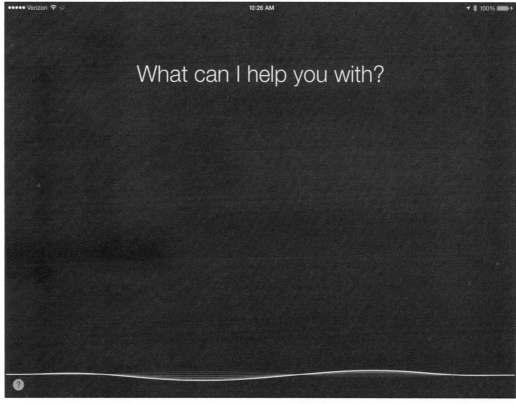

*Figure 6-1: **Siri is available to you at the press of the Home button.***

ask many questions that Siri can look up for you. In all cases, you start to use Siri with the following actions:

1. Press and hold **Home** until the Siri wavy line appears. After two beeps, a notice will pop up asking what Siri can help you with, as you can see in Figure 6-1.

2. Before a second pair of beeps and while there is still a wavy line, tell Siri what you want. For example, I asked "What does HTML mean?" Here is the result:

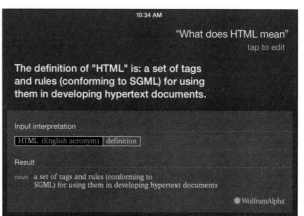

3. Another example is to ask Siri, "What will the weather be like this weekend?" Here is the response:

4. If you hear the second pair of beeps or see that the wavy line has disappeared, simply tap the microphone and you hear the opening beeps again.

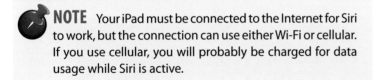
NOTE Your iPad must be connected to the Internet for Siri to work, but the connection can use either Wi-Fi or cellular. If you use cellular, you will probably be charged for data usage while Siri is active.

While you can use practically any words and any phrasing to talk to Siri, some words and phrases and techniques work better than others. Here are some pointers on how best to talk to Siri:

- Talk naturally as you would to another person, using common words generally understood by most people.

- Be clear and concise, using as few words as possible.
- Always ask what you want, never what you don't want.
- To add punctuation, such as a question mark, say the punctuation at the end of the sentence or question.
- Try to be in a location with as little background noise or music as possible.
- It is very helpful to give Siri as much information about yourself as you can in your entry in Contacts, as discussed in "Set Up Siri." If you provide this information, Siri will know what you mean by "work" and "home," and if you add people like "mother," "brother," or "partner," Siri can respond to those terms.

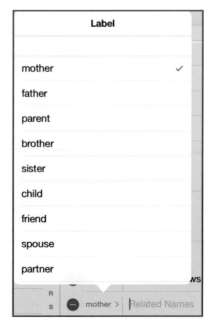

- Siri can help you use her. For example, if I ask Siri to text my son and I haven't added his name to my contact information, Siri will ask for his name and then ask me if that can be added to my contact information.

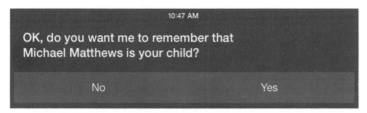

- If you ask Siri what she can do for you, you will get a scrollable list of commands and questions you can say or ask based on the standard apps on an iPad.

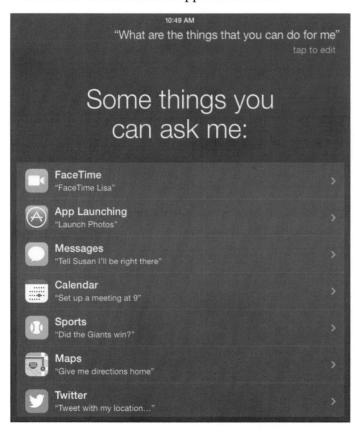

- Siri can only give you location-related information, like "Where is the nearest post office?" if you have a cellular-enabled iPad and if you have allowed Siri to use your current location. Apple says that it doesn't track or store your location.
- You can use a headset, such as the Apple EarPods, with Siri, using the call button, or center button on the EarPods, to summon Siri.

In the following sections we'll look at using Siri with a number of the iPad's apps. In all cases, if Siri is not displayed, press and hold the **Home** button to bring up Siri. If the Siri microphone is on the screen, tap the microphone to get Siri's attention. The following sections will assume that Siri is ready and waiting for you to say something.

Simply try any common phraseology and see how Siri responds. You can always try again, and Siri will often help you get what you need.

Use Siri to Set an Alarm

Siri can set, change, and cancel an alarm with these statements:

- "Set an alarm for tomorrow at 6:30 AM."

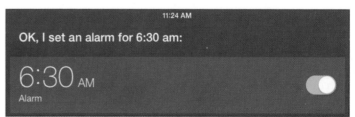

- "Change my alarm to 7 AM."
- "Set an alarm for weekdays at 7 AM" (see Figure 6-2).
- "Cancel my alarm at 7 AM" (this will cancel the 7 AM alarm for all weekdays).

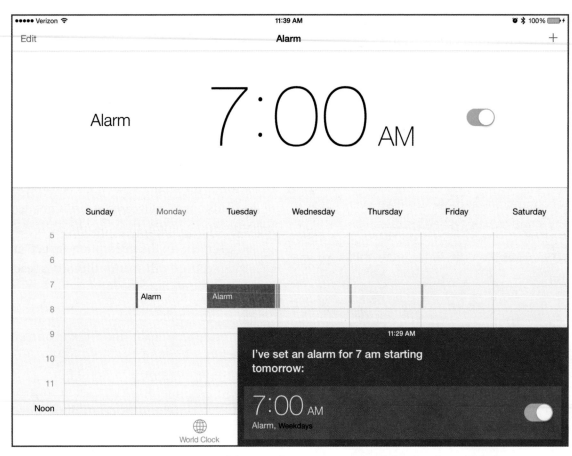

*Figure 6-2: **Siri can't set an alarm for days of the week, but you can use "weekdays" and "everyday."***

The term "tomorrow" can be replaced with tomorrow's specific day of the week, such as "Monday," given that tomorrow is Monday. Finally, you can use "turn on" in place of "set" and "delete" instead of "cancel."

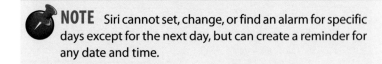

NOTE Siri cannot set, change, or find an alarm for specific days except for the next day, but can create a reminder for any date and time.

Use Siri to Add Calendar Events

Siri can create, change, cancel, and find calendar events with these statements:

- "Set up an appointment with Scott Smith for Wednesday at 2 PM."

- "Schedule lunch with Carole at noon on September 29th."
- "Cancel the appointment with Scott Smith on Wednesday."
- "Change the lunch with Carole to 1 PM on the 29th."
- "When is my lunch with Carole?"

Use Siri to See a Map and Get Directions

Siri is particularly valuable for providing hands-free information and directions while you are driving, but be sure to keep your eyes on the road. Here are some of the questions you can ask Siri:

- "Where am I"?

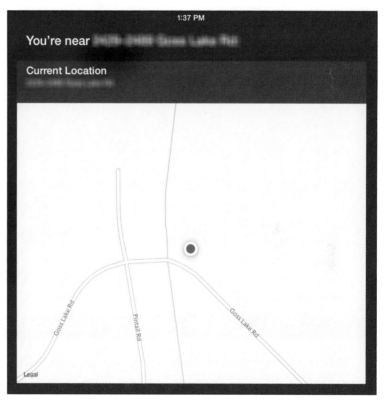

- "Show me the location of the Pink Door in Seattle."

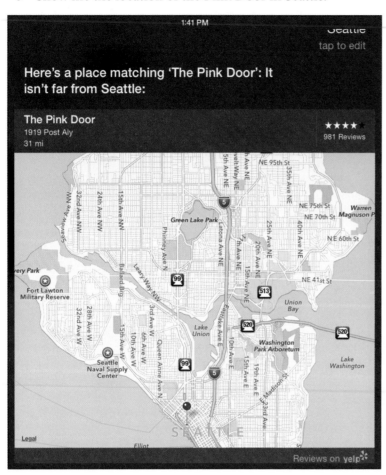

- "Where is Cimarron, New Mexico?" Siri could not initially answer this question. When I rephrased it, "Show me where the city of Cimarron, New Mexico is?" I got a map.

- "How do I get to Castle Rock, Washington?" This gets me a map, and by tapping the directions icon (the set of lines in the bottom middle), it gives me the list of directions, as you see in Figure 6-3.

- "Read me the directions to Castle Rock, Washington." This gets me verbal directions based on the changes in my GPS location.

Use Siri to Search the Web

Searching the Web is one of Siri's many strengths. Here are some of the many ways you can query the Web:

- "Search for Greek restaurants north of Seattle." Figure 6-4 shows the results.

- "Google all-electric automobiles."

- "Search the Web for QuickSteps books."

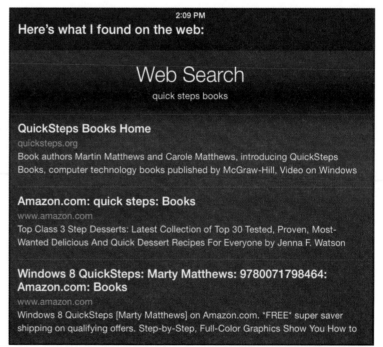

- "Show me the website for Taylor Thermometers."

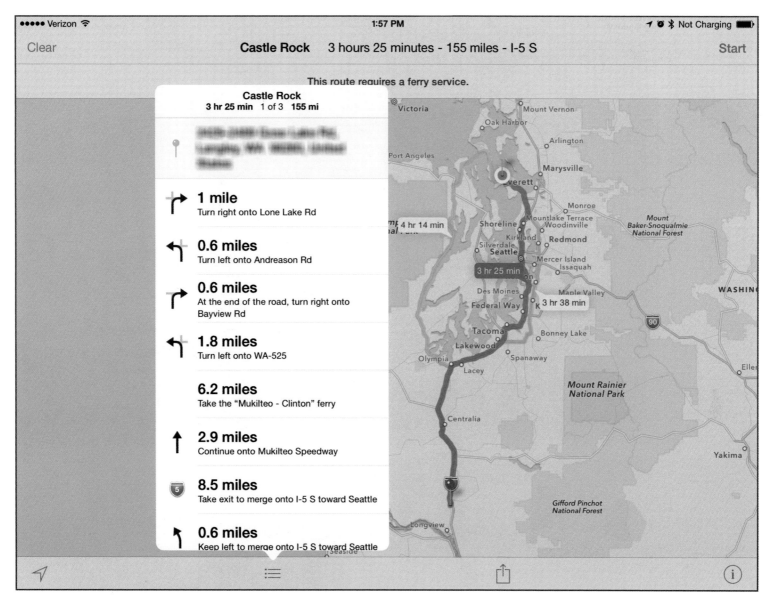

Figure 6-3: *Siri can save a lot of time typing in search parameters.*

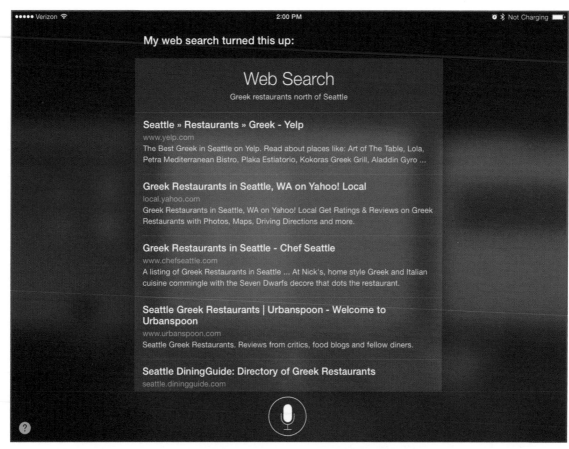

Figure 6-4: *Using Siri is often faster and easier than opening Safari and typing a query.*

Use Siri to Play Music

You can quickly play any music on your iPad, as well as skip a song and pause or stop play. You can say:

- "Play Santana."
- "Play Twilight Time.

- "Pause the song."

- "Stop."
- "Skip this song."

Use Siri to Locate Contacts

Depending on your Contacts list, Siri may find some ambiguities and give you a choice. For example, if I say "Find Roger," Siri comes back with this response:

If you have identified your family—wife, son, mother, for example—you can have Siri search on any of those. For example, I can say, "What is my wife's new mobile number?" and get this response:

Use Siri to Check for and Send Texts and Email

Siri is a pretty good stenographer when it comes to checking on and sending texts and email, but not perfect, although in my case, operator error is also a problem. Here are some examples:

- "Check for email from Tim Connor" gives me a list of emails dating back a year. If I say, "When was my last email from Tim Connor?" I get the last message from him.

- "Send a text to my wife asking when we should have dinner" produces a valid text message to my wife, but with a literal transfer of the message I requested—an error on my part.

- "Send an email to my wife" causes Siri to ask "What is the subject?" After answering that, Siri asks for the message. With that, she asks if I am ready to send. If so, I say "yes," and the message is sent. (Note that Siri doesn't know the difference between "weeks" and "week's.)

Getting Information with Siri

You can get a lot of information with Siri. You saw one example earlier in this chapter with questions about the weather and closest post office. Here are some other examples:

- "What is the current Dow average?" Siri responds with the correct information. Siri can do this for any widely traded stock. If she can't immediately find the price of the stock in question, she will ask you if you want to search the Web for the stock.

- "What is the traffic on I-5 north of Seattle?" Siri responds with, "Here is the traffic around Seattle," and provides a map of the Seattle area (see Figure 6-5) that shows the traffic congestion with a dotted red line next to roadways and construction with orange markers.

- "What is the name of the conductor of the Seattle Symphony?" Siri automatically searched the Web and returned a page with the correct answer.

- "What is the department store chain headquartered in Seattle?" Siri responded saying, "I found 15 department stores in Seattle," and listed them.

- "Where is the nearest Acura dealer?" Siri provides this response:

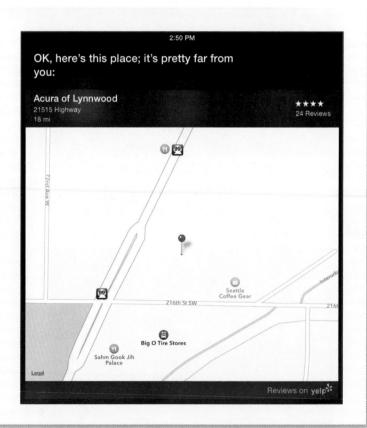

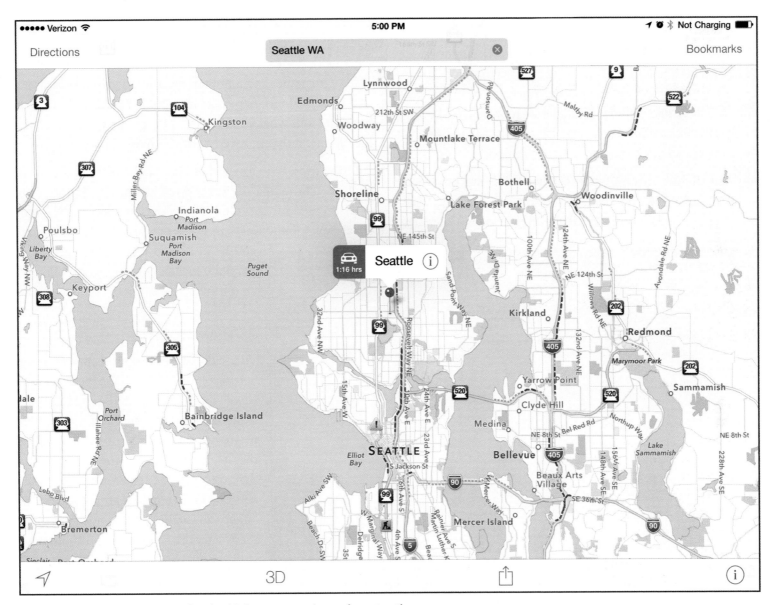

Figure 6-5: Siri can get you maps showing highway congestion and construction.

DICTATING

Dictating on your iPad is separate from using Siri, but is related. Like Siri, dictating uses the Internet to connect to Apple servers where the voice recognition is done. You must be connected with either Wi-Fi or cellular for dictating to work. Unlike Siri, though, dictation allows you to pause as long as you like and it does not talk back to you or answer questions.

You can dictate in any writing app where the onscreen keyboard has a microphone in the bottom left, as you can see in Figure 6-6. This includes Mail, Safari, Messages, Calendar, Contacts, Reminders, Notes, and Pages, among others. The key is the microphone in the onscreen keyboard, although some apps work better than others. In Contacts, with many short fields with names and numbers, dictation does not work as well as it does in Notes. Expect in any app that you may need to go back and edit what you dictated. On the other side, dictation has significantly improved from iOS 6 to iOS 7.

As you dictate, you can add punctuation by saying the words, such as "comma," "period," "question mark," "quote…end quote," "cap" for a capital letter, "exclamation mark," "new paragraph," "new line," and others. Talk slowly and clearly and be in a quiet place. Use a headset, if possible, such as the Apple EarPods, with a built-in microphone.

*Figure 6-6: **Dictation can quickly get information into your iPad, but it may need editing.***

▷▷ Use Dictation

To use dictation, you must turn on Siri in Settings | General as described earlier in this chapter. Then open the app where you want to use it, tap where you want the text to go, tap the microphone, and begin to dictate. As you dictate, the sound wave at the bottom of the screen will expand and contract vertically (the amplitude will get larger and smaller). The louder you speak, the greater the amplitude. If the amplitude is filling the vertical space, as you see in the first illustration that follows, you are probably talking too loud. If you don't see more than the default sound wave, as you see in the second illustration, you are probably talking too softly. The ability to clearly understand your speech depends on having a moderate volume.

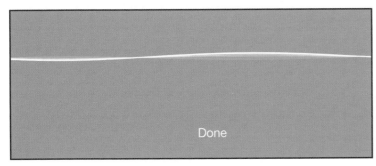

Here are two examples of using dictation, as best as I can present it in a book without you hearing my dictation.

Dictate a List in Notes

Here is a list of items I want to do to prepare for an upcoming vacation trip in Europe. I've left out the quote marks for clarity:

Trip to Europe To Do List newline

One Get and read the best travel books comma Rick Steves question mark newline

Two Layout an itinerary period newline

Three Make air comma hotel comma rental car reservations period newline

I tried this several times and here is result of the final time:

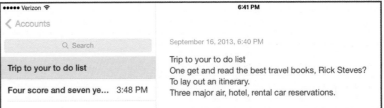

As you can see, dictating this list has its issues. I learned several things during the process:

- Speak slowly and enunciate clearly.
- Periodically pause to give the computer a chance to process the words.
- Break up what you are dictating into smaller chunks.
- Touch the screen to complete a section and see the result.
- Don't expect perfection. Most people can type more accurately and faster.

Dictate Paragraphs in Notes

Keeping the previous points in mind, I opened Notes, created a new document, and proceeded to dictate the second paragraph of the U.S. Declaration of Independence. The results are shown in Figure 6-7. The results are pretty good. Some of the mistakes are mine—I forgot the commas after "life" and "liberty."

▷▷ Select, Change, and Move Text

As you type (or especially dictate) text, it is more than likely that you will want to or need to change the text that has been entered. To change text, you must first select what you want to change. You can identify where you are in a string of text by

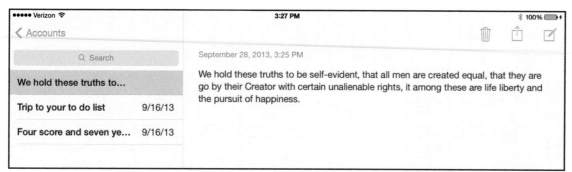

Figure 6-7: **Dictating on the iPad is very promising.**

the blue *insertion point* on the right end of what you just typed or dictated. The task is to place the insertion point on the right end of the text that you want changed—and remember that your tool to do this is your finger, which is huge compared with the text on the iPad. Thankfully, Apple has provided a number of tools to help you do this.

 NOTE The techniques described in the "Select, Change, and Move Text" section with Notes also work similarly with the other text-related standard apps on the iPad, including Mail, Messages, Contacts, Calendar, and Reminders.

Select Text

Let's start with the text pictured in Figure 6-7 and see how to select it to make the necessary changes and how to select and move it where you need it.

- Approximately place the insertion point by touching and holding on the piece of text to be changed. A magnifying glass will appear with the insertion point in it.

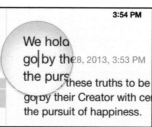

- **Precisely place the insertion point**, while still holding your finger on the text to be changed and displaying the magnifying glass, by slightly moving your finger left or right to move the insertion point exactly where you want it—this is not always easy.

–Or–

Lift your finger and swipe across the text in either direction with one finger to move the insertion point one character.

–Or–

Lift your finger and swipe across the text in either direction with two fingers to move the insertion point one word.

–Or–

Lift your finger and swipe across the text in either direction with three fingers to move the insertion point to the beginning or end of the current line.

- **Select a word** by double-tapping it.

–Or–

a. Touch and hold on a word until the magnifying glass appears and then release your finger to display the Select menu.

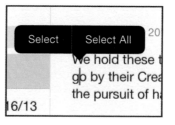

b. Tap **Select** to select the word and display the Cut/Copy menu.

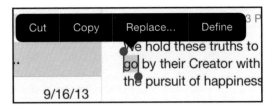

- **Select everything** by following the previous step a. and then tapping **Select All**.

- **Select more than a word** by selecting a word and dragging the end points (the darker blue circles) in either direction as needed.

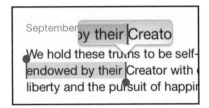

Change Selected Text

- **Cut, copy, and paste text** by selecting what you want to work with and, in that process, displaying the Cut/Copy menu. Then:

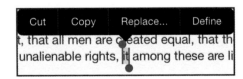

- **Remove the text** from its current location by tapping **Cut**.

- **Leave the text** in its current location by tapping **Copy**.

- **Replace the text** with a suggested word.

- **Place the text** at a new location by selecting the location and tapping **Paste**.

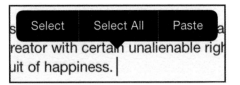

 **NOTE** Many external keyboards have COMMAND, OPTION, and arrow keys that make selecting and moving in text much easier. See "Use an External Keyboard" QuickFacts next.

 QuickFacts

Using an External Keyboard

An external keyboard, such as the Apple Wireless Keyboard or the Logitech Ultrathin Keyboard Cover, has additional keys not available with the onscreen keyboard, including the COMMAND, OPTION, and arrow keys. You can beneficially use these keys while editing text and elsewhere. Here are some of the ways that the extra keys can be used to move the insertion point and do other editing tasks:

- **Move a character at a time** using the arrow keys by themselves.

- **Move a word at a time** by pressing and holding the **OPTION** key while pressing the arrow keys.

- **Move to the beginning or end of a line** by pressing and holding **COMMAND** (**CMD**) while pressing the arrow keys.

- **Select text and expand the selection** by pressing and holding **SHIFT** while pressing the arrow keys.

- **Delete to the beginning of the line** by pressing and holding **COMMAND** (**CMD**) while pressing **DELETE**.

Check Spelling

By default, the iPad checks your spelling as you enter text. (If you don't want that, you can turn it off, from the Home screen, by tapping **Settings | General | Keyboard | Check Spelling On/Off**.) When you misspell a word, the iPad places a red dotted underline beneath it librty . Tap the word and, if it can, Pages will offer suggestions for the misspelled word. If you want one of the suggestions, tap it.

Share and Print Notes

If you want to share your notes with others, you can use the Share icon and the Share menu, as explained in earlier chapters.

Kathleen Landel

I use my iPad to separate my work life from my personal and household life. Since I'm on the desktop computer at home working for much of the day, I like being able to grab my iPad, which I can take anywhere, and catch up with my family and household computer tasks.

I keep in touch with my son and husband using messaging and email. We share photos, articles, and web links with each other, which helps keep us connected in spite of our busy lives. Several times a day I use the app to check our shared Google calendar. The iPad share feature makes it so easy to share any content. I especially like taking my iPad when I visit my elderly parents to share family photos with them.

After a busy day I relax with my iPad by reading *The New York Times* and other news media. I love seeing what is up with far-flung family and friends on Facebook, posting happy birthday wishes, and sharing old family photos. I keep up with my favorite public radio and television shows, like *This American Life, RadioLab,* and *Masterpiece Theater,* at my convenience. I've even improved my Scrabble skills playing online, and I always have several competitive games of Dice with Buddies going with my son and nephew.

Some of my other favorite apps include:

- **CalenMob**   I can make appointments and keep up-to-date on our family Google Calendar anywhere.
- **Bank App**   I can check my credit union balance, transfer funds, and even make deposits.
- **Printer App**   I can print an email, attachment, or a favorite article wirelessly from anywhere in the house.
- **3M Cloud Library**   This app allows me to download books from my local library system in any format.
- **PDFReaderLite**   I can read and save PDF articles from my research on the Internet.
- **Calculator HD**   This is a great, multifeatured calculator.

Chapter 7

Listening to and Reading on the iPad

In the first six chapters, I've primarily covered how to get the most productive use out of your iPad. In this and the next two chapters, you'll see how to relax and enjoy your iPad. In this chapter we'll look at getting, organizing, and listening to music from several sources and then how to get, organize, and read electronic books (eBooks) and other documents, also from various sources.

LISTEN TO MUSIC

Music has always been a powerful part of human history and it remains so in this mobile digital age. People may not agree on the type of music they like, but the majority of people like to listen to some form of it, and the iPad supports that in spades. Here we'll look at getting music from two sources (iTunes and your computer), organizing it into playlists, and then listening to it.

⏵ Get Music from iTunes

Apple has made a very substantial business of selling music online through iTunes, which makes available for purchase and download a significant part of popular music—over 28 million songs when this was written. iTunes is easy to use to search, open, preview, and buy music that you want to listen to.

 TIP In addition to music, at the iTunes Store you can buy movies, TV shows, and audiobooks. The general discussion here on how to use iTunes applies equally to all the types of media that are available through it. We'll talk more about videos and movies in Chapter 8.

Set Up iTunes

iTunes comes as a standard part of the iPad, and using it requires little more than opening it. You must, of course, have an Apple ID, but you most likely have that, as described in Chapter 1. Take a brief look at the iTunes settings.

From the Home screen, tap **Settings | iTunes & App Store** to open those settings.

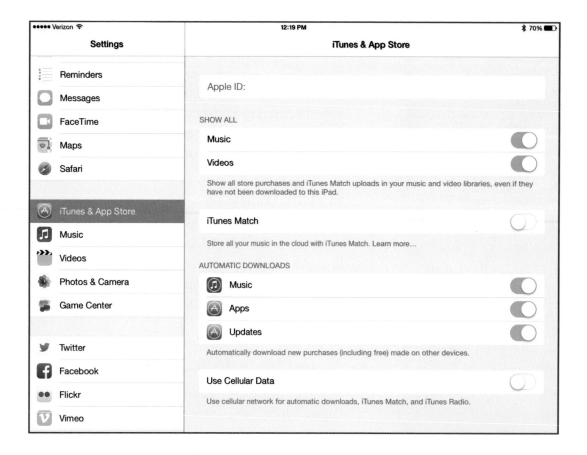

- Show All allows you to determine if you want to show in iTunes and the App Store all of your purchases and iTunes Matches (see next item) for both music and videos. The default is to show them.

- See the "Understanding iTunes Match" QuickFacts to determine how to set the iTunes Match option.

- The three Automatic Downloads options allow purchases on other devices, such as an iPhone, to be automatically downloaded to your iPad. These are on by default, and under most circumstances, you want to leave them that way.

- If you have a cellular iPad and have a limited data plan, you probably do *not* want to use cellular to do the automatic downloads between Apple devices and for iTunes Match. This is the default, which you probably want to leave.

Understanding iTunes Match

iTunes Match is an Apple subscription service currently costing $24.99 per year that provides a copy on iCloud of all your music, including what you have downloaded from iTunes, purchased from other sources, and copied from CDs. The music that you purchase and download from iTunes automatically goes up onto iCloud, but music from other sources does not and therefore has to be separately transferred to multiple devices. With iTunes Match, Apple replaces your music from other sources with the most recent versions and at the highest available fidelity. With all your music on iCloud, you can listen to it on any device with iCloud, including PCs.

With iTunes Match, all of your music collection is scanned and, for those items not downloaded from iTunes, Apple's library of over 28 million songs is reviewed for a match. If it is found, the Apple copy is placed in iCloud for you to use. In the unlikely event that the song is not found, your copy is placed in iCloud. You can have up to 25,000 songs in iCloud, more if you buy them from the iTunes Store, that can be played on up to ten devices.

To use iTunes Match:

1. Open iTunes on your computer (not iPad).

2. Click **Store** in the menu bar and then click **Turn On iTunes Match** to open a page in iTunes explaining iTunes Match.

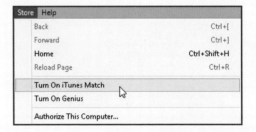

3. If you want to go ahead, click **Subscribe For,** currently, **$24.99 Per Year**, enter your Apple ID and password, and click **Subscribe**. Your music, either your copy or Apple's, will be placed in your account on iCloud and you will see an iCloud icon appear next to the piece in your iTunes library.

4. On your iPad Home screen, tap **Settings | iTunes & App Store | iTunes Match On/Off** to turn it on if it is off.

Become Familiar with iTunes

Take a quick look around iTunes and get familiar with the interface. Open it by tapping iTunes on the Home screen. The iTunes screen that opens (see Figure 7-1) has two sets of selectors. At the bottom of the screen there are the primary categories of Music, Movies, TV Shows, and Audiobooks. For each of the first four categories at the bottom there is a set of genres, or subcategories, at the top of the screen. The last three items on the bottom reverse the positions and put the major categories on top of the screen, as you can see in Figure 7-2. Top Charts provides a different way of looking at the iTunes library based on popularity. Genius provides suggestions based on what you have purchased, and finally, a list of what you have purchased.

Figure 7-2: *The quantity of music that is available on iTunes is mind boggling.*

Search iTunes

The key hurdle in using iTunes, of course, is finding the music that you want to buy. iTunes gives you several ways of reviewing what is available.

1. When you first open iTunes, All Genres is selected in the upper selection bar. This provides a smattering of recent popular albums and songs of different types.

2. To hone in on a particular genre, tap the other buttons across the top to review their music.

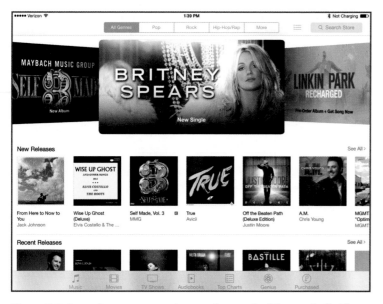

Figure 7-1: *As seniors, we may not recognize much of the music that is displayed, but iTunes has our music also.*

3. The final button on the right provides a number of additional genres, including several such as Classic Hits and Classical, that may be of more interest to our age group.

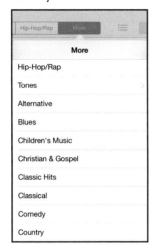

4. On the far upper right is a search box in which you can enter album, artist, and composer names, as well as categories of music. For example, to search for the music of my youth and young adulthood, I entered "Music of the 50s and 60s" and was amazed at all that I got, as you can see in Figure 7-3.

Preview and Buy Music

Once you have found the music you may want, the next step is to preview it and make sure it is what you really want and, if so, to buy it. To preview and potentially buy an album or song that you have found:

1. From the iTunes page that you found earlier—for example, the result of my "Music of the 50s and 60s" search shown in Figure 7-3—tap an album or song you are interested in. I tapped **Cruisin' To The Hits Of The '50s And '60s**.

2. You get an overview, review summary, price, and list of the songs on an album or an individual song. Tap any of

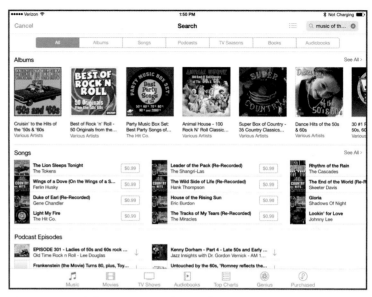

Figure 7-3: ***Don't limit your searches to albums or artists, but try unique categories you might think of.***

the songs to have a 90-second preview of the song played on your iPad.

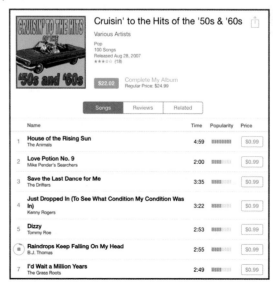

3. When you find a song or album that you want to buy, tap the price, tap **Buy Song** `BUY SONG`, enter your Apple ID password, and tap **OK**. You will see your song downloading, and when it is done, the word "Play" `PLAY` replaces the price. The first time you buy something from the iTunes or App Store you will be asked to agree to Apple's Terms of Sale (a 34-page) document that you can have emailed to you).

 CAUTION! Once you have purchased one song or album, you do not have to re-enter your Apple ID password during this session, making it easier and faster to make purchases—maybe not always a good thing.

⏩ Transfer Music from a Computer

If you have had a computer for any length of time, you probably have put some music on it, either by downloading the music or by copying CDs you have to your computer (called "ripping" CDs). The major way to get music from other iTunes sources to your iPad is through your computer, and to do that you need to have iTunes installed on your computer. You may already have iTunes on your computer, but just in case, we will review that here, then look at collecting the music you have on your computer, ripping CDs to iTunes, and finally transferring and syncing your music between your computer and your iPad.

Get iTunes on Your Computer

iTunes is available for download for either a Mac or a PC from Apple.com.

1. Open the browser on your computer and type <u>apple.com</u> in the address box.

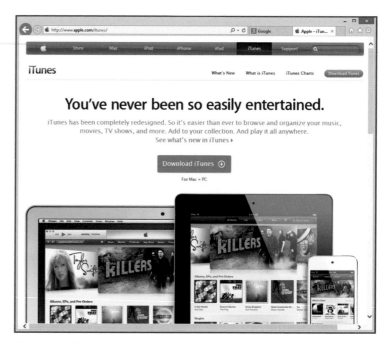

*Figure 7-4: **iTunes on your computer can be your complete media (music, movies, and TV) resource.***

2. Click **iTunes** in the bar at the top and then click **Download iTunes** (see Figure 7-4) | **Download Now** | **Run** (you don't have to enter your email address at this point).

3. When you see the Welcome To iTunes message, click **Next**, select the options you want (I add iTunes to my desktop, do not use it as my default player, but do automatically update it and use the default folder), and click **Install** | **Yes** | **Finish** to complete the installation. iTunes will appear on your computer as you see in Figure 7-5.

Collect the Music on Your Computer

To get the music on your computer to your iPad, it must first reside in iTunes on your computer. Begin by finding the music

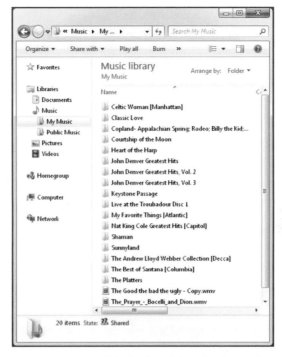

Figure 7-5: *iTunes is, of course, biased to the iTunes Store, but you don't have to use it.*

Figure 7-6: *My Music is the default location for music on a PC, but it can be anywhere.*

on your computer. On recent Windows computers (Vista, 7, or 8), it is probably located within Libraries/Music/My Music, as you see in Figure 7-6. With that knowledge:

1. From iTunes, on the first time you use iTunes, click **Scan For Media**, as you saw in Figure 7-5. This will pick up the easily recognized music. On my computer it picked up most of the 18 albums I have.

2. Still in iTunes on your computer, click **File | Add Folder To Library**. Navigate to the folder that contains your music (most likely Libraries/Music/My Music).

3. Click the top album, press and hold **SHIFT**, click the bottom album to select them all, and click **Select Folder**.

4. You may be told that one or more of the songs you are adding to iTunes needs to be converted to a different format. Click **Convert**. The process of converting and

adding your music to iTunes may take several minutes, depending on how big your library is.

Rip CDs to iTunes

To rip or add music from a CD to iTunes:

1. Place the CD in your computer's CD drive.

2. Depending on your computer and whether iTunes is running, various messages will pop up. If iTunes is not running, you will see these messages and will need to take these steps:

- **Windows 7** A single message pops up. Click **Import Songs Using iTunes**.

- **Windows 8** Two messages appear. Tap or click the first and then tap or click **Import Songs iTunes**.

- **iMac OS X Mountain Lion** The CD will display on the desktop. Open iTunes and click **Import CD**.

3. If iTunes is running when you insert a CD, you will get a message asking if you want to import the CD into your iTunes library. Click **Yes**.

iTunes will open, displaying the CD you inserted and its songs, as shown in Figure 7-7. If iTunes wasn't open when you inserted the CD, click **Import CD** on the far right.

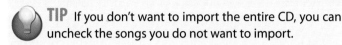 **TIP** If you don't want to import the entire CD, you can uncheck the songs you do not want to import.

4. If you are asked about import settings, unless you have a special need, accept the default, and click **OK**.

5. As the CD is being imported, you'll see the status at the top and a white checkmark in a green circle, as shown in Figure 7-8.

6. When you are done importing, remove the CD from the computer.

Figure 7-7: **When you insert a CD into a computer, you can play the CD or import it or individual songs.**

Figure 7-8: **Music that you have imported into iTunes gives you virtually the same fidelity as playing the music directly from the CD.**

Transfer and Sync to iPad

To transfer music from your computer to your iPad, plug your iPad into a Universal Serial Bus (USB) port on your computer and unlock the iPad, if necessary. If your iPad and iTunes on your computer are using the default setup, iTunes will immediately begin transferring your music on the computer to the iPad, as you can see in Figure 7-9. The process is called "syncing" because music on the computer that is not on the iPad will be transferred to the iPad, although the opposite is not true—music on the iPad but not on the computer will not be transferred to the computer, although music on the iPad will be available to play through iTunes on the computer but not physically reside on the computer.

If the syncing did not take place automatically, in iTunes on your computer, click on the name of your iPad under Devices on the left, and then click **Sync** in the lower-right corner.

*Figure 7-9: **iTunes on your computer provides the primary conduit of information between your computer and your iPad.***

In either case, when you are done, the music in iTunes on your computer should be the same as the music on your iPad.

Get Music from Other Sources

Apple would like you to believe that iTunes is the be-all and end-all of music acquisition on your iPad. If you go to the App Store and search for "music players," however, you will find over 100 apps that facilitate downloading and playing music on your iPad. These apps generally include a built-in browser that lets you search for legal, free music that you can download and then a player that will play this music. The free music is generally in the MP3 format and is from lesser-known artists and composers. I discuss getting and using such an app in the next section.

> **CAUTION!** If you search hard enough, you can probably find top-rated artists and composers for free on sites that are probably illegally offering the music. I would not download this music for two reasons. First, you can get in legal trouble because you are violating the copyright laws. Second, if the site doesn't care that they are violating the law in facilitating your downloading the music for free, what might they be including in the package you download that can steal information from your iPad and harm your data? I strongly recommend staying a long way away from such sites.

Amazon provides another source of music that you pay for and either can download to your computer and then over to your iPad, or you can store it on the Amazon Cloud and then download the Amazon Cloud player for the iPad. In some cases, Amazon is cheaper than the iTunes Store (the album *Cruisin' to the Hits of the '50 and '60s* discussed earlier in this chapter is $24.99 on iTunes and the MP3 version on Amazon is $9.49), but that is not universally true. In some cases, Amazon only offers CD versions of the music, which is more expensive than iTunes' electronic version. We'll briefly look at how an Amazon Cloud purchase and app works later in this chapter.

Use a Non-Apple Player

As was mentioned earlier, there are over 100 music player apps in the App Store. A few of these are shown in Figure 7-10. I will use the MP3 Music Downloader to demonstrate how a third-party iPad app downloads and plays music from the Internet. I have only looked at two such apps, and even that was only a cursory look, so my choice of the MP3 Music Downloader is

*Figure 7-10: **Many of the music players only give you a minimal app, and you have to upgrade at a price to get the full-featured player.***

not a recommendation and should not be considered even a knowledgeable choice, although from the bit that I have used it, it works well, is full featured, and doesn't hound you to upgrade. Here is what I did:

1. From the Home screen, tap **App Store | Search box**. If needed, clear the Search box. In the Search box, type <u>music players</u>, and press **RETURN**.

2. Select the music player you want to download, tap the price twice | **Install App**, enter your Apple ID password, tap **OK** twice | **Open**.

3. In most cases, a browser opens. In the Search box, type <u>free music</u> and press **RETURN**. Three sites that I believe to be safe are:
   last.fm/music/+free-music-downloads/
   freemusicarchive.org/
   freeplaymusic.com/ (great for music that is free to use on websites)

4. Select a site and use its commands to find and then select the music you want. Some sites allow you to preview a piece and then download it when you are ready.

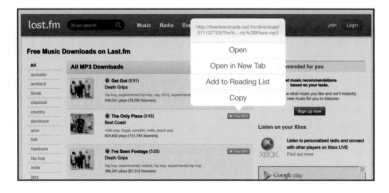

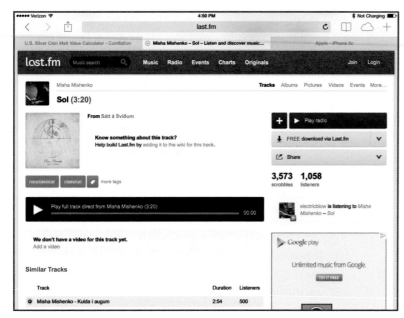

2. In Amazon's search box, tap the **All** down arrow | **Music**, and type the music you are searching for.

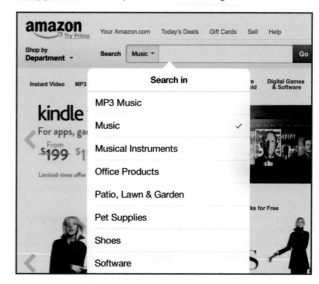

*Figure 7-11: **Most of the players combine a browser with a file system with the actual player.***

5. When you have selected the song you want, tap the Play button to listen to it, as you can see in Figure 7-11.

Use the Amazon Cloud Player

The Amazon alternative allows you to buy popular music by top-rated artists, sometimes at a discount, and then either download it to your computer and then transfer it to your iPad, or store it on the Amazon Cloud and then use an Amazon Cloud player to listen to the music. The option of using your computer was discussed earlier in this chapter. Look here at using the Amazon cloud.

1. On your iPad's Home screen, tap **Safari**. In the address box, type amazon.com, and press **Go**.

NOTE Amazon sells CDs, which they ship to you and you can play them and rip them on your computer and, once ripped, transfer to your iPad. Amazon also sells MP3 electronic files, which you can download to your computer and transfer to your iPad, or put them on the Amazon Cloud and play them with the Amazon Cloud Player on your iPad. With most CDs, you can also have them put on Amazon Cloud at no extra cost.

3. When you find what you are looking for (I searched for and found the same album I searched for on iTunes—*Cruisin' to the Hits of the '50s and '60s*—see Figure 7-12), tap the album, review the content, and when you are ready, tap **Buy**. Enter your Amazon ID and password and continue to complete the purchase.

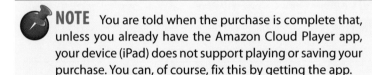

MP3 Songs					
To view this content, download Flash player (version 9.0.0 or higher)					
Disc 1:					
Song Title	Artist	Time	Popularity	Price	
▶ 1. House Of The Rising Sun	The Animals	4:59	‖‖‖‖‖‖‖‖‖‖	$0.99	Buy MP3
▶ 2. Love Potion No. 9	Mike Pender's Searchers	2:00	‖‖‖‖‖‖‖‖‖‖	$0.99	Buy MP3
▶ 3. Save The Last Dance For Me	The Drifters	3:35	‖‖‖‖‖‖‖‖‖‖	$0.99	Buy MP3
▶ 4. Just Dropped In (To See What Condition My Condition Was In)	Kenny Rogers	3:22	‖‖‖‖‖‖‖‖‖‖	$0.99	Buy MP3

*Figure 7-12: **When an Amazon album is displayed, you can preview a song by tapping the arrowhead on the left of a song.***

NOTE You are told when the purchase is complete that, unless you already have the Amazon Cloud Player app, your device (iPad) does not support playing or saving your purchase. You can, of course, fix this by getting the app.

4. To get the Amazon Cloud Player app, either:

Thanks, Martin S Matthews!

✓ Purchase completed. View your order details

✓ Available in Cloud Player

⚠ This device does not support saving Amazon MP3 purchases to your device.

Cruisin' To The Hits Of The '50s & '60s
Various Artists
$9.49

Play your music in Cloud Player

› Get the Cloud Player app for iPhone, iPad, iPod touch, and Android

› Continue shopping

Need download help? Click here.

- Tap **Get The Cloud Player App** on the purchase completed page, and tap **iPad | Get The App** to open the App Store displaying the Amazon Cloud Player.

–Or–

*Figure 7-13: **Amazon Cloud Player will also play other music it sees on your iPad.***

- Tap **App Store** from the iPad's Home screen and search for Amazon Cloud Player.

- Then, in either case, with the Amazon Cloud Player displayed, tap **Free | Install App**, enter your Apple ID password, tap **OK**, and tap **Open** when it is done.

5. When the Amazon Cloud Player opens (see Figure 7-13), enter your email address, enter your Amazon password, and tap **Sign In**. You will see the music you have purchased for the Amazon Cloud. Tap the albums and songs you want to play.

⏩ Create Playlists

A playlist is a list of songs from various albums that you want to play together in sequence. Selecting the playlist plays all the songs on it. You can create a playlist in Music, in third-party music players, and in the Amazon Cloud Player. The process of creating a playlist is similar in all cases—basically select the songs you want on a playlist and give it a name. Here is how you do it in the iPad's default Music player.

1. From the iPad's Home screen, tap **Music | Playlists** on the bottom left. If you have purchased several individual songs on an album, they will be shown as a playlist under the album's name.

2. To create a new playlist, tap **New Playlist** in the upper-right corner, type a name, and tap **Save**. This will open a list of all the songs on all the albums you have either imported from your computer or purchased on iTunes, as shown in Figure 7-14.

> **New Playlist**
> Enter a name for this playlist.
>
> [   ]
>
> Cancel   Save

3. Either swipe up or use the alphabetic index on the far right to scroll through the list so you can find the songs you want.

4. Tap the songs you want on the playlist. When you have selected all the songs you want, tap **Done**. The list of songs on your playlist will appear.

5. Tap **Edit** in the upper left to go into edit mode, as you see in Figure 7-15.

> **NOTE** Only playlists that you create on the iPad can be edited. Playlists that you bring over from your computer cannot be edited.

6. To delete a song on the list, tap the white bar in the red circle and then tap **Remove** Remove . Drag the grip strip on the far right to reposition songs within the list.

Figure 7-14: You can also add songs from both the Albums and Artists pages using the buttons at the bottom of the page.

*Figure 7-15: **You can change a playlist by opening a playlist as if to play it and tapping Edit in the upper-right corner.***

7. To add a song to the list, tap the plus sign in the upper right and repeat Steps 3 and 4. When the list is the way you want it, tap **Done | Playlists** in the top-center area. Your new playlist will appear on Music's Playlists page.

Listen to Music

You can listen to music on your iPad using iPad's Music app and using any of the third-party music players, including the Amazon Cloud Player. Music is the iPad's built-in player and has a number of features to fulfill that function, as you see in Figure 7-16. On more recent iPads, unless it has been moved, the Music icon is on the right end of the dock at the bottom of the screen.

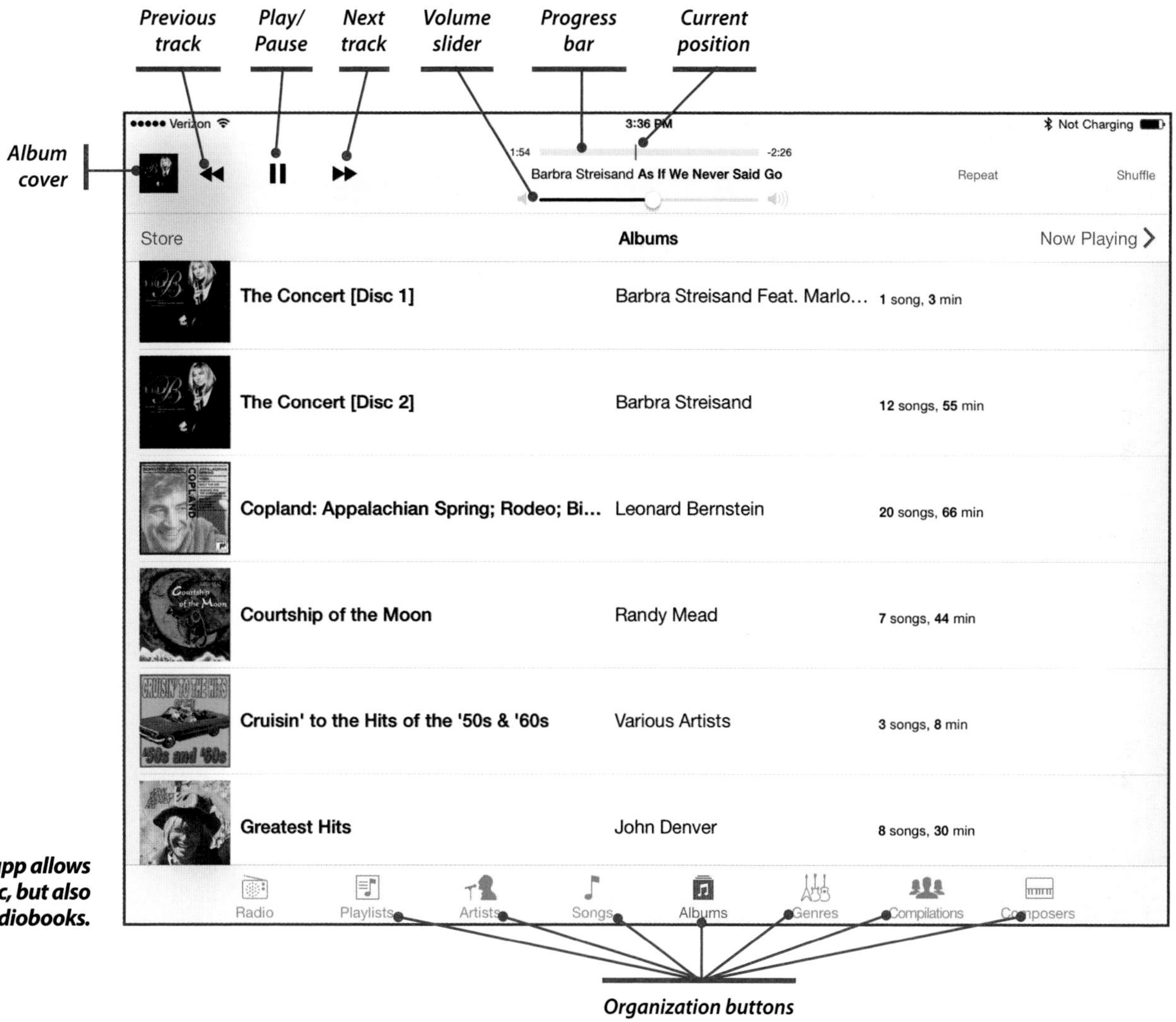

Figure 7-16: *The Music app allows you to play not only music, but also podcasts and audiobooks.*

Music's controls include:

- **Player controls** with Previous and Next to step through an album one track at a time in either direction, and Play and Pause to start and stop playing the current song.

- **Now Playing** to enlarge the cover, provide enlarged player controls, and provide two additional controls as shown in Figure 7-17.

  - **Return to library** leaves the album display and returns to the library display.

Return to library   **Song list**

Figure 7-17: *The Now Playing screen may be considered more attractive than the library image.*

- **Song List** displays the list of songs in the album.

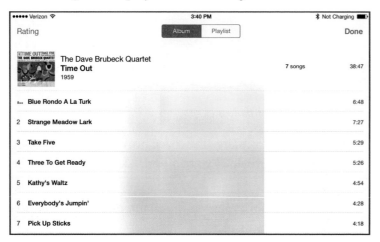

- **Repeat** repeats the current song.

- **Current position** shows where you are currently at in the song that is playing. You can drag the red position marker (also called a "playhead") in either direction to move what is currently playing.

- **Progress bar** provides the span for marking the current position in a song that is playing. The number of minutes already played and remaining are at either end of the progress bar.

- **Shuffle** rearranges the list of songs in an album and plays them in a random order.

- **Volume slider** can be dragged left or right to lower or raise the volume of the music being played.

- **Organization buttons** open different organizational views of your music library.
- **Store** immediately opens the iTunes Store.

Set Up Music

Open Music's settings from the Home screen by tapping **Settings | Music**. Options include:

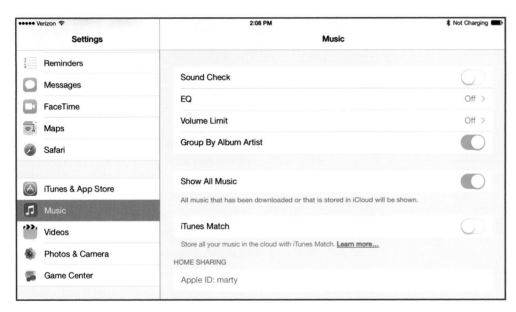

- **Sound Check**, when turned on, levels out volume highs and lows.
- **EQ** allows you to select preset equalizer settings for various types of music.
- **Volume Limit** lets you set a maximum volume limit, which you might want to use with headphones.
- **Group By Album Artist** groups albums by one artist together.

- **Show All Music** provides for the display of all music that has been downloaded to the iPad or stored on your iCloud account.
- **iTunes Match** sets up the storing of all of your music on iCloud including music you have ripped from CD and downloaded from other sources. See the "Understanding iTunes Match" QuickFacts earlier in this chapter.
- **Home Sharing** displays the Apple ID used with Home Sharing. See the "Use Home Sharing" QuickFacts later in this chapter.

Play Music

Actually playing music is, at this point, anticlimactic and you probably have, with touch so obvious, figured it out. It, of course, varies a bit, depending on the view you have on the screen.

1. From the Home screen, tap **Music**. The most common view to open is the Album view, shown earlier in Figure 7-16.
2. From Album view, tap the album you want to play to open the list of songs.
3. On the list of songs, tap the song you want to play. The progress bar and its controls will open, as you see in Figure 7-18, and the song will begin. The entire album will play if you don't interrupt it.
4. Tap **Pause** in the player controls on the left to temporarily stop playing the music. Tap **Play** to start playing again where you left off.

Figure 7-18: *Some headphones, such as Apple's EarPods, allow you to adjust the volume remotely on the wire to the headphones.*

Figure 7-19: *The audio controls in the Control Center provide an alternative to opening the Music app.*

5. Tap **Previous** or **Next** to go to the previous or next song or track in the album.

6. Tap **Now Playing** in the top right to open the Now Playing view shown earlier in Figure 7-17.

7. If you open in or select **Artists** instead of Albums, you still get albums but they are organized by artist name, so Steps 2 through 6 apply. The same is true with Playlist, except that "playlist" replaces "album."

8. If you open in or select **Songs**, you get a long list of all the songs on your iPad, as you saw earlier in Figure 7-14. It is organized (sorted) by song title and you can jump down or up the alphabet by tapping the letters on the far right. Steps 3 through 6 apply here.

Use the Audio Controls

If you are playing music while also using another app, like reading a book or magazine, you can quickly get to a set of audio controls in the Control Center without having to open the Music app and possibly losing your place in what you are reading, as you can see in Figure 7-19. Here is how you can display the audio controls:

From any open screen on your iPad, swipe up from the bottom of the screen.

Listen to iTunes Radio

With the release of iOS 7 and iTunes 11.1 on both PCs and Macs in the fall of 2013, Apple debuted iTunes Radio, a competitor of Pandora and other streaming (the music is sent to you as you are listening to it) Internet "radio" stations. iTunes Radio provides over 250 stations dedicated either to particular types or genres of music or groupings of music such as the current top 100 songs or The Beatles Radio. You can also create your own station, which is stored on iCloud, so you can listen to it and any of the other stations anywhere you have iTunes including your iPhone, iPod, and your PC or Mac computer.

NOTE iTunes Radio is itself free, but there will be occasional ads to listen to, and you are reminded that you can buy the current song for your own library by clicking the price associated with it. If you sign up for iTunes Match (explained earlier in this chapter) you will be spared the advertising.

When you first open iTunes Radio a welcome message appears. You can tap **Learn More** to read a brief overview of iTunes Radio, or you can tap **Start Listening** to explore iTunes Radio, which opens as you see in Figure 7-20. Across the top are

Figure 7-20: iTunes Radio provides a great way to sample a very wide variety of music.

featured stations. On the bottom are a couple of suggested stations for you based on the music you have. To use iTunes Radio on your iPad:

1. From within Music, tap **Radio** in the bottom-left area. Scroll either list of stations by swiping from right to left.

2. Select a station to listen to by tapping it. The station will begin playing. Tap **Now Playing** in the upper-right area to see the cover of the current song.

3. Tap the info icon (i) for more information about the current song and to create a new station based on the current artist or current song. You can also tune the current station to play only the top hits, a variety of related music, or

explore some variations off the
theme of the current station.
Finally you can choose to allow
explicit tracks and if and how
you want to share this station
with others.

4. There are several ways to start
a station of your own. In Step
3 you saw how to start a new
station based on an artist or a
song you are currently playing.
You can also tap New Station
(the red plus sign) on the
iTunes Radio page shown in
Figure 7-20. On the screen that opens you can:

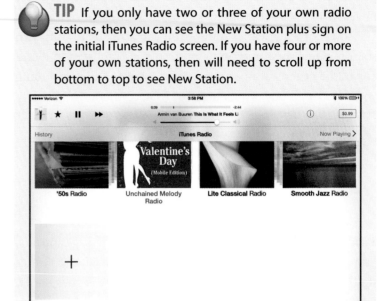

TIP If you only have two or three of your own radio
stations, then you can see the New Station plus sign on
the initial iTunes Radio screen. If you have four or more
of your own stations, then will need to scroll up from
bottom to top to see New Station.

• Enter an artist, genre, or song on which to base a
station. For example, I entered "Unchained Melody"
and got five alternative songs and one artist. I then pick
the one that is closest to what I had in mind. (Actually
none of the suggestions were what I had in mind—the
Platters recording.) A new station is created and the first
selection begins playing.

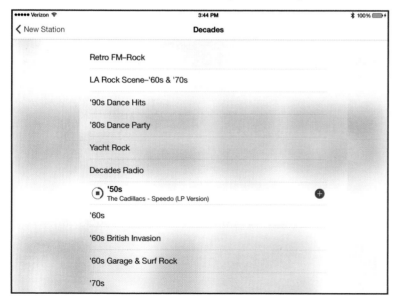

- Alternatively, tap a selection and then follow it through to get the music you want. For example, I tap "Decades" and then tap "'50s" followed by tapping "'60" to hear a medley of song snippets to help me decide if I like that choice. If I do, I tap the plus sign on the right.

5. You can see and return to music you have recently listened to by tapping **History** in the upper-right area of the iTunes Radio page you saw in Figure 7-20. A list of the songs is displayed as you can see in Figure 7-21. Tap a song to hear it again and/or tap the price of the song on the right to add it to your library.

6. To change or delete a radio station you have created, tap **Edit** on the left of the My Stations heading. Tap the station you want to work with. You can add artists, songs, and/ or genre that you want more of or don't want to hear. Alternatively, you can tap **Delete Station** and then tap **Delete** to remove the station.

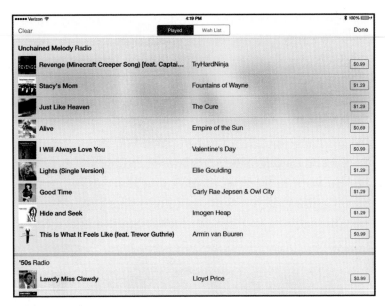

Figure 7-21: *On iTunes Radio it is easy to focus on the music that you like.*

Using Home Sharing

You do not have to download everything in iTunes on your computer to your iPad in order to listen on the iPad to all the music on your computer or on other computers on your home network. Apple's Home Sharing allows you to do this, but it must be enabled on all the computers with which you want to share media. You can share not only music, but also videos, movies, and TV, which will be discussed in Chapter 8. Begin by enabling Home Sharing on your computer, then enable it on your iPad, and finally on any additional computers. iTunes must be installed on each device where you will also need to enable Home Sharing with the same Apple ID and password.

1. On your computer, open iTunes and in the menu bar click **File | Home Sharing | Turn On Home Sharing**.

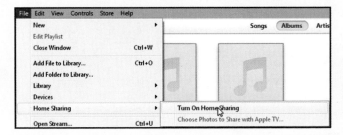

2. Type your Apple ID and password, and click **Turn On Home Sharing** (see Figure 7-22).

Figure 7-22: *Using Home Sharing allows you to keep only what you are currently listening to on your iPad.*

3. On your iPad, from the Home screen, tap **Settings | Music**, and, under Home Sharing, type the Apple ID and password used on your computer, and tap **Return**.

4. If you already have an Apple ID shown in Music settings and it is not the same as you used in iTunes on your computer, tap the **Apple ID | Sign Out**. Then do Step 3 with the correct ID.

5. From the iPad's Home screen, tap **Music | More** (in the bottom-right area) **| Shared** and either *computer name* **iPad** to utilize the music on your iPad or *computer name* **Library** to access the music on that computer.

6. Add other computers to Home Sharing by installing iTunes and turning on Home Sharing as described in Steps 1 and 2.

READ ON THE iPAD

Reading on the iPad, especially with the Retina display, is a real joy, comfortable, easy on the eyes, and offers more to read than a person could do in several lifetimes. Many newspapers are available both in Safari and in their own apps. Next, there are a large number of magazines, again both online and in their own apps. Then there is the iBook app that comes with iPad with which you can buy books and read them. Finally, there are a number of third-party eBook readers available in the App Store, along with thousands of free books that you can read and a great number more that you can buy.

Read Using Safari

There is a great deal of material to read on the Internet that is available directly in Safari without another app. This includes web pages themselves, blogs (web logs, or ongoing writing about a particular subject), newspapers, and magazines. Here are examples of web pages and blogs (newspapers and magazines are very similar).

Read Web Pages

There are a number of websites with a lot of written material, for example, CNN.

1. From the Home screen, tap **Safari**.

2. Tap in the address box at the top center of the screen, and tap the **X** on the right end of the box to remove its contents.

3. Type cnn.com and tap **Go**. CNN's home page will open.

4. When you see an article you want to read, tap **Full Story** to open a page with that story.

President Barack Obama greets New Jersey Gov. Chris Christie in Asbury Park, New Jersey, on Tuesday, May 28. "Down the shore, everything's all right," Obama declared on his return to the New Jersey coast seven months after Superstorm Sandy caused billions of dollars in damage there. View photos of the Jersey Shore reopening this weekend and Obama's visit to New Jersey in October.

Jersey Shore reunion for Obama, Christie

(CNN) -- "Down the shore, everything's all right," President Barack Obama declared Tuesday on his return to New Jersey's devastated coast seven months after Superstorm Sandy caused billions of dollars in damage there.

*Figure 7-23: **The built-in reader in Safari is a significant asset to reading webpages.***

5. Tap **Reader** (the stack of lines) at the left end of the address bar. The article will appear in a well-formatted, easy-to-read page (see Figure 7-23).

Read Blogs

Blogs are an ongoing series of articles by one or more authors, generally on a single topic. You can search for and read a blog on the iPad.

1. In Safari, clear the address bar, type google.com, and tap **Go**.

2. In Google's search box, type blogs about ipad and tap **Search**.

3. You may have to go through several pages by tapping links on each page to get to an article you want to read. In this case, you normally do not have the reader available, so you must read directly from the webpage, as you see here.

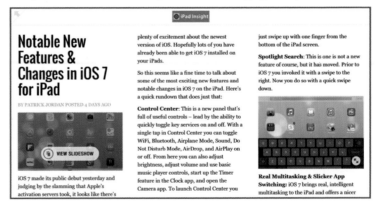

Read Using Dedicated Apps

A number of major sites, especially newspapers and magazines, have their own dedicated reader apps to more fully control the reading experience.

Use a Newspaper App

Here is how to get and use *The Seattle Times* app, as an example:

1. From the Home screen, tap **App Store**.

2. Tap in and clear the search box, and then type <u>Seattle Times</u> and tap **Search**. *The Seattle Times* App appears.

3. Tap the price and then tap **Install**. As needed, enter your Apple ID and any identifying words or characters for the site. When the installation is done, tap **Open**.

4. *The Seattle Times* app opens with an actual image of the front page, as you can see in Figure 7-24.

5. Double-tap an article to open it in a reader, such as that shown in Figure 7-25.

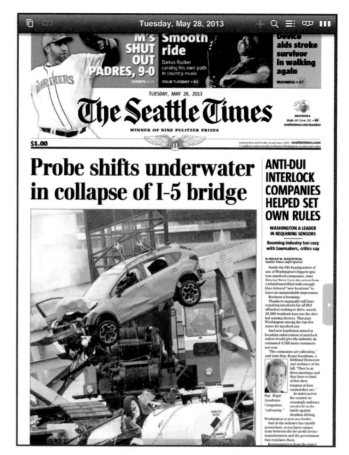

*Figure 7-24: **A number of newspapers give you an actual image of their front page, as if you were reading the real paper.***

Use Newsstand and a Magazine App

The Newsstand is a holder for certain newspapers and magazines whose app has been customized so that the publication goes

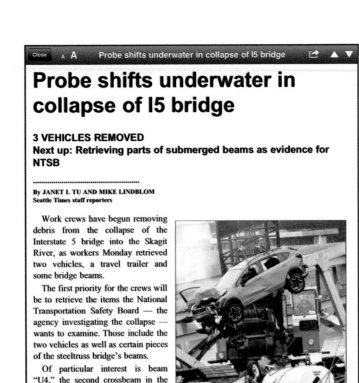

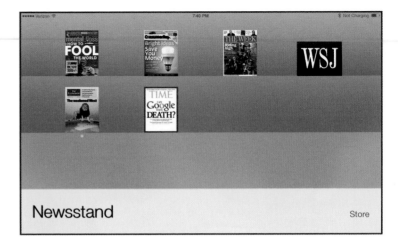

Figure 7-25: *Many dedicated readers are as good as, if not better than, the Safari reader.*

2. Tap **Store** on the bottom-right corner of the Newsstand. The App Store will open and display several magazines, as you can see in Figure 7-26.

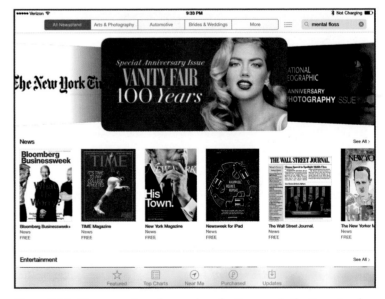

Figure 7-26: *A large number of magazines don't appear in the Newsstand Store, but are available and also work with Newsstand.*

into the Newsstand (the Newsstand itself is not an app). One such magazine is *National Geographic*. Here's how to get it:

1. From the Home screen, tap the Newsstand icon to open the Newsstand.

3. To locate a magazine you don't immediately see, tap and clear the search box in the upper-right corner, type the magazine name, and tap **Search**. A set of magazine apps will appear.

4. Tap *National Geographic* in either the original set of magazines if it appeared in Step 2, or as a result of a search in Step 3.

5. Tap **Free**, tap **Install**, and then tap **Open**. A page opens showing recent copies of the magazine where you can buy individual issues or subscribe for a year.

6. Tap your choice, tap **Buy**, type your Apple ID password, and tap **OK**. Tap **Download** and the magazine will download and then be displayed, as you see in Figure 7-27.

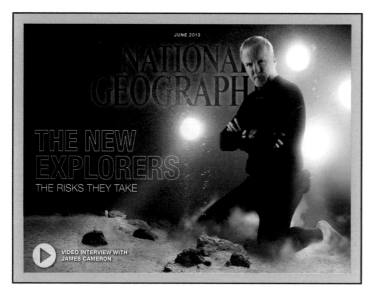

Figure 7-27: Reading **National Geographic** *on an iPad is a terrific experience. The photography is spectacular, and the interactive graphics and videos are stunning.*

 TIP Some magazines automatically download new issues and sometimes automatically charge you for that new issue, depending on your subscription arrangement with them. By tapping **Settings | iTunes & App Store** you can turn off the Automatic Downloads Updates.

Read Using iBooks

One of the great assets of the iPad is the ability to comfortably read books and store a number of books to read. With just the iPad, you can carry a small library around with you; add to that the iBookstore and the iCloud, and you have an endless supply of reading material. The iBooks app is not only a container and organizer for your books, as is Newsstand for magazines, but it is also an excellent reader, a portal to the iBookstore, and a means to fully annotate your books with bookmarks, highlighting, and notes.

Get and Set Up iBooks

Start your iBook experience by getting it and setting it up the way you want.

1. From the Home screen, tap **App Store**, tap and clear the search box, type <u>ibooks</u>, and tap **Search**. In the iBooks description that opens, tap **Free** twice, tap **Install App**, type your Apple ID password, tap **OK**, and tap **Open**.

2. Press **Home** and tap **Settings | iBooks** to open the iBooks settings.

3. Review the settings and consider if you want to change any of them:

- **Full Justification**, when enabled, aligns the text to the margins on both the left and right edges by spreading out the characters and words. The alternative is to have a ragged right edge with consistent character and word spacing.

- **Auto-hyphenation**, when enabled, allows splitting words on the right margin to facilitate justification without drastic changes to the character and word spacing.

- **Both Margins Advance**, when enabled, allows you to advance to the next page on the right by tapping the left margin as well as the right margin. Otherwise, tapping the left margin will take you back one page.

- **Sync Bookmarks** and **Sync Collections**, when enabled, syncs your bookmarks, notes, and current page information, as well as the way you have organized your books into collections across your iOS devices such as iPhones and iPods.

- **Show All Purchases**, when enabled, displays book purchases that you have removed from your iPad but that are kept on iCloud.

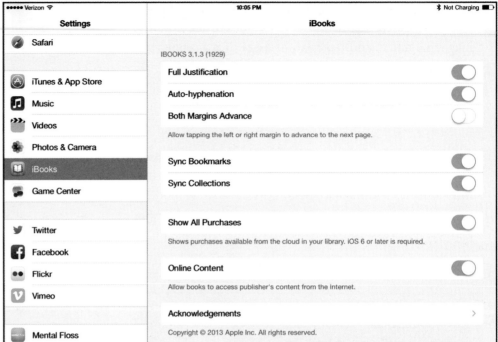

- **Online Content**, when enabled, allows the book you are reading to go online and access content from the book's publisher.

- **Acknowledgements** is Apple acknowledging the people that contributed to iBooks.

4. Press **Home** to leave Settings.

Search and Buy from the iBookstore

The iBookstore is like the iTunes Store except that it is for books. Here is how to buy or acquire (some are free) one or more books:

1. From the Home screen, tap **iBooks** and tap **Store** in the upper-left corner. The iBookstore will open as you see in Figure 7-28.

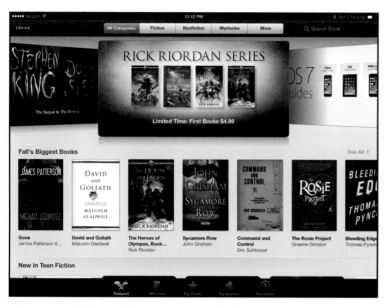

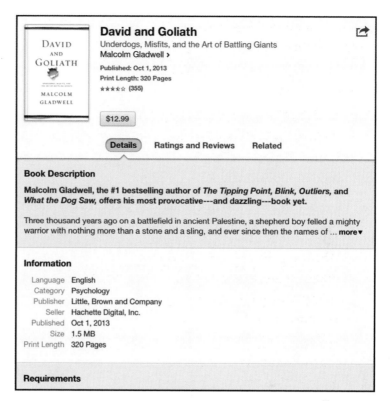

Figure 7-28: *Only a small percentage of the books that are available are shown on the initial iBookstore screen. Look at the other categories and search for what you want.*

2. Swipe from right to left the various lines of books. Swipe up to review various categories of books. You might want to explore the categories "Great Books for $3.99 or Less" and "Free Books." You can also use the search box to search for specific books, authors, or categories.

3. When you find a book you are interested in, tap it to open detailed information about it. If desired, tap **More** to read a lengthier description.

4. If you want to read a sample of the book, tap **Sample**. The book will appear on your bookshelf with the word "Sample" on the cover. Some samples are quite extensive. Dan Brown's *Inferno*, pictured here, which is a 480-page book, has a 117-page sample.

5. When you are ready to buy a book, tap the book's price | **Buy Book**, enter your Apple ID password, and tap **Return**. The book will appear in iBooks.

Use iBooks

While the principal purpose of iBooks is to facilitate the reading of books, it also provides for the acquiring, organization, display, and disposal of books. The functions that can be performed in iBooks include:

- **View books** either in the standard bookshelf view shown in the previous section or in a list view, shown next, by tapping the stack of lines icon in the upper-right corner.

- **Sort List View** by tapping one of the sort methods at the bottom of the list view screen.
- **Arrange books** on the bookshelf by touching and holding on a book while dragging it to another location.

- **Search for a book** by scrolling to the top (swiping from top to bottom) of the bookshelf or book list; tapping in the search box; entering the keywords such as author, title, or subject; and tapping **Search**.

- **Delete books** in either view by tapping **Edit** in the far upper-right corner and tapping the book or books you want to delete to place a white checkmark in a blue circle on the book(s). When you are ready, tap **Delete**. You then can tap either **Delete This Copy** to delete the copy on your iPad or **Delete From All Devices** to delete copies from your iPad as well as any copies on your other iOS devices. Finally, tap **Done**. The book will remain available to you in iCloud (see the icon in the upper-right corner of the book). Tap the book to bring a copy back onto the iPad.

- **Organize books** by putting your library into collections or categories that you set up. You saw earlier how you can have iBook put your library into its categories in List view, but with Collections, you can put your library into your own categories (called "collections") that appear in both Bookshelf and List views. Here's how:

1. Tap **Collections** at the top left of either the Bookshelf or List view, and tap **New**. Type the name of the new collection and tap **Done**. Repeat this for additional collections.

2. Tap **Edit** on the far upper right, tap the books you want in a collection so they have a checkmark, tap **Move** in the far upper left, and tap the collection in which you want to place the selected books. The collection will open in a separate bookshelf or list.

3. Return to the original bookshelf by tapping **Collections | Books**.

4. Swipe the bookshelf to either the left or right to display other collections.

Read a Book

Using iBook to read a book is quite easy, but iBook also provides the means to do much more than just read in terms of enlarging the page, changing the font size, jumping to a particular page, jumping to the table of contents, looking up the definition of a word, and adding a bookmark. Not all books that you read in iBooks have exactly the same features, but many have those that are described here.

- From iBook, if needed, swipe the bookshelf to open the collection and then tap the book that you want to read. The book will open. If you have never read any of the books on the iPad before, the book will open to page 1. If you have previously read some of the book on the iPad or other iOS device with which you are sharing the book, the book will open to where you were last reading, as shown in Figure 7-29.

  - **Turn a page** by tapping in the left margin or swiping from the left edge to go back a page, or by tapping in the right margin or swiping from the right edge to go forward a page.

  - **Display the controls** (see Figure 7-30) by taping virtually anywhere on the page, although Apple recommends toward the center of the page.

  - **Return to the library** by tapping the **Library** button Library in the upper-left corner.

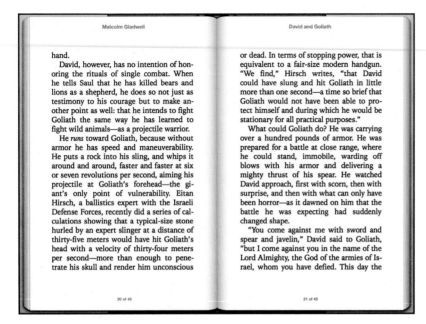

Figure 7-29: *The iPad provides an excellent and easy reading experience.*

- **Display the table of contents** or a list of bookmarks or your notes by tapping the **Contents** icon 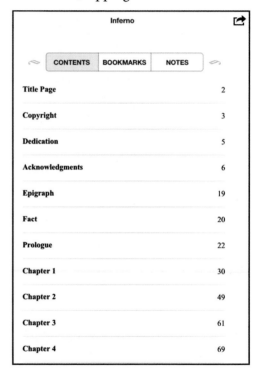 and then, if not Contents, tapping either **Bookmarks** or **Notes**.

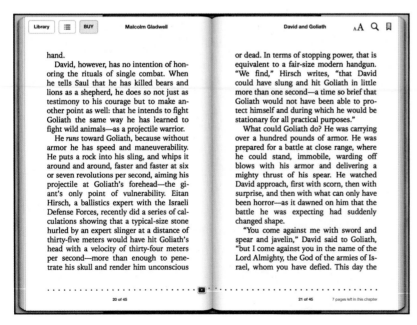

Figure 7-30: *The controls, which can be displayed or not, provide easy manipulation of a book, much more so than a paper book held in your hands.*

- **Change the font and size** by tapping the **Fonts** icon ₐA to open the Fonts menu where you can change the brightness using the slider at the top, decrease or increase the font size by repeatedly tapping the smaller or larger "A," change the font by tapping **Fonts** and tapping a font, and choose a different theme by tapping **Themes** and tapping a color and/or theme.

- **Search the text** by tapping the **Search** icon Q to open the Search box. Type a word to search for and tap **Search**.

- **Add a bookmark** by tapping the **Bookmark** icon on the far right. Tap the icon again to delete it. Since iBook keeps track of where you are currently reading, bookmarks are for other purposes you might have. See a list of bookmarks by tapping the **Contents** icon | **Bookmarks**.

- **Go to another page** by dragging the slider at the bottom of the page in either direction.

Annotate a Book

For those who like to annotate the books they read, reading in iBook has to be a real asset. Besides leaving bookmarks, as discussed earlier, you can:

- **Select text**, any amount of it, by double-tapping some of what you want to select and then dragging the end points to enclose all of the text you want to select. When you do that, a menu appears that allows you to get a definition, highlight, make a note, or search the selection.

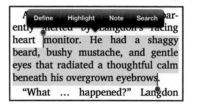

- **Magnify a word** by touching and holding on a particular word. A magnifying glass will appear above the word and allow you to move your finger to exactly select what you want. When you lift your finger, the word(s) will be underlined in red.

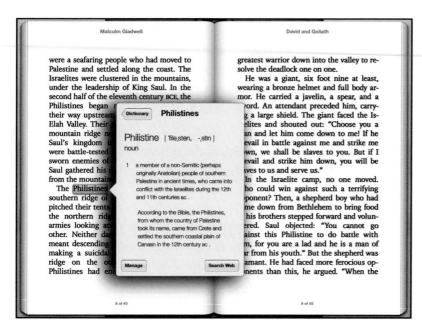

Figure 7-31: *The ability to immediately look up words as you are reading can be helpful.*

- **Define a word** by selecting it and tapping **Define**. A dictionary entry will appear and define the word, as shown in Figure 7-31. If that is inadequate, you can tap either **Search The Web** or **Search Wikipedia** for further information.

- **Highlight text** by selecting it and tapping **Highlight**. In the Highlight menu that opens, tap one of the five colors, the underline ⒶⒶ, or add a note. By default, the highlight will be the highlight color you last used, or, if you have not used highlight before, it will be yellow. You can both highlight and add a note at the same time. Close the highlight menu by tapping anywhere outside of the highlight.

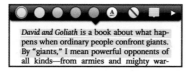

- **Add a note** by selecting the text to be noted and tapping **Note**. A blank note will appear where you can type the note you want. When you are finished, tap outside the note or highlight. The note will disappear and a little yellow icon will appear in the margin 🗒 .

- **Remove highlight or a note** by tapping the highlighted text or note and tapping the remove highlight icon 🚫. If you have a note, you will be told that the note will also be deleted and you can tap **Cancel** or **Delete**; otherwise, just the highlight will be removed from the text and you are returned to the normal page.

- **Search** by selecting a word and tapping **Search**. The same search panel opens as shown earlier with the Search icon at the top of the page.

▷▷ Read Using Third-Party Readers

When you search the App Store, you will see that there are a number of third-party readers for books, magazines, and newspapers. Two of the better-known readers are Amazon's Kindle reader and Barnes & Noble's Nook, which allow you to read the many documents created for these devices.

Use the Kindle Reader

Amazon says that the Kindle app will give you access to over a million books and hundreds of newspapers and magazines.

1. From the Home screen, tap **App Store** and tap in and clear the search box. Type <u>Kindle</u> and tap **Search**. The Kindle information will be displayed.

2. Tap **Free** twice | **Install App**, type your Apple ID password, and tap **OK** | **Open**.

3. If available, enter your Amazon ID and password or register with Amazon, and tap **Register This Kindle**. If you have previously purchased Kindle books, they will appear.

4. To purchase books for the Kindle reader, open Safari, type <u>Amazon.com</u> in the address box, and tap **Go.** Search for the book you want, select the Kindle edition, and complete the purchase. The book you purchased will appear in your Kindle library.

5. Tap the book you want to read, and it will open in the reader. It looks and operates like iBooks. You can:

   - **Turn a page** by tapping in the left margin or swiping from the left edge to go back a page, or by tapping in the right margin or swiping from the right edge to go forward a page.

   - **Display the controls** (see Figure 7-32) by tapping toward the center of the page. The controls, from left to right, are used to go to various places within the book as shown next; change the brightness, font, font size, color, and layout of a page; search the book for a word or phrase; open a notebook of your notes and bookmarks; analyze the people and terms on a page (this is a unique feature); add a bookmark; with the slider at the bottom of the screen, jump to any page in the book; and return to the last page read.

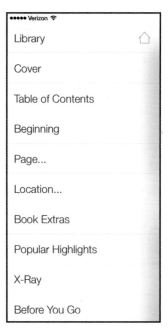

   - **Select a word** by pressing and holding on it. A magnifying glass will appear to help you select it. When you remove your finger, the definition of the word will appear at

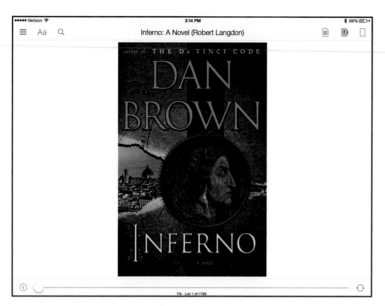

Figure 7-32: **The Kindle reader is very similar to iBook.**

the bottom of the page (if you haven't already, you will have to first download a dictionary for Kindle) and the highlighter will open where you can add a highlight, a note, or share the information via Twitter or Facebook.

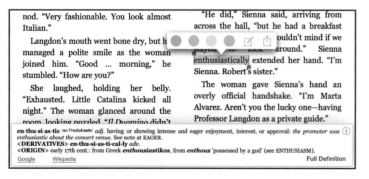

Use the Nook Reader

Barnes & Noble says that Nook reader gives you access to over three million books, including over a million free books.

1. From the Home screen, tap **App Store** and tap in and clear the search box. Type <u>Nook</u> and tap **Search**. The Nook information will be displayed.

2. Tap **Free** twice | **Install App**, type your Apple ID password, and tap **OK | Open**.

3. If you have a Barnes & Noble or Nook account, tap **Sign In**, select your country, tap **Yes** to accept the Nook end-user agreement, tap **Submit**, enter your email address and your password, tap **Sign In**, and proceed to Step 5.

4. If you do not have a Barnes & Noble or Nook account, press **Home**, tap Safari, type <u>barnesandnoble.com</u> in the address box, and tap **Go**. In the Barnes & Noble website, tap **Sign In** at the top center. Type your email address, tap **No**, and tap **Secure Sign In**. Enter the requested information and tap **Create Account**. Return to Step 3 and register your Nook reader.

5. To purchase books for the Nook reader, open Safari, type barnesandnoble.com in the address box, tap **Go**, and tap **Nook Books**. Search for the book you want, select the Nook edition, and complete the purchase. The book you purchased will appear in your Nook library.

6. Tap the book you want to read, and it will open in the reader. It operates much like iBooks and the Kindle reader. You can:

- **Turn a page** by tapping in the left margin or swiping from the left edge to go back a page, or by tapping in the right margin or swiping from the right edge to go forward a page.

- **Display the controls** (see Figure 7-33) by tapping toward the center of the page. The controls, from left to right, are used to return to your library of books; open the table of

contents, list of bookmarks, or list of annotations; go to a particular page number; change the font size, font, color, line spacing, and margins; change the brightness; search the book for a word or phrase; see information about the book; add a bookmark; and with the slider at the bottom, jump to any page in the book.

- **Select a word** by pressing and holding on it. When you remove your finger, the definition of the word will appear at the bottom of the page and a menu of options will open where you can add a note or a highlight, look up the word in a full-featured dictionary, or search for the word in the book.

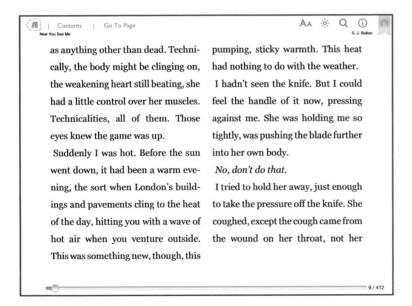

Figure 7-33: *The Nook has a slightly different look, but it operates similarly to other e-readers.*

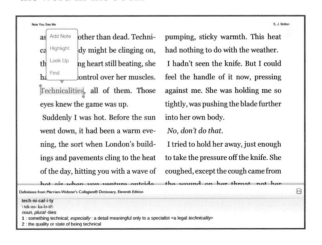

Using Public Libraries

Many public libraries, even smaller ones, have programs for lending eBooks on the Internet. You need a library card and that is about all. There are differences among libraries on how the eBook lending works, and you'll need to explore your own local library. To give you an example, I'll demonstrate how my regional library's program operates. It is the Sno-Isle Libraries and covers Snohomish and Island Counties in the northwest corner of Washington state. Here's what I did to get onto my library's program:

1. Open Safari | Google. In Google's text box, I typed Sno Isle Libraries. This got me the Uniform Resource Locator (URL) for the library, and by tapping the link, I opened its home page, which you can see in Figure 7-34.

2. I tapped **Electronic Media** and got a list of six eBook and eMagazine services. I tapped one of the services (OverDrive) and tapped **All Fiction**. There were 17,822 titles available.

3. I did a search on Dan Brown's *Inferno*. The library had 39 electronic copies, none were immediately available, and 82 people were in line waiting for it, as shown in Figure 7-35. Also, it was available for Kindle and two other formats I was not familiar with.

4. After looking at several more books, I found one I could immediately borrow. I tapped **Borrow**, entered my library card number, tapped **Sign In | Download**, selected a service (Kindle), and then tapped **Confirm & Download**.

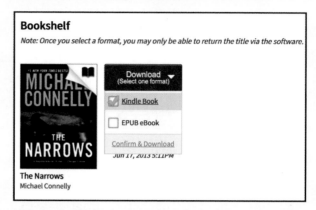

5. The Amazon website opened and confirmed that I had gotten a Digital Library Loan that expired in two weeks (upon request, this can be lengthened to three weeks). In Amazon, I had to tap **Get Library Book** and make sure that the iPad was the selected device.

6. I opened the Kindle reader app, tapped the **Sync** icon, and the library book appeared in the Kindle's library. Tapping the book opened it so it could be read. A loaned library book looks and reads exactly like a purchased book, except that it will disappear in a limited time, usually two to three weeks.

USE MAPS

iPad's Maps is one of its most useful and practical apps, as well as being fascinating and even fun. You can quickly find where an address is located as well as get directions to it. You can also see where you currently are and get information about your current area, as well as find out about points of interest and local establishments. You can see this in a standard map view, shown in Figure 7-36, in a 3-D satellite view, and in a hybrid view where the street names, points of interest, and establishments are overlaid on the satellite view, as you can see in Figure 7-37. If that wasn't enough, you can view the satellite and hybrid views straight up and down, where you can better see the streets, or at an angle where you can better see the buildings. Maps has

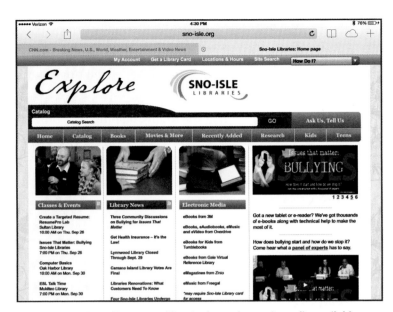

Figure 7-34: *Many, if not most, libraries have electronic media available for loan.*

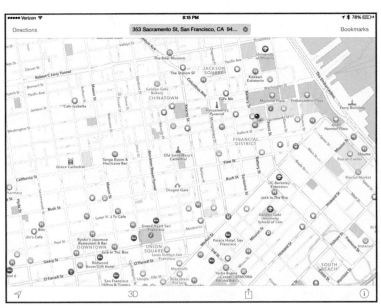

Figure 7-36: *Maps standard map view provides a great amount of information and is similar to a paper map.*

Figure 7-35: *Like paper books, libraries have a limited number of copies of eBooks and sometimes there are long waiting lists for them.*

Figure 7-37: *Maps hybrid satellite view, while harder to use as a map, is fascinating to look at.*

two primary purposes: to find out where something is located and to get directions to a location.

> **NOTE** Maps requires an Internet connection, either Wi-Fi or cellular, and voice driving directions requires a cellular connection that will incur data usage. To get your current location you must give permission for that. While maps are relatively accurate and quite useful, they are not perfect and you must allow for some error.

⏩ Explore Maps

Maps can be fun to explore, but are also very useful to find out where something is located.

1. From the Home screen tap **Maps**. Maps will open and show you where you are currently located with a blue dot in a white circle, as you can see in Figure 7-38.

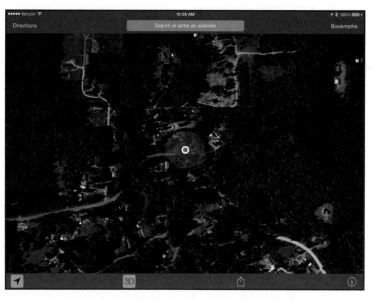

Figure 7-38: **You can always find your current location in Maps.**

2. You can change what you are seeing:
   - Move around a map by dragging it with a single finger.
   - Change the orientation of the map by rotating it with two fingers.
   - Return to the North at the top by tapping the compass in the upper-right corner, which only appears when you have rotated the map.
   - Zoom in by double-tapping with a single finger or by spreading two fingers apart.
   - Zoom out by tapping with two fingers or by bringing together two fingers.

3. Search for a location by tapping in the search box at the top of the screen and typing an address; the name or type of an establishment; or a landmark, area, town, city, zip code, or region. Maps may suggest a destination as you are typing. If you want the suggestion, tap it.

4. Tap **Bookmarks** in the upper-right corner to use the address of a contact, bookmarks you have created in Maps, or recent locations you have entered into Maps.

5. Touch and hold on a location on the map to drop a pin there, identify it, and mark it for future reference. Tap the info icon ⓘ and find out more information about that location.

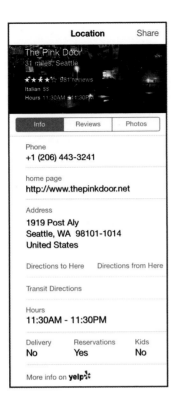

6. Tap **Reviews** on some info drop-downs to see what others think about a restaurant or other establishment. With other options you can get directions, create a contact, see photos, add a bookmark, and review related apps.

7. Tap one of the many icons on the map to get information about that location or establishment.

8. Tap the arrowhead in the lower-left corner to see your current location.

9. Tap **3D** in the lower-middle-left area while in Standard Maps view and zoom in to see a shadow of the buildings in that area.

10. Tap the Share menu icon in the lower-middle-right area to send map information of either your current location or a selected location to others using AirDrop, Message, Mail, or other means.

11. Tap the info icon in the lower-right corner to change the map view, drop a pin in the center of the map, print a map on a selected local wireless printer, report a problem with the map, or show traffic on local streets using increasingly thicker red dashed lines for increasing traffic congestion and yellow dotted lines for construction.

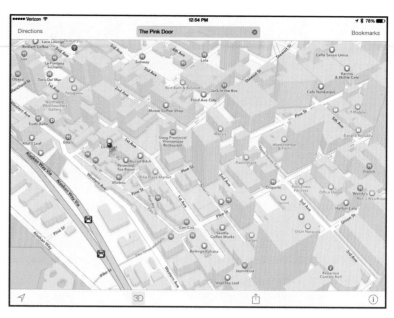

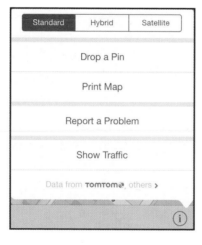

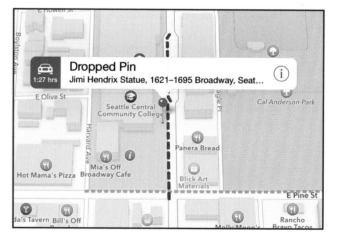

12. Press the **Home** button and tap **Settings | Maps**. Here you can control the volume of voice navigation, choose whether distance is in miles or kilometers, labels in English, and whether directions are for driving or walking.

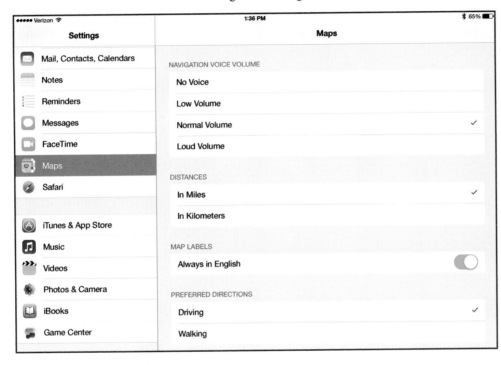

▷▷ Get Directions

It is one thing to locate a place or an establishment, but it might still be difficult to get there. Maps can show you how to get to a destination with alternative routes on a map, with a set of written instructions, and can give you turn-by-turn voice instructions.

1. From the Maps screen, tap **Directions** in the upper-left corner to open the Directions menu.

Alternatively you open directions by tapping the automobile symbol on a pin you dropped or appears when you touch and hold on a map feature or the map itself. You can also tap **Directions To/From Here** in information dropdowns.

2. At the top of the Directions menu select whether you want directions for driving, walking, or using transit.

3. Enter or select the starting and ending locations and tap **Route** to display the route on the map. The recommended route will be shown in dark blue, while alternative routes will be shown in lighter blue with the approximate driving times shown with each route, as you can see in Figure 7-39.

4. Start getting voice directions by tapping **Start** in the upper-right corner. The voice directions will begin and then pause until it detects that you have completed that step. You can

stop the voice directions by tapping **End** in the upper-left corner, change the volume by tapping the loudspeaker in the lower-right corner, or display written directions by tapping the stack of lines at the bottom-middle of the screen.

5. Tap **Clear** in the upper-left corner, to remove a route from the map.

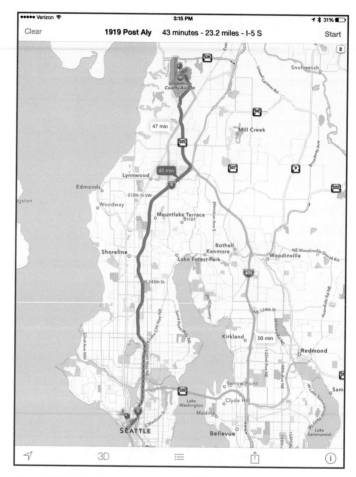

Figure 7-39: Routes on a map are useful for overall information, but you will often also need turn-by-turn directions in by voice or written.

Bob Dent

My use of the iPad is not very broad, but I read a lot on it. Some subscriptions I read solely on the iPad even though I also get a paper version. *The New Yorker* magazine is an example of this. Another is a newspaper I get from the United Kingdom where I have recently canceled the paper version because it gets hung up in the mail. One reason that both *The New Yorker* and the UK newspaper are particularly good on the iPad is that their articles tend to be contiguous, all in one place, instead of jumping around the magazine. Newspapers generally, though, are not so easy to read on the iPad, and I tend to prefer the real thing.

I do like reading books on the iPad and have read a number of them there. I make a decision on whether I want to give a book to someone and, if not, I buy it for the iPad. I carry the iPad everywhere I go, generally in place of the laptop I used to carry, so the books and magazines are with me whenever I have a moment. One drawback to the iPad, though, is that I can't leave it on the beach like I would a book. I'm pretty sure it would disappear in a short time when I go for a swim.

I go online with Safari occasionally. For example, I use airline sites to keep track of flights when I travel. I haven't downloaded a boarding pass to either my iPad or iPhone, even though I could, principally because the paper boarding pass seems more secure. I have used Google Maps a bit, and I have done a little writing, generally in email messages to myself that I will put into real documents or letters on my iMac when I get home.

I find the iPad is handy, intuitive, and easy to use. Friends I have from Microsoft use iPads and agree it's easy and intuitive. Our family has now gone fully to Apple products after many years of Microsoft products. Both my wife and I have replaced our laptops with iPads for our mobile and travel needs.

Chapter 8

Working with Photos and Videos

The iPad is truly a multimedia device. In the last chapter you saw how well it handled literature and music. In this chapter you'll see how it does an equally good job with photos and videos, and in addition it can take and edit photos and videos. We'll look at how to transfer these to and from your computer, as well as how to take, edit, and view them on the iPad.

WORK WITH PHOTOS

There are many reasons why you want photos on your iPad, from the simple fact that you like them or want them for the wallpaper on the Home screen, to using them to illustrate points in a document, or to display them in a photo essay. Whatever the reason, the iPad makes it easy to acquire, take, edit, store, and use photos. All of these actions are discussed in this section.

▷▷ Transfer Photos from Your Computer

Much like music, you get photos from your computer through iTunes to your iPad. If you don't have iTunes on your computer, see the previous chapter for how to get it. With iTunes available, use the following sections to collect and transfer the photos on your computer.

Collect Photos on Your Computer

To get photos to your iPad from your computer, they must first reside in iTunes on your computer. Begin by finding the photos. On recent Windows computers (Vista, 7, or 8), they are probably located within Libraries/Pictures/My Pictures. On a Mac, they are probably in iPhoto. Both My Pictures and iPhoto are shown in Figure 8-1.

1. In Windows, open Windows Explorer or File Explorer in Windows 8 and navigate to Libraries/Pictures/My Pictures; in a Mac, open iPhoto, and see if the photos that you want on your iPad are there. If so, go on to Step 2. If not, search

your hard drive for the pictures you want and move them to My Pictures in Windows or iPhoto on the Mac.

 NOTE You don't have to move your photos to My Pictures or iPhoto if you really don't want to; it just makes life simpler. If you don't use My Pictures or iPhoto, then in iTunes, change Sync Photos From My Pictures or iPhoto to the folder you are using for your photos.

2. Plug your iPad into your computer, open iTunes on your computer, click your iPad in iTunes, and click **Photos** in the top options on the right. The Sync Photos From pane will appear in either the PC or Mac, as you see in Figure 8-2.

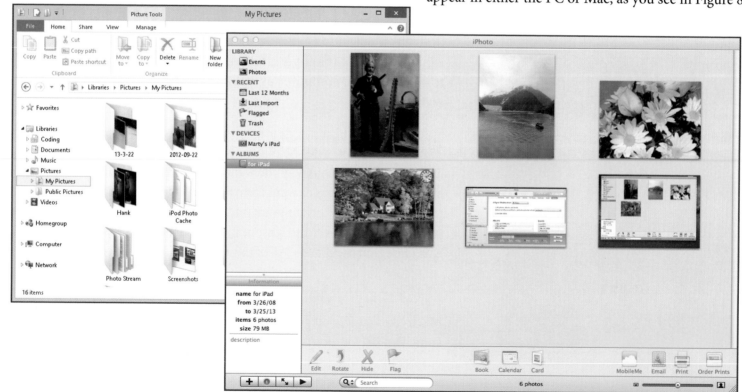

Figure 8-1: **Photos are often in My Pictures on a PC and in iPhotos on a Mac, but they can be anywhere.**

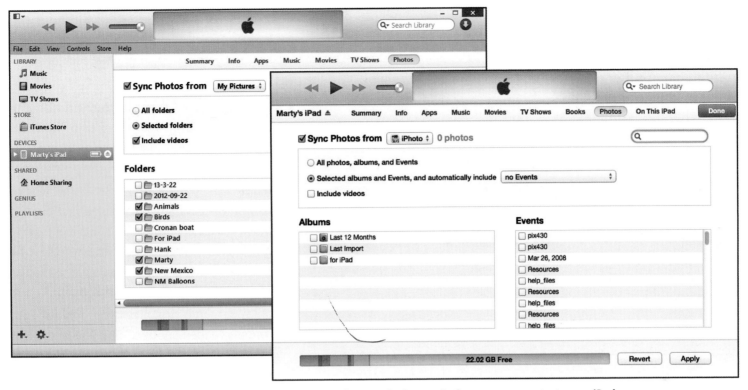

*Figure 8-2: **iTunes on your computer provides the primary conduit for transferring media from your computer to your iPad.***

3. Click **Sync Photos From**. If you don't use My Pictures or iPhoto, then click the two-way arrow, click **Choose Folder**, and select the folder you are using for your photos.

4. Click either **All Folders** or **Selected Folders** (Albums on a Mac) (I recommend the latter due to the limited storage on the iPad) and whether you want to include videos. If so, click that option. If you choose Selected Folders or Albums, click the ones you want transferred to the iPad.

Transfer Photos to Your iPad

Transferring photos from your computer to your iPad at this point is pretty simple—click **Apply**. You will see a message at the top of iTunes saying that your computer is syncing with your iPad. "Syncing," you may remember, is keeping the same media content on both devices.

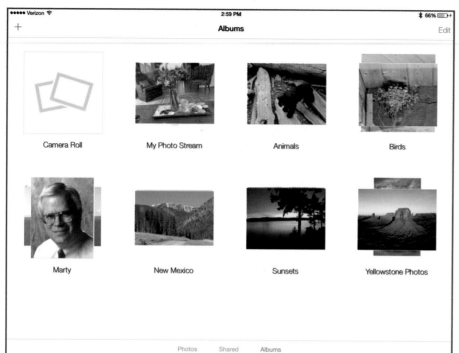

Figure 8-3: *The Photos app on your iPad provides organization of your photos through albums.*

Organize Your Photos

The Photos app provides three primary ways of looking at, or views of, your photos, each of which has further categorization:

- **Photos**, which takes all your photos and automatically organizes them into Moments (by date and time), Collections (by location for more recent photos with geocoding), and Years.

- **Shared**, which, if you have set up an iCloud account, displays Shared Streams that contain photos you share with the other devices that are on your iCloud account or shared with specific people. We'll talk about these later in this chapter in the QuickFacts "Using Photo Stream."

- **Albums**, which organizes your photos into groupings called "albums" that you create. For the photos that you brought across from your computer, each album is a folder that you had on your computer, as you saw earlier in Figure 8-3. The album named Camera Roll in Figure 8-3 appears when you take pictures with your iPad's camera or take screen captures. See discussions later in this chapter on both taking pictures and capturing screens.

 Use the Photos App

On your iPad, from the Home screen, tap **Photos**. A screen of the photos from your computer should open, as you see in my case in Figure 8-3. If the syncing did not take place, in iTunes on your computer click your iPad under Devices on the left and then click **Sync** in the lower-right corner. When completed, the photos that you selected in iTunes on your computer should be the same as the photos on your iPad.

TIP *Screen captures, or "screenshots," are images of what is currently on the iPad's screen. All of the iPad screen images in this book are screenshots from my iPad. You take a screenshot by pressing and holding the **Sleep/Wake** button while pressing the **Home** button. The screen will go blank for a fraction of a second and you will hear a "click" sound. The images will go into the Camera Roll album and, if enabled, into your Photo Stream.*

Figure 8-4: **Within an album you can see and select individual photos.**

Work with Photos

You can work with your photographs in either the Albums or Photos view. The objective, though, is to get to an individual picture. Here, we'll start with albums.

1. In Photos, if it isn't already selected, tap **Albums** at the bottom (at the top in iOS 6 and earlier) of the Photos screen.

2. Tap an album to open it and see the photos.

3. Tap a photo to enlarge it, as shown in Figure 8-4.

4. Drag either the photo itself or the photo selection bar at the bottom of the screen to view other photos.

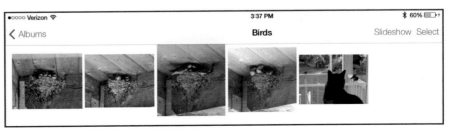

5. Tap a photo to redisplay the controls at the top and bottom.

6. Tap the **Share** icon 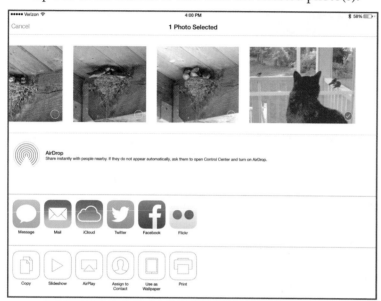, select any additional photos in the album by tapping the circle at the bottom of a photo, and tap one of the actions to take with the selected photo(s).

7. When you are ready, tap **Cancel**, if you are still in the Share screen, then tap the album name on the far left to close the photo and return to the display of the album's photos. There you can select another photo or tap **Albums** to return to the album screen.

Work with Albums

As you read earlier, folders on a PC or albums on a Mac that you downloaded from your computer become albums on the iPad. After you have taken pictures or captured screens, the iPad creates an album for these items called Camera Roll. In addition, you can create as many albums as you like.

1. To add another album from the album screen, tap the plus sign on the upper far left, type an album name, and tap **Save**. In the Photos screen that opens, tap the photos that you want to add to the new album. Tap **Done** when you are ready.

2. Tap **Edit** on the upper far right of the Albums screen. Here you can:

- **Move an album** by pressing and holding on an album and then dragging it where you want it.
- **Delete** an album that you have created on the iPad (you can't delete an album that you brought over from your computer) by tapping the **x** in the upper-left corner of the album and then tapping **Delete Album**.

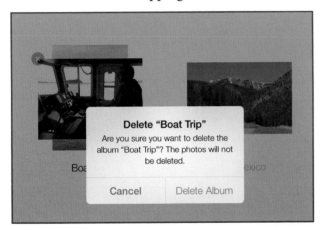

- **Rename** an album that you have created on the iPad by double-tapping the name and using the onscreen keyboard to make the changes you want.

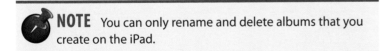

NOTE You can only rename and delete albums that you create on the iPad.

3. Tap **Photos** to open a screen of your photos and, if needed, go to the Moments display. Tap **Select** and then tap the photos that you want to share, delete, or add to other albums, as shown in Figure 8-5.

- Tap the **Share** icon to open the Share menu where you can attach a photo to a message or email; send it

to iCloud, Twitter, Facebook, or Flickr; and copy, print, or perform other actions on it.

- Tap **Add To** to add selected photos to albums that were created on the iPad. You can't add to albums that you brought over from folders on your computer.
- Tap **Delete** (the recycle bin) to delete selected images that you have taken or copied on your iPad that don't also exist on your computer or another device. Tap **Remove From Album** to complete the process.
- Tap **Cancel** to stop any operation you have started.

4. Copy a photo by pressing and holding on it until the word "Copy" appears, tapping **Copy** and then opening an album you created in iPad. Then either press and hold on an existing photo and then tap **Paste** to paste the copy to the

Figure 8-5: *Photos lets you work with your photos in one place, independent of their albums.*

left of the existing photo, or press and hold on a blank area of the album and tap **Paste** to paste the copy to the right of the last existing photo.

TIP There are a number of third-party photo editing apps in the App Store that provide many more features than those available in Photos. Search "photo editing" and you will see over 100 apps that are available.

Edit Photos

With a single photo displayed, tap **Edit** on the upper-right corner to perform a number of operations, as shown in Figure 8-6:

- Tap **Rotate**  once for each 45 degrees of counterclockwise rotation that you want.

- Tap **Enhance** to apply an automatic enhancement, generally brightening.

- Tap **Filters** (in iOS 7 and later only) to apply one of eight filters, which you can choose from the option displayed across the bottom of the screen.

- Tap **Red-Eye** and tap each eye in which you want to remove red-eye.

- Tap **Crop** and drag the corners in toward the center to crop the photo on two sides, as shown in Figure 8-7.

- Tap **Aspect Ratio** at the bottom center, and tap a size to have the cropped image fit a certain size such as 3 × 5 or 5 × 7. Tap **Reset** to return to the image before it was cropped. Tap the yellow **Crop** in the upper-right corner to complete the cropping. The yellow word "Crop" does not show until up you actually indicate you want to crop the picture by dragging one or more of the corners.

  - Tap **Cancel** to stop whatever editing function is currently underway.

  - Tap **Undo** to remove the last edit you performed.

  - Tap **Revert To Original** to do that.

Set Up a Slideshow

A slideshow displays the photos in the current album one after the other. From the Album view, tap **Slideshow** to create one. The Slideshow Options menu will open. See "Review Photos & Camera Settings" later in this chapter.

*Figure 8-6: **Edit Photo allows you to make several overall changes to a photo.***

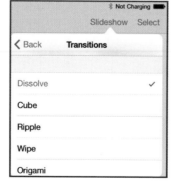

Figure 8-7: ***Cropping lets the photo better focus on the primary subject.***

- Tap **Transitions** and review the various transitions that are available. Try several to see which one you like and then use it.

- If desired, tap the **Play Music** on/off switch, tap **Music**, and then select the piece you want to play in the background.

- Tap **Start Slideshow** to do that.

 **QuickFacts**

Using Photo Stream

Photo Stream is a component of iCloud that allows you to share recent photos that you have taken on your iPad with other devices that share your iCloud account. Of course, you must have set up and enabled an iCloud account as described in Chapter 1. Also, Photo Stream must be enabled in Settings, as described in "Review Photos & Camera Settings" later in this chapter.

Photos that you take with Camera or screenshots (see earlier Tip) that you capture on your iPad go into the Camera Roll album and then, if it is enabled, are automatically uploaded to your Photo Stream on iCloud after you leave Camera (see Figure 8-8). The photos can then be viewed on all the devices that share your iCloud account, including PC and Mac computers. On your iPad you will also see photos taken or captured on your other iCloud-enabled devices. You can keep up to 1,000 photos on your Photo Stream, and they won't count against your total iCloud storage.

It's easy to manage your Photo Stream:

1. From the Home screen, tap **Photos**, if necessary, return to Albums, tap **My Photo Stream** in the top center, and tap **Select** on the top right.

2. Tap the photo(s) that you want to share, delete, or save to your iPad.

3. Tap the **Share** icon at the top left to open the Share menu and add the photo(s) to an email, message, Shared Photo Stream (see the next section), Twitter, Facebook, your Camera Roll, print, copy, or perform other actions on it.

4. Tap **Add To** to save the photo(s) to an existing album that you have created or to a new album.

5. Tap **Delete** (the recycle bin) to remove the photo(s) from your Photo Stream on your iPad. This does not delete the original photo.

Shared Photo Stream

Shared Photo Stream is a separate photo stream that you share with other people not on your iCloud account but who have iOS 6 or later or OS X Mountain Lion or later devices (recent iPhones, iPads, iPod touch, and Macs). To create a Shared Photo Stream:

1. From most Photos screens, tap **Shared** at the bottom of the screen to open Shared Streams.

2. Tap the plus sign in the upper-left corner to open and name a new stream you are creating.

3. Tap **Next** and enter the email address(es) of the people you

want to share with. Tap the plus sign in a circle to enter additional email addresses.

4. When you are ready, tap **Create**.

5. Tap the new stream and tap the plus sign to open Photos. Tap the photos you want to include in your new Photo Stream.

6. Tap **People** to invite additional people and decide how you want to manage the Photo Stream.

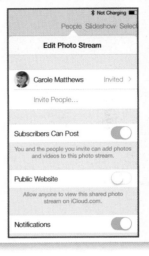

Figure 8-8: *Photo Stream shares the photos you take on one of your iCloud devices with your other iCloud devices.*

Review Photos & Camera Settings

Review the settings that are available for Photos from the Home screen by tapping **Settings | Photos & Camera** (see Figure 8-9):

- **My Photo Stream** allows you to turn on or off the basic Photo Stream capability. See the "Using Photo Stream" QuickFacts.

- **Photo Sharing** allows you to turn on or off the Shared Photo Stream capability. See the "Using Photo Stream" QuickFacts.

- **Summarize Photos** allows you to choose a compact summarized view for Collections and Years.

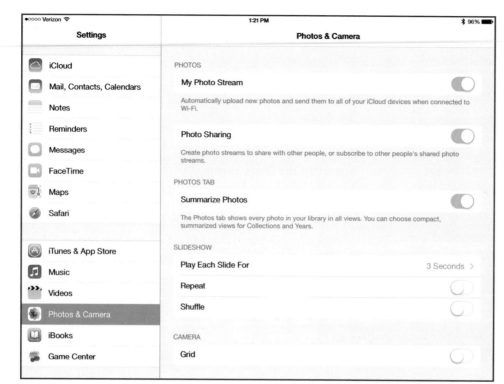

Figure 8-9: As with all settings, try the Photos & Camera settings to see if they suit you.

Take Photos on the iPad

I bet you have already figured out how to take a picture with your iPad.

1. From the Home screen, tap **Camera**. An image of what the camera is looking at will be displayed.

2. Press the Camera button in the middle of the right side of the screen. That is all there is to it. Your picture will appear at the end of the Camera Roll album, as you can see in Figure 8-10.

After taking a couple of pictures with just these two steps, you are going to want to change the focus, zoom in or out, use a grid to align the objects you are photographing, jump to the Camera Roll and jump back to Camera, and switch from the back to the front camera.

- **Play Each Side For** allows you to set the number of seconds, from 2 to 20, that each slide plays in a slideshow.

- **Repeat** allows you to turn on or off the playing of a slideshow.

- **Shuffle** allows you to turn on or off the random mixing of slides in a slideshow.

- **Camera Grid** allows you to turn on or off a grid for better aligning a photo. This does not show in the final picture.

- **Keep Normal Photo** saves a normal photo when an HDR (High Dynamic Range) series of photos are taken that blend the best parts of three separate exposures.

Change Focus

The iPad's cameras have automatic focus capability and, by default, aim that capability at the center of the image on the screen. In Camera, when you hold the iPad still, preparing to take a picture, a small white square briefly appears in the center of the image showing where the focus is aimed. As you move the iPad and change the image, Camera will refocus and the little white square will briefly reappear to show you what it is focusing on, as you see in Figure 8-11. At any time you can touch the screen to tell the iPad to focus on that spot. You'll see the little white square appear where you touched the screen.

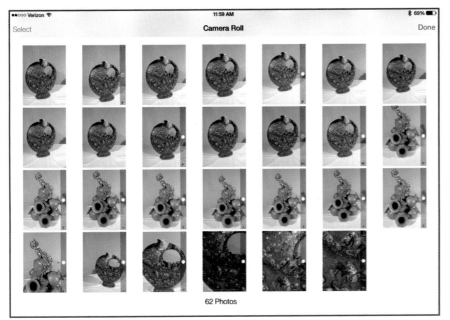

Figure 8-10: *The Camera Roll album is one long stream of photos you take or capture.*

Zoom In or Out

Camera has the standard iPad zoom capability where you can zoom in (enlarge the image) by spreading two fingers apart on the screen and zoom out (reduce the image) by bringing two fingers together (pinching) on the screen. When you start to use your fingers to zoom in or out, a slider control appears on the bottom of the screen (see Figure 8-12). You can drag the slider in either direction to accomplish the zooming.

Use a Grid

As you try to compose a picture, it is sometimes hard to align the object you are photographing within the frame of the picture. To help with that, Camera allows you to turn on a grid that you can use for aligning objects on the screen, as you saw in Figure 8-12.

Figure 8-11: *Camera's focus is optimized within a small white square on the screen.*

Figure 8-12: *You can zoom in or out using either your fingers or the slider control at the bottom of the screen.*

Turn on or off the grid by tapping **Settings | Photos & Camera | Camera Grid** as described earlier in the chapter. The grid appears on the screen but will not show up in the photo.

Jump to the Camera Roll

As you are taking pictures, you will probably want to quickly look at your latest picture to see if you got what you wanted. You can do that by tapping the thumbnail image of your last snapshot in the lower-right corner. That takes you to the full-screen image of your last photo (see Figure 8-13). Use your finger to scroll from left to right to see previous photos. You can also use any of the Camera Roll controls you learned about

Figure 8-13: **One of the best features of the iPad's camera is the ability to quickly see a larger size image of what you just took.**

earlier in this chapter. If the controls disappear, tap the screen to redisplay them. When you are ready to return to the Camera, tap **Done** in the upper-right corner.

Switch from Back to Front

The iPad has two cameras, one on the back with a higher resolution that is meant for taking the majority of pictures and videos, and one on the front that is primarily for FaceTime conversations. You can switch between the two by tapping the camera and circular arrows icon in the upper right.

Take a Square Photo

The normal photo taken by the iPad is rectangular. iOS 7 gives you the option to make the photo square. In the command bar on the right, drag **Square** up to the yellow dot. You will see the elongated sides shorten to form a square.

✓ QuickFacts

Moving iPad Photos to Your Computer

As you take pictures or otherwise collect them on your iPad, you likely will want them also on your computer. You can do this by simply plugging your iPad into your computer.

Move to a PC

When you plug your iPad into a PC computer, an AutoPlay message pops up giving you several options about what to do with your iPad information. All are good options, but I like to control where information is put on my computer, so I choose

Open Device To View Files. The other options don't give you the same degree of control.

1. On a PC, in the AutoPlay dialog box, click **Open Device To View Files**. This opens the Windows Explorer (File Explorer on Windows 8) displaying the internal storage of your iPad.

2. To drill down to your photos, double-click **Internal Storage** to open it. Double-click the **DCIM** file folder to open it, and then double-click the final file folder. This opens the Camera Roll album on your iPad, displaying the photos it contains, as you see in Figure 8-14.

3. Use the File (Windows) Explorer as you normally would to move the iPad's photos on the right to folders on your computer on the left.

Move to a Mac

On a Mac, when you plug your iPad into the computer, iTunes may open it if that is your default setting. Close iTunes, open iPhoto, click your iPad, click the photos you want to import onto your Mac, and click **Import Selected**, as shown in Figure 8-15. Click either **Delete Originals** or **Keep Originals**. Use the Finder as you normally would to move the iPad's photos to where you want them.

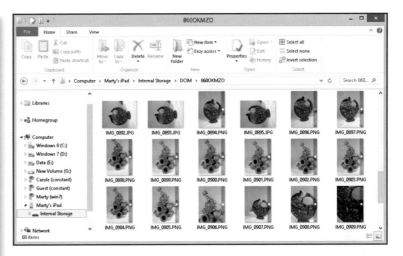

Figure 8-14: *Getting photos from your iPad is just like getting pictures from another folder on your computer.*

Figure 8-15: *On a Mac, you need to use iPhoto to initially get photos off the iPad.*

ⓘ Use Photo Booth

The iPad's Photo Booth app lets you have fun with photos you take much like the photo booths you see at a fair or other public place. Photo Booth uses either camera on the iPad to take a picture with one of nine effects (including "normal") that you can see in Figure 8-16.

1. From the Home screen, tap the Photo Booth icon to open the app. You will see the nine options that can be used in a photo as shown in Figure 8-16.

2. Tap one of the effects to use it, compose your picture, and tap the round button at the bottom center of the screen to take the photo, as you see in Figure 8-17.

Figure 8-17: **You can get some really strange effects in Photo Booth.**

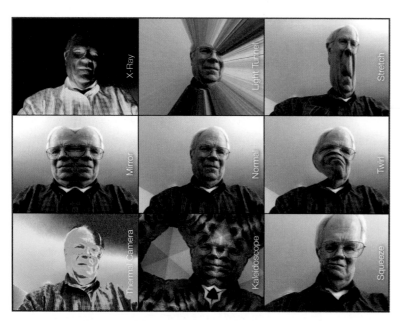

Figure 8-16: **Photo Booth lets you distort a photo you take in one of eight ways.**

3. Tap the icon on the bottom left ▣ to return to the nine alternatives, or switch cameras by tapping the icon on the bottom right.

4. Once you have selected an effect you want to use, tap one of the thumbnails of the photos you have taken that appear at the bottom of the screen to display the full-screen photo. Tap the screen to make the controls reappear.

5. Delete the selected picture by tapping the recycle bin icon in the bottom-left area of the screen.

6. Tap the Share icon at the bottom-left corner of the screen and then tap one of the actions—**AirDrop**, **Message**, **Mail**, or **Copy**—or one of the other options to carry out the action.

7. Tap the screen to return to the active camera.

WORK WITH VIDEOS

You iPad provides an excellent way to watch, record, and edit videos. The newer iPads with the Retina display actually provide a higher-resolution display than the newer high-definition (HD) TVs (the iPad Retina display resolution is 2,048 × 1,536 pixels vs. 1,920 × 1,080 pixels in an HD TV). This makes the iPad a great video, movie, or TV viewing experience on a small screen. One of the best uses of this is to load several movies and/or TV series on your iPad and take them with you on a long airplane flight—you will be entertained for many hours.

You can get videos to watch on your computer through online purchase (such as from the iTunes Store), through rentals and subscription services such as Netflix, and through libraries.

With the iPad's cameras you can also record videos in much the same way as you take a photo on an iPad, do some limited editing with the default apps, and download apps for more comprehensive video editing.

▷▷ Transfer Videos from Your Computer

Transferring videos from your computer to your iPad is similar to moving photos in that they must first be in iTunes, but videos have some peculiarities. Most importantly, you need to make sure that your videos are in an acceptable format, such as .mp4, .m4v, or .mov. Several video formats, such as .avi and .wmv, both of which are common on Windows PCs, cannot be moved into iTunes or onto the iPad, and iTunes does not help you convert them. Also, videos that use Adobe

Flash, which is common on YouTube, will not work in iTunes and on the iPad (although you can get apps that will play Flash videos).

 NOTE You can get third-party apps for the iPad that will play .avi and .wmv movie files, but you can't transfer the movies through iTunes without first converting them to an acceptable format. To use the third-party players, you must download the videos through Safari or as an email attachment. See "Download Videos" later in this chapter.

Convert to MP4

You will need to convert your .avi and .wmv files to the .mp4 format. Unfortunately, there is not an easy way to do that. You need to find, download, and run a conversion program. If you do a Google search on "free avi to mp4 converter," you will find a number of offerings. Several will start out by telling you they are free and then have some gotcha, like a watermark with the converter name in the middle of each frame, or you are forced to also download other software you don't want, or you are hounded to buy the "pro" version, or they just don't work very well. I have quickly tried four products with varying results (take these comments as a starting place and do some research; software changes quickly):

- **Wondershare Video Converter Ultimate** (Wondershare .net) was the easiest to use and did a good job of video conversion, but the free version left a watermark with the word "Wondershare" and their logo in the middle of each frame. To fix that, you need to buy the full product.

In June 2013 this sold for $28.99 on TigerDirect.com and $49.95 on Wondershare.net (on their home page they say $59.95, but if you get the free version and then look at upgrading, it is $49.95).

- **Free Video Converter** (dvdvideomedia.com) was moderately easy to use, but kept running into problems with longer files. In four trials it never finished a longer test file, although shorter files were fine.

- **Handbrake** (handbrake.fr) was difficult to use and I never got a satisfactory result. Others, though, recommend this product.

- **Any Video Converter** (any-video-converter.com) was fairly easy to use and did a reasonable job of converting, although it had problems converting and stitching together an eight-segment video. After converting, a message pops up recommending upgrading, and during downloading,

the AVG toolbar was installed against my wishes and I had to remove it through the Control Panel. There are Pro and Ultimate versions, which in June 2013 cost $29.95 and $44.95, respectively, on any-video-converter.com.

Move Files to Your iPad

With several .mp4 videos on your computer that you want on your iPad, the next step is to move them there.

1. Locate the video files on your computer and open the folder that contains them. On a Windows PC, the normal place for videos is Libraries/Videos/My Videos. On a Mac, it is often iPhoto.

2. Open iTunes on your computer. Under Library on the left, click **Movies**, and then click **Home Videos** in the upper right. It may be that if your videos are in the standard My

Videos or iPhoto folders they will automatically appear here in iTunes.

3. If you don't see your videos in iTunes, you have two ways to get them there:

- Arrange the window containing your videos and the iTunes window so you can see them both at the same time and then drag your videos from their original window to iTunes.

- In iTunes open the **File** menu in the upper left (if you don't see the File, Edit, or View menus, click the black and white square in the far upper-left corner, and click **Show Menu Bar**) and click **Add Folder To Library**.

4. Once your videos are in iTunes on your computer, plug your iPad into your computer, click your iPad under Devices, click **Movies** in the upper menu bar, and click **Sync** in the lower right.

5. On your iPad's Home screen, tap **Videos**. You should see the ones you brought over from your computer.

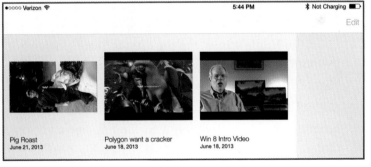

Download Videos

There is an almost unlimited availability of videos that you can view on your iPad. "Videos," in this case, includes movies, TV shows, music and personal videos, and video podcasts.

You can download videos from iTunes and many additional sources on the Internet. When you download a video, you may have it permanently, although in the cases of rentals and library loans, what you downloaded will disappear after a set time. You can also *stream* videos, which means that it is sent to you in small bites as you view it. Streaming, though, requires that you have a faster and stable Internet connection. Look at what is available and how to use videos from the iTunes Store and then what is available on the Internet in general, with and without additional apps.

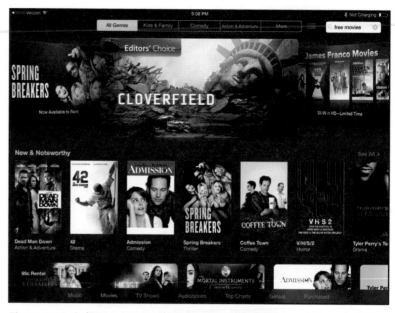

 TIP For many movies on iTunes you can choose to rent or buy the movie. If you buy the movie, you can permanently keep it and watch it as many times as you wish. If you rent a movie, you have 30 days to begin watching it and then 24 hours to finish watching it from the time you click play.

Figure 8-18: *In iTunes you can get movies to rent or buy, and there are often special deals.*

Download with iTunes on Your iPad

Using iTunes on your iPad to get videos is similar to using it to get books, although it takes a lot longer.

1. From the Home screen, tap the **iTunes Store** icon and on the bottom menu bar toward the left, tap **Movies** to see a number of movies displayed, as shown in Figure 8-18.

2. See additional videos within an individual category, generally a row, by swiping it to the left. See additional categories by swiping up.

3. Tap a video to see additional information and view trailers of it. Tap a trailer to view it.

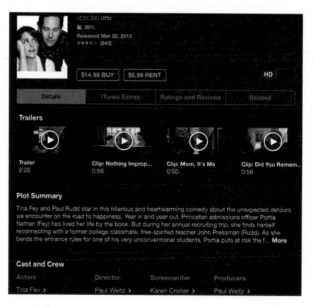

4. Tap either the **Buy** price or the **Rent** price (if it is available), select **HD** (high definition and up to twice the size of the file if it is available) or **SD** (standard definition and a much smaller file), and tap **Buy Movie** (or **Buy Video**) or **Rent Movie**, enter your Apple ID password, and tap **OK** to complete the process. You will see the word "Downloading" where the amount was. If you tap **Downloads** in the lower-right corner you will see the progress of the downloading.

5. Tap outside of the information box to close the added information.

6. When the downloading has finished, press **Home**, tap **Videos**, and tap your video to play it.

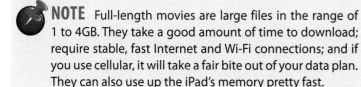

NOTE Full-length movies are large files in the range of 1 to 4GB. They take a good amount of time to download; require stable, fast Internet and Wi-Fi connections; and if you use cellular, it will take a fair bite out of your data plan. They can also use up the iPad's memory pretty fast.

Download with iTunes on Your Computer

If you have a fast Internet connection and a slower Wi-Fi connection to your iPad and you are having trouble downloading movies directly to your iPad (as I have had), you can download the video with iTunes on your computer and then transfer it to your iPad when plugged into your computer.

1. On your computer, open iTunes and click **iTunes Store | Movies**. Review the movies that are available and click the movie that you want to rent or buy.

2. Click the rent or buy amount, select **HD** or **SD**, and click **Rent** or **Buy** two more times to confirm the transaction. The movie will begin downloading, as you will see at the top of the iTunes window. After a few moments you will get a message that you can begin watching the movie if you wish.

3. When the movie has completed downloading, click your iPad | **Movies** to see your downloaded movie ready to move to your iPad, as shown in Figure 8-19.

4. Click **Move** to move the movie to your iPad and then click **Apply** to make that happen. You will see a "Transferring Movies" message at the top of iTunes. Transferring will take a whole lot less time than downloading. When it is complete, on your iPad Home screen, tap **Videos** and then tap either **Rentals** or **Movies** to see the movies you just downloaded on your computer and transferred to your iPad.

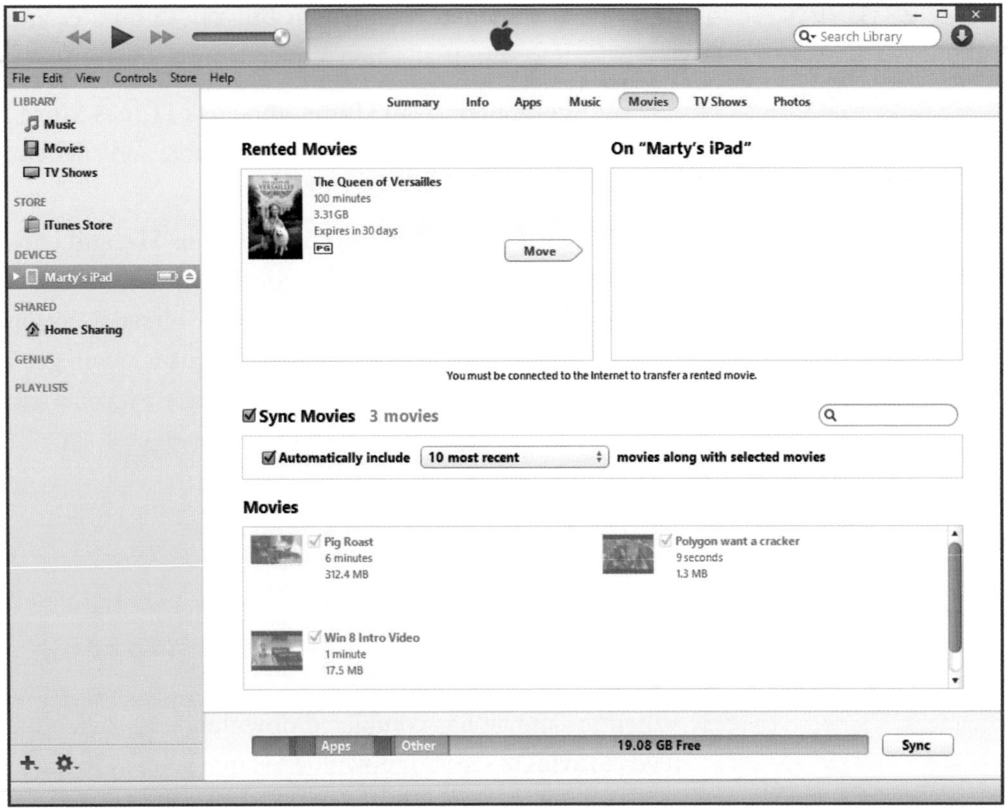

![iTunes window showing Movies sync settings with Rented Movies, The Queen of Versailles, and a Movies list including Pig Roast, Polygon want a cracker, and Win 8 Intro Video]

Figure 8-19: **Downloading videos to your computer first can help solve problems downloading to your iPad.**

Download Videos with Other Apps

In addition to iTunes you have other ways to get and view videos from the Internet, and you have several choices of how and with which tools you do that. The first choice is whether you want a general-purpose player or a video service with an

app like Netflix or Hulu where they supply the videos you watch. Another choice is how you want to watch the videos:

- Download them to your iPad so you can take them with you, say on an airplane flight, and don't have to worry about your Internet connection being interrupted

- Stream them to your iPad as you watch the video so you don't have to take room in the iPad's memory and don't have to wait for a download to complete

Many video players allow you to both download videos and stream them. If you do a search for "video players" on the App Store, you will see over 200 of them. If you then do a Google search of iPad video players, you will find a number of sites that rank the players with many differences of opinion. Here are three alternatives that I have found that serve my purposes:

- **OPlayerHD Lite** is a free general-purpose player for both downloaded and streaming videos with a built-in browser that most reviewers agree is among the best of all players and definitely at the top of the free players. The

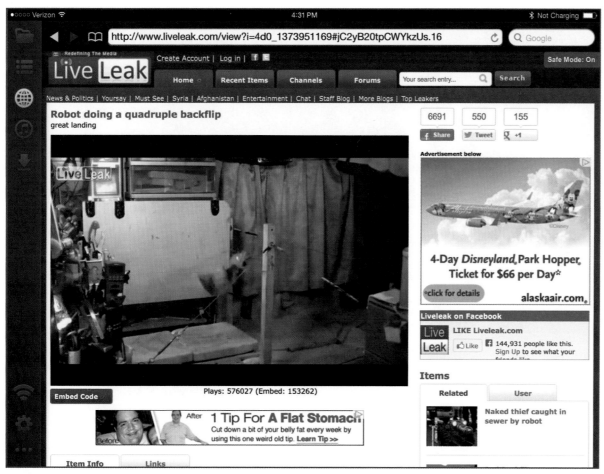

Figure 8-20: **OPlayerHD Lite has a complex interface, but allows you to search for, download, and play videos.**

only penalty for being free is a small ad. You can use the browser to search for and download videos and then view them, as you see in Figure 8-20.

- YouTube is a free player for free streaming videos that have been put up on YouTube by millions of different people and organizations.

You can watch YouTube from Safari, but flash videos on YouTube will not play in Safari. The YouTube player app, shown in Figure 8-21, will play flash videos and is optimized for quickly downloading and playing the short video clips.

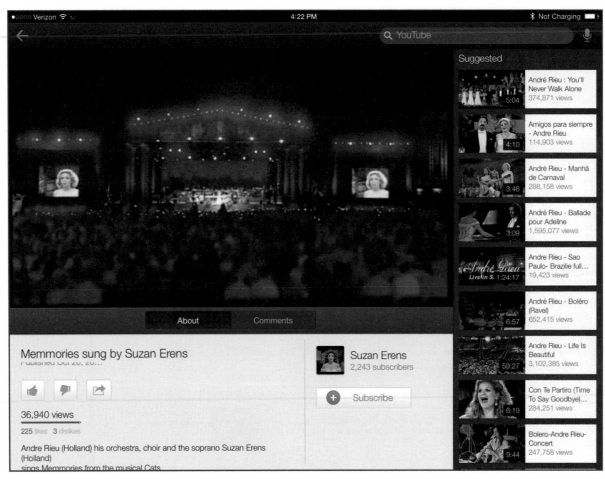

Figure 8-21: *YouTube is famous for the millions of videos clips about almost any subject.*

- **Netflix** is a video rental service to which you pay a monthly fee of currently $7.99 in the United States to stream all the videos (both movies and TV shows) you can watch in a month (see Figure 8-22). Netflix has hundreds of thousands of movies and TV episodes you can watch instantly. One monthly subscription, which can be canceled at any time, will allow you to watch not only on your iPad, but also on your TV, with an Internet connection, and on your smart phone or Android device.

Figure 8-22: *The Netflix service allows you to stream as many videos as you like, but unless you get DVDs, you can't store them on your iPad.*

⟩⟩ Make Videos

The iPad's cameras take videos as well as photos, and you do this very much like you take a photo.

1. On the Home screen, tap **Camera** and slide the **Video** option down to the yellow mark on the left of the screen, as you can see in Figure 8-23.

2. Aim the camera where you want to begin the video capture, press the red button on the right side, and then pan the iPad (move it from left to right or from right to left) to capture what you want in the video. A timer above the button shows you how long you have been shooting.

Figure 8-23: *Capturing video is almost exactly the same as taking a picture, except that you can pan the iPad to capture more.*

Edit and Share Videos

As you take videos, you may notice that you have frames on either the beginning or end of the video that you want to remove. The iPad provides a simple video editor that lets you trim frames from either end of a video clip, but not remove frames in the middle of it. You can also delete a video or share it with others in various ways.

1. From the Home screen, tap **Photos**, if needed tap **Albums**, tap **Videos** or the album you are using for your videos, and tap the video you want to work with. It will open and have features you saw in Figure 8-24. If you don't see the series of frames at the top of the screen, tap the video.

3. When you are done capturing, press the red square that has replaced the red button. You can then view what you just shot by tapping the thumbnail of your video at the bottom right.

4. Tap the triangle in the middle of the screen to play the video, as you can see in Figure 8-24. Videos you produce are kept in Photos, not in Videos, but in the Videos album.

5. You can start playing a video anyplace in its duration by tapping in the sequence of frames at the top of the screen, or you can drag a finger across the frames to quickly or slowly view the video.

Figure 8-24: *While the iPad is not easy to handle when capturing a video, due to its size, it can be handy to take a short video when you have other things you also want to do with an iPad.*

2. To trim an end of the selected video, tap either end of the series of frames so it becomes enclosed in a yellow border. Drag toward the middle from either end until

the frames you want to trim have become dim, as you see in Figure 8-25. Tap **Trim** in the upper-right corner and then tap either **Trim Original**, so you will only have a clip

without the frames you trimmed, or **Save As New Clip** to create a new clip without the trimmed frames and still have the original clip with the frames.

3. To delete the entire video, tap the recycle bin in the lower-right corner and then tap **Delete Video**.

Figure 8-25: **You can only remove the frames at the beginning or end of a video clip.**

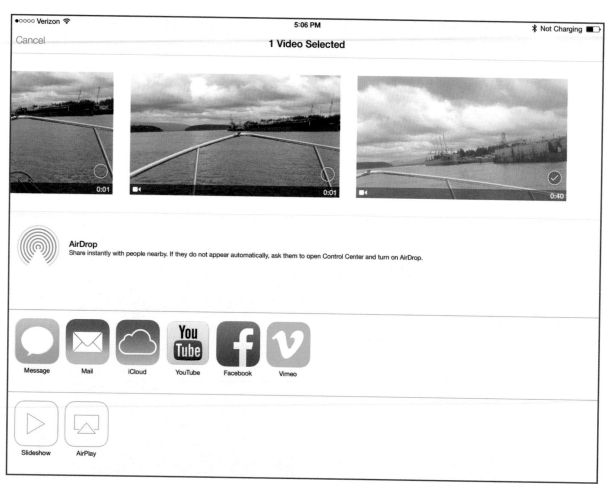

Figure 8-26: *You can share your videos in the normal ways.*

4. To share a video with other people, tap the **Share** icon in the lower-left corner of the screen and then tap the method (Message or Mail) or service (YouTube, Facebook, or Vimeo) that you want to use (see Figure 8-26). Note that YouTube and Vimeo are unique to videos. In both cases, you must have an existing account to upload videos.

USE FACETIME

FaceTime makes the iPad (or an iPhone or iPod touch) into a video phone where you can contact someone and have a face-to-face conversation with them—a video chat. To use

Figure 8-27: **Use the initial FaceTime screen to compose the look you want for the call.**

2. Select the person in your contact list that you want to call and then tap the **FaceTime** icon (the camera) in the person's Contact data. The other person will appear on your screen with your picture inset in a corner. You can begin talking as you normally would. The iPad's microphone is pretty good and you shouldn't have to lean in.

FaceTime, you need to have an Apple ID and either a Wi-Fi or cellular connection to the Internet. Note, though, that in using a cellular service for FaceTime you may incur data charges.

To make a FaceTime call:

1. Tap the **FaceTime** icon on the Home screen. The FaceTime screen will appear with your contacts on the right side, as you can see in Figure 8-27.

3. Drag the small image of you to any of the four corners.

4. When you are done with the call, tap the screen, and then tap **End**.

5. You can show the person you are talking to what you are looking at by tapping the switch camera icon ▣ to activate the other camera in the iPad and then aiming the iPad at what you want to show.

6. You can also mute the iPad's microphone if, for example, you want to take a call on another phone, by tapping the mute icon ▣ .

7. If you want to resume a FaceTime call, tap **Recents** and then tap the call you want to resume.

Chapter 9

Socializing and Playing Games

The iPad has a practical and useful side, as you've seen with Safari, email, messaging, and scheduling. It also has an entertaining side: listening to music; reading books, magazines, and newspapers; and taking and viewing photos and videos. Finally, as you'll see in this chapter, it has a socializing and fun side: interacting with your family and friends, and playing games. While this is a lighter aspect of the iPad, it is no less important, and in this chapter you'll see how to get connected and use Twitter and Facebook, as well as explore the Game Center and find, download, and use third-party games, some of which are multiplayer games where you can interact with your friends.

FOLLOW TWITTER 🐦

Twitter is a social networking service on the Internet that allows you to post very small messages, called *Tweets*, of no more than 140 characters. Twitter says it is an information network of 140-character messages. You can choose to follow this stream of messages, or Tweets, on any topic and from any individual. You can also choose to add your own Tweets, which anyone can read. You can read the public postings of anyone else and sign up to be a follower of anyone. Twitter has a very large user base, with over half a billion active registered users who produce over 50 million Tweets per day and over two billion Twitter search engine queries per day. (Statistics from StatisticBrain.com as of 5-7-2013.

▷▷ Enable and Explore Twitter

You must register with Twitter before you can use it. You can access Twitter from Safari at twitter.com or you can download for free the Twitter app from the App Store. The app is tailored to your iPad, so begin by downloading the app and then registering with Twitter. Next, locate some information and contributors who you want to follow. Finally, post Tweets of your own and build a following.

Download and Register with Twitter

1. From the Home screen, tap the **App Store**. Clear the Search box. Type <u>twitter</u>, and tap **Twitter** in the search results.

2. Tap **Free | Install App**, enter your Apple ID password, and tap **OK**. The Twitter app will be downloaded. Tap **Open** to display Twitter, as you see in Figure 9-1. If you want, tap **OK** to allow Twitter to use your current location.

3. If you don't have an existing Twitter account, tap **Sign Up** and enter the requested information. Otherwise, enter the email address and password for your existing Twitter account. Tap **Don't Allow** or **OK** to allow notifications.

4. Tap **Follow Your Friends** and then tap **OK**, if you wish, to allow access to your contacts. A list of your contacts who are on Twitter will be displayed. Tap **Follow** for each person you want to follow, or tap **Follow All** to do that. Tap the **Next** arrow to display a list of your contacts who are not on Twitter and whom you can invite to join Twitter and follow you. Tap the **Next** arrow to display a list of people who your friends are following and are suggested as people you might want to follow. Tap **Follow** for each one you want to follow, or tap **Follow All** to do that.

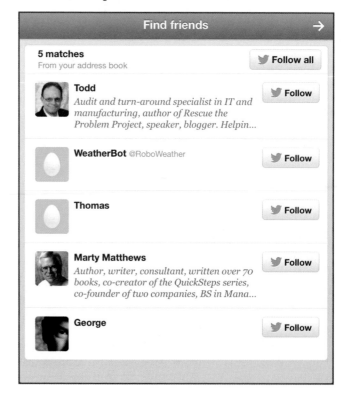

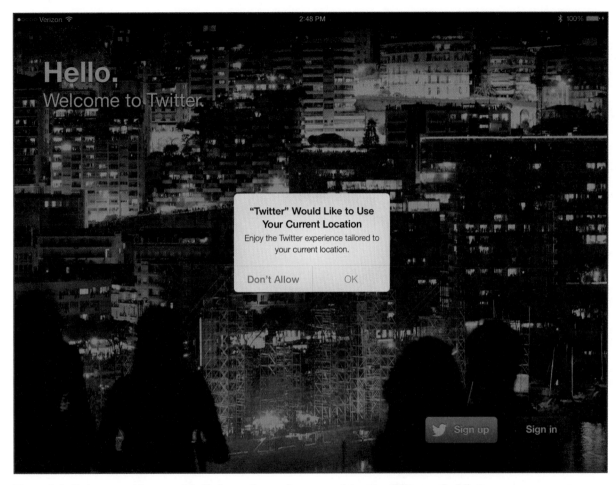

Figure 9-1: **Twitter provides a world of information; only you can determine if it is worthwhile to you.**

5. You are asked if you want to add your photo to your Twitter account, and you are given the option of taking a photo with the iPad or choosing an existing photo. If you choose the latter, you are asked if you want to allow Twitter access to your Photos. Tap **OK** or **Don't Allow** (if you choose Don't Allow, you will need to take a photo and insert it unless you choose not to have a photo on Twitter). Select the photo

you want, move and scale it, and tap **Use | Finish**. Your Home page opens displaying recent Tweets of those you are following, similar to Figure 9-2.

Locate Tweets to Follow

In setting up Twitter, you've added the people in your contact list who you want to follow, but it is likely that you want to

Figure 9-2: **Some people seem to do nothing but Tweet, while others hardly do anything.**

follow others in areas that you are interested in. As I am writing this, Apple's iOS 7 is in beta testing and I am interested in what people are saying about it. Also, I like to cook, so I am interested in new and unique recipes. I can search on both of these topics to see who is Tweeting on them.

1. Tap the **Search** icon [Q], type what you want to search for, and then tap the result you want to explore. In my case, I type and tap "iOS 7" to get the screen shown in Figure 9-3.

2. Scroll down the Tweets until you see one you might want to follow and then tap it. The selected Tweet will expand.

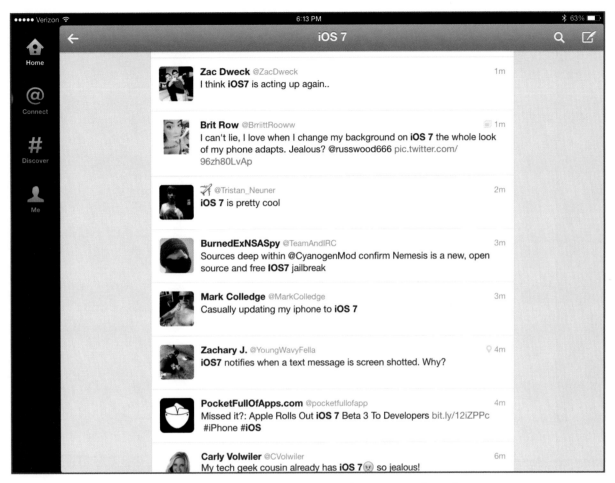

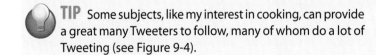

*Figure 9-3: **Depending on the subject, you may get a large number of Tweets to go through.***

3. Tap **Follow** if you want to follow this Tweeter or subject.

4. Repeat the first three steps for as many subjects as you want to follow.

TIP Some subjects, like my interest in cooking, can provide a great many Tweeters to follow, many of whom do a lot of Tweeting (see Figure 9-4).

Figure 9-4: A major task with Twitter is to separate the wheat from the chaff. Thankfully, there is a 140-character limit.

Search Categories

If searching on a name, keyword, or phrase does not get you what you want, or you just wonder what else is there in Twitter, use the #Discover option to review one or more of the suggested Tweets and open the huge list of categories in which to browse.

1. From within Twitter, tap **#Discover** in the left column. This opens a list of suggestions, based on what else you are following, for you to consider.

2. Tap one of the suggestions to explore it further. It may lead you to a website, and that may lead you to other sites, as shown in Figure 9-5.

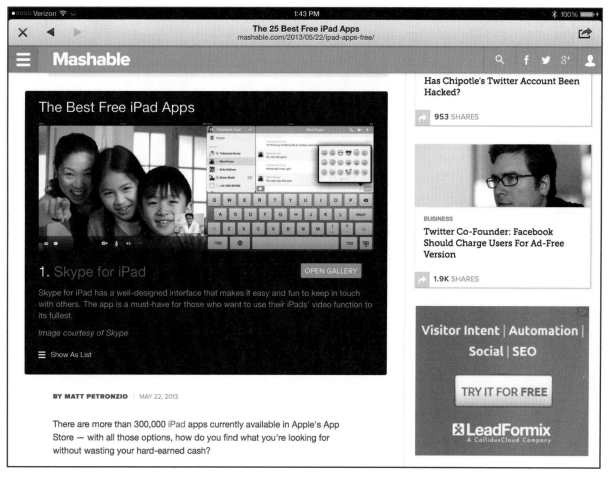

Figure 9-5: **Exploring one suggestion can lead to a totally unrelated site you want to follow.**

3. When you have explored a path as far as you want, return to Twitter by tapping the **X** in the upper-left corner and then tapping the left arrow, also in the upper-left corner.

4. When you have looked through the suggestions as much as you want, scroll to the bottom of the Discover screen and tap **Browse Categories** to open the mother lode of possibilities (see Figure 9-6). Tap one of the major categories, such as **News**, and then scroll down the many options under that category, tapping **Follow** as desired.

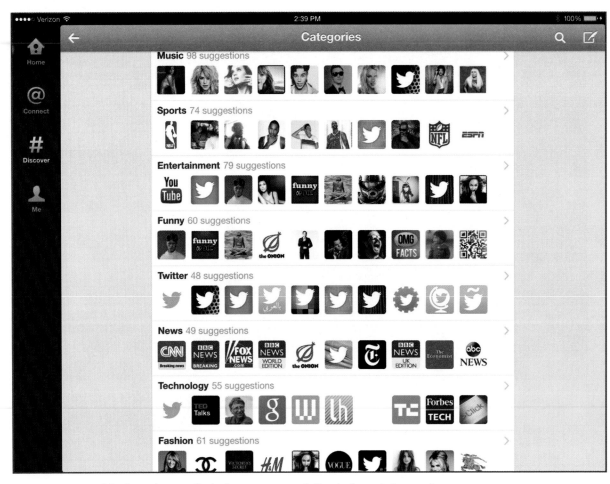

Figure 9-6: *One of the best places to find what you want to follow is through Categories.*

▷▷ Post Tweets and Build a Following

While reading the Tweets of others can be interesting, beneficial, and even exciting, there is an equally compelling use of Twitter to get your thoughts and comments out to the world. You can do this by posting your own new Tweet, with and without photos, by replying to the Tweets of others, and by retweeting what others have posted.

Post a Tweet

Posting Tweets is no harder than posting a text message, except that you are limited to 140 characters, and, of course, you must figure out what to say.

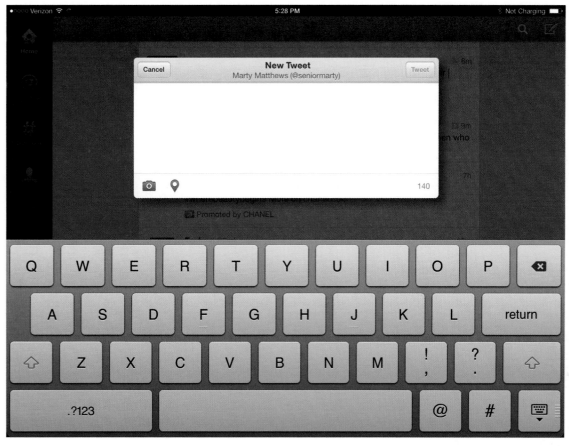

Figure 9-7: *You can Tweet about anything, but consider what would be of interest to others.*

1. On any Twitter page, tap the **Tweet** icon  to open the New Tweet dialog box, as you see in Figure 9-7.

2. Type whatever you want to say in the text box. Notice the number in the lower-right corner, which starts at 140, is decreasing as you type, telling you the number of characters you have left.

3. When you are ready, tap **Tweet** in the upper-right corner to post on Twitter.

4. If you are not already there, tap your Twitter Home screen and you will see what you posted.

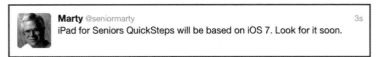

Tweet with Photos and Add Your Location

You may have noticed two icons in the lower-left corner of the New Tweet dialog box. These allow you to add a photo to your Tweet and to add your location.

1. Open a New Tweet dialog box as described in the previous section, and enter a Tweet as you have previously.

2. Tap the **Photo** icon in the lower-left corner and tap either:

- **Take Photo** to open the iPad's Camera app where you can take a photo as described in Chapter 8.

- **Choose Existing Photo** to open the gallery of existing photos that are available on your iPad where you can open an album and choose a photo.

3. Tap the **Location** icon to be asked if you want to add your current location to your Tweets. Tap **Enable** to do that, or tap **Cancel** to not add your location.

4. When the Tweet is ready, tap **Tweet** to send it.

Reply to Tweets and Retweets

You can reply to the Tweets of others and you can retweet Tweets you find that might interest your followers.

From the list of Tweets on your Twitter Home screen, tap a Tweet you want to reply to or retweet. The enlarged Tweet appears with a series of icons on the bottom right.

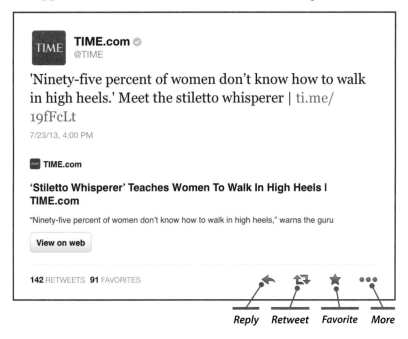

- Tap the **Reply** icon and enter a Tweet as you would normally.

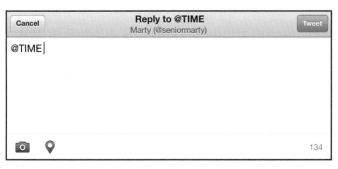

- Tap the **Retweet** icon and tap **Retweet** to create a new Tweet that is nothing more than the original Tweet that goes to your followers with a green Retweet symbol in the upper-right corner.

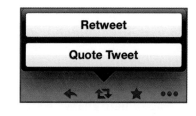

- If you tap the **Retweet** icon after tapping **Retweet**, you can undo your last retweet.

- After tapping the **Retweet** icon, you can alternatively tap **Quote Tweet** to create a new Tweet that contains the full original Tweet, not leaving much room for any comments.

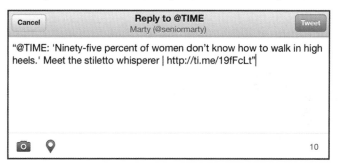

- Tap the **Favorites** icon to indicate a Tweet is one of your favorites.

- Tap the **More** icon to take various actions with the link to the existing Tweet or to mail the Tweet.

Tailor Twitter Settings

You can change Twitter settings in both the iPad's settings and in Twitter.

1. From the Home screen, tap **Settings | Twitter**. Tap your account to change your password and/or description. Tap **Find Me By Email** to allow people to search Twitter and find you using your email address. Tap **Done** to leave your account settings.

2. Also in iPad Settings you can add another Twitter account, either existing or new; update your possible Twitter followings based on changes to your contacts; and allow Twitter to use your Apple account.

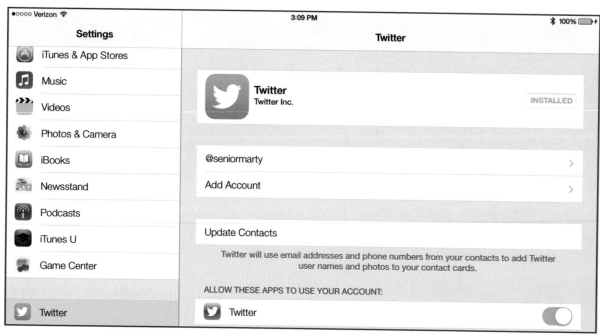

3. While in iPad Settings, tap **Notification Center | Twitter** and choose the notification settings for Tweets that are correct for you. Return to the Home screen when you are finished.

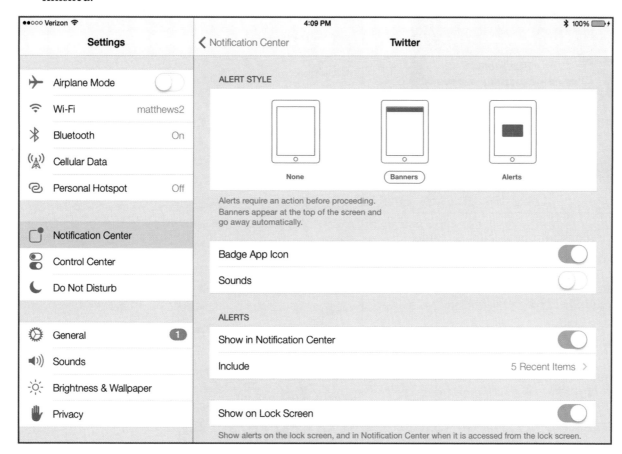

4. Tap **Twitter | Me** and tap the **Settings** icon.

5. Tap **Edit Profile** to change your photo, header image, name, location, website, and bio. Tap **Save** when you are ready.

6. Tap **Settings** to change your font size, image quality, sound effects, and connect tab. Tap **Done** when you are ready.

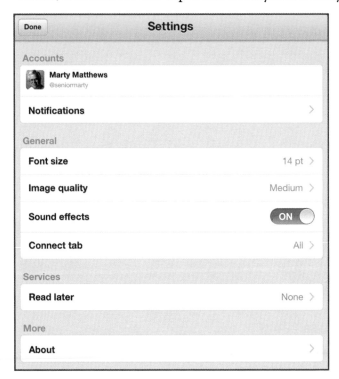

7. Tap **Sign Out** and then tap it again to completely leave Twitter. The next time you want to use Twitter, you will have to sign in again.

EXPLORE FACEBOOK

Facebook is the largest social networking site by a large margin, with over 1.15 billion active users worldwide as of March 2013 according to Wikipedia. Facebook allows people 13 and older to connect with their friends and share comments, pictures, and videos. To do that, each user, after registering, creates their own webpage and identifies the friends that they want to share with.

You can limit sharing to just your friends, or have a public page that anyone can view. You can send invitations to people to be your Facebook friends, and you will likely receive invitations from others to be their friends. Making full use of Facebook is a book-length subject, and my wife, Carole Matthews, has written one, *Facebook for Seniors QuickSteps,* published by McGraw-Hill Education.

⏩ Start Using Facebook

Like Twitter, you can use Facebook either through Safari or with the Facebook app, which you can download for free from the App Store. Also, like Twitter, I recommend using the app because it can then use the full page and is a little faster. Once you get Facebook open, if it is for the first time, you can immediately start using it by posting comments, photos, and videos. You will want to add friends who can see and respond to what you have posted. Finally, you may want to customize your page.

Download and Register with Facebook

1. From the Home screen, tap the **App Store**. Clear the Search box. Type facebook, and tap **Facebook** in the search results.

2. Tap **Free | Install App**, enter your Apple ID password, and tap **OK**. The Facebook app will be downloaded. Tap **Open** to display Facebook.

3. If you don't have an existing Facebook account, tap **Sign Up For Facebook** and enter the requested information. Otherwise, enter the email address and password for your existing Facebook account. Facebook will open.

Use Facebook

If you have an existing Facebook account, your current Facebook page will open; otherwise, you are asked where you want to start, as you can see in Figure 9-8.

Figure 9-8: *You can start using Facebook by posting a status or comment, posting a photo, or checking what is in your local neighborhood*

2. Tap **Photo** to add one. Tap either **Take Photo Or Video** or **Choose From Library**, and either take a photo as you normally would or select a photo from those on your computer, and then tap **Post**.

1. Tap **What's On Your Mind** and enter a status or comment that you would like to share with others. When you have completed entering the comment, tap **Post**. Your status or comment will appear on your page.

3. Tap **Check In**. Facebook will ask if it can use your current location. If that is acceptable to you, tap **OK**; otherwise, tap **Don't Allow**. If you allow the use of your current location, Facebook will display a list of businesses that are close to you.

4. Tap the three bars in the upper-left corner to open the list of options, or "bookmarks," you can select in the left column, as you can see in Figure 9-9, which also shows a photo I added in Step 2 (my desktop companion).

5. Tap your name at the top of the left column to open your Timeline or Wall, shown in Figure 9-10.

6. Tap **About** in the top-left corner of your Timeline and then tap **About** again to open your profile page where you can enter information about yourself (see Figure 9-11). Also, you can tap any of the other options across the top of that page to add photos and location information; music, movies, TV shows, and books you like; and add notes and keep an activity log.

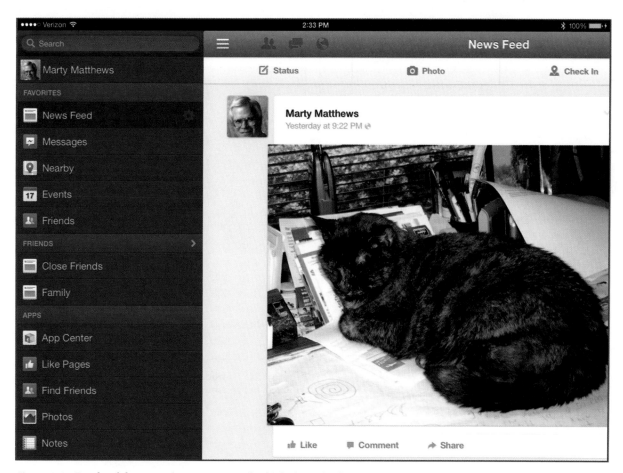

Figure 9-9: Facebook has two views, News Feed, which shows both your and your friends' comments and photos, and Timeline, which is also called your "Wall."

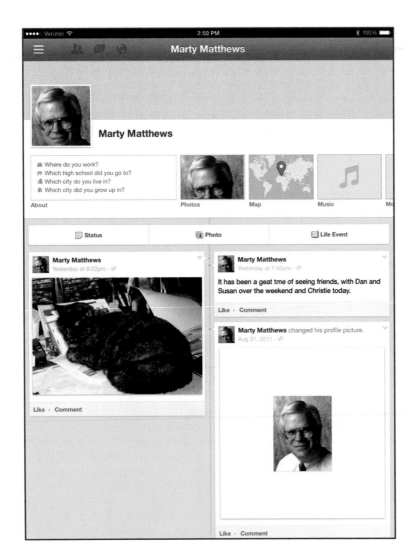

Figure 9-10: **The Timeline or Wall view shows your posts as well as those your friends post specifically to you in chronological order.**

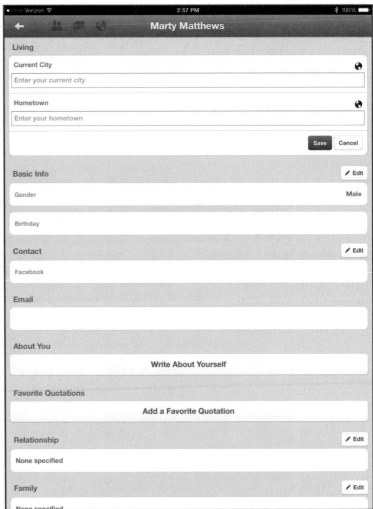

Figure 9-11: **Facebook invites you to publicize a lot of information about yourself, but you might want to consider what you want everyone to know.**

Add and Contact Friends

Posting comments and statuses on Facebook doesn't do a lot for you without a set of friends who will see them. If you add a few friends to start, the number of your friends will quickly grow as you get suggestions to add friends of friends and others will request that you be their friend as they learn you are on Facebook.

1. In the list of options on the left, tap **Find Friends** to see several ways to add friends. If you are just starting out, you will probably not see any people under Suggestions, Requests, or Filters.

2. Tap **Search | Name Or Email** and type a friend's name or email address (an email address is preferred because if you enter a name, you then must search through all the people on Facebook with the same name—probably a lot). Finally, tap **Search**. (See illustration shown at right.)

3. When you see a friend you would like to add, tap that friend's name to open their page and then tap **Add Friend**. You will see the label "Add Friend" change to "Friend Request Sent."

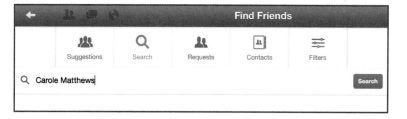

4. Tap the return arrow in the upper-left corner twice to return to the Find Friends page and then tap **Contacts** to see a list of email providers. Tap your email provider, enter your email address and your password, and tap **Find Friends**. A list of people will appear. Tap **Add** opposite the people you want to be your friends.

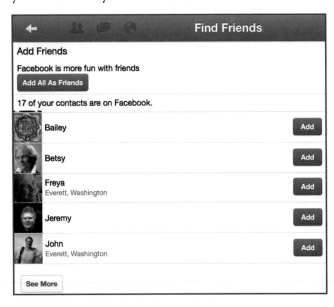

5. After adding several requests for friends, tap **Suggestions** and you will see that you now have a number of suggestions based on the requests you have made and who their friends are. Tap the **Add Friend** icon on the right of the people you want to be your friends. Your friends will receive a request in their email, like this:

6. After your friends have had a chance to see their email and respond, you will see them in the right column on your News Feed page. If you tap the **Notification** icon in the title bar, you will also see the friends who accepted your requests (see Figure 9-12).

7. To say hello and thank a friend for responding, tap **Write On** *friend's* **Timeline**. Your friend's Timeline will appear. Tap **Write Post** to open a dialog box and write a message. Tap **Post**. Your message will appear in your friend's Timeline.

▶▶ Manage Your Facebook Account

Facebook can disseminate a lot of information about you, and it is important that you use the controls that Facebook provides to place the limitations you want on who can see what.

Figure 9-12: *You will be surprised at how fast you will add friends.*

While there are a couple of settings for Facebook in the iPad's settings, they are not significant. The settings you need to pay attention to are in Facebook in either Account Settings or Privacy Settings, which give you the same options.

1. In Facebook, if you don't see the column of options on the left, either swipe the screen from left to right, or tap the three bars in the upper-left corner.

2. Drag or scroll the list of options up and tap **Account Settings** to open the Facebook Settings shown in Figure 9-13.

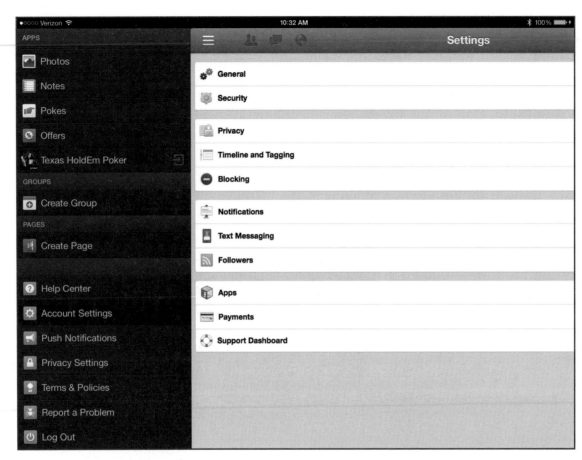

Figure 9-13: **Become really familiar with the Facebook Settings and make sure they are set to your liking.**

3. Tap **General** and tap any of the fields, Name, Email, or Password; make the desired changes; and tap **Save**. You can also deactivate your account by tapping that option, answering the questions, and tapping **Deactivate** again if you are sure you want to deactivate the account.

4. Tap the **Return** arrow in the upper-left corner and tap **Security**, tap the option below, and follow the instructions for the specified result:

- **Secure Browsing** uses a secure Internet connection (https) when it is available.

- **Login Notification** sends either a text message or an email when your Facebook account is accessed from a device that you haven't used before.

- **Login Approvals** requires a security code to access your Facebook account from a browser you haven't used before.

- **Third Party Authenticator** sets up a third-party app to generate Facebook security codes used for Login Approvals or to reset your password.

- **Trusted Contacts** identifies friends to whom you give a security code that they can give you if you forget it and allow you to access your Facebook account.

- **App Passwords** sets up an app password to use in place of your normal Facebook login password that will allow you to securely log in to apps that cannot receive security codes.

- **Recognized Devices** reviews and possibly removes devices that are recognized by your Facebook account.

- **Active Sessions** reviews and possibly removes current sessions that are accessing your Facebook account.

5. Tap the **Return** arrow in the upper-left corner and tap **Privacy**, tap the option below, and follow the instructions for the specified result. For many of the options, you can choose among Public, Friends Of Friends, Friends, and Only Me.

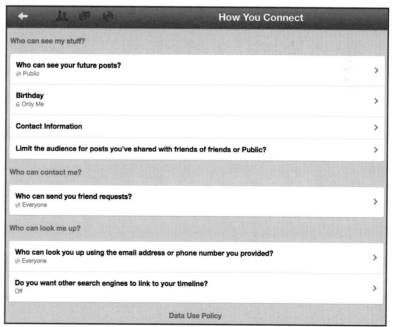

- **Who Can See Your Future Posts** lets you choose who can see your posts.

- **Birthday** lets you choose who can see your birthday.

- **Contact Information** lets you choose who has access to your physical and email addresses.

- **Limit The Audience For Posts** lets you limit the access to the old posts on your Timeline.

- **Who Can Send You Friend Requests** lets you say Everyone or just Friends Of Friends can send you friend requests.

- **Who Can Look You Up Using Your Email Or Phone Number** lets you choose who can do that.

- **Do You Want Other Search Engines To Link To Your Timeline** lets you choose whether to do that. If this is on, everybody, whether on Facebook or not, can find what is posted on your Timeline.

6. Tap the **Return** arrow in the upper-left corner and tap **Timeline And Tagging** to manage who can post to your Timeline and to see where you have been tagged or suggested to be tagged in your Timeline. A "tag" is where someone posts a picture where you have been tagged.

7. Tap the **Return** arrow in the upper-left corner and tap **Blocking** to add a name or email address of a person who you want to block from seeing things you post on your Timeline, inviting you to an event or group, starting a conversation with you, or adding you as a friend.

8. Tap **Notifications** to manage the notifications you get in Facebook that are generated from Facebook, email, iPad Notifications, or text messages.

9. Tap **Text Messages** to activate receiving text messages in Facebook. By default, it is turned off.

10. Tap **Followers** to allow followers to see more than your public posts.

11. Tap **Apps** to manage the apps you use.

12. Tap **Payments** to see the total of payments you have used and the currency it is in.

13. Tap **Support Dashboard** to see the history of your support from Facebook, Inc.

▶▶ Explore the Rest of Facebook

As you can see by the many options in the left column (when it is displayed with the three-bar icon in the upper left or by swiping from left to right), there are many elements of Facebook I haven't discussed, and even for those I have, only the fundamentals have been covered. For a full discussion of Facebook, I recommend *Facebook for Seniors QuickSteps* by Carole Matthews and published by McGraw-Hill Education. On your own, I recommend that you select each of the options on the left and explore what you can do with it. This is especially true with the App Center, where you can find many additional activities you can do with Facebook and social networking such as playing games, sharing mutual interests such as travel, and dating. In your exploring, use common sense to protect yourself as discussed in the "Protecting Your Online Identity" QuickFacts later in this chapter.

By looking at only Twitter and Facebook, I have only touched on social networking apps, although far and away the most popular ones, especially for seniors. If you are interested in business and job networking, I recommend looking at LinkedIn, and if you want to share a common interest, I recommend Pinterest, which you can do as an app in Facebook or directly as an iPad app.

Talk to your friends and associates about what they are using and possibly try out other social networking apps.

PLAY GAMES

Almost everybody likes to play games. They are a great time filler, and they test our ability and skill. If you looked at Facebook apps, as suggested earlier in this chapter, you saw a great many games. In addition to that, the iPad Apps Store offers a large number of games you can directly play, as you can see in Figure 9-14, and the iPad's Game Center allows you to compete with others in multiplayer games and to keep track of how you are doing in the games you play. The Game Center is separate from the games themselves, so we'll discuss them first.

Protecting Your Online Identity

It is a wonderful thing to be able to find and exchange information with people with similar interests. Social networking facilitates these communications so that we connect with broader webs of people, and with people we simply do not know. In today's world, though, it is wise to be "street smart" when it comes to the streets of the Internet. Here are a few hard-and-fast rules for keeping your identity to yourself and your information private:

- Make sure your password is reasonably difficult to figure out, by using combinations of numbers, letters, and special characters. Protect your passwords for the various applications you use, such as Facebook; don't share them with others. Change your password periodically.

- Be wise about the information you put on the Internet. For example, share only that information you are comfortable with unknown persons knowing. Don't put highly personal information or photos in Facebook, for instance. Even if you think you are only sharing with friends, you may be surprised with whom they share.

- If you are in a forum or blog that is publicly available, don't put information that could cause your identify or your home to be compromised—don't put your address or even your town or city name. Put a city close by, for instance. Don't use your last name, or use a fake ID. Be very aware of the information you are sharing and make it minimal. (However, there are some sites that require you to enter your correct information. In this case, you'll have to enter your real data *if you really want to use the site,* but be stingy when you can.)

- Don't click links from unknown persons. These can be programmed to gather information from you or your computer.

- Keep your computer browser software up to date so that the latest advances in security are on your computer. Equally important is making sure your antivirus or Internet security software is current.

- Be very wary about meeting people in person or sharing personal information with strangers in unprotected sites.

Social networking can be fun and a great way to meet people and interact with them. Just keep in mind that you want to be "street smart" while you are having that great time.

Figure 9-14: ***Games in the iPad's App Store offer you almost unlimited entertainment.***

⮞⮞ Download and Play Games

There are literally thousands of iPad games. Many are free, or at least start out free, and many more cost something from 99 cents on up. Just to find a game you want is a major undertaking, and to make sure it is well thought of and fun to play takes considerable research. There are many different types of games, such as action games, board games, card games, kid games, puzzle games, racing games, strategy games, and trivia games. You can limit yourself to free games, knowing that many "free" games get you hooked during free play and then have various ways to get you to pay something. While we'll discuss several games here, I suggest that you do some initial research by typing <u>best iPad games</u> (see Figure 9-15) or <u>best free iPad</u> <u>games</u> into Google or Bing and reading through the reviews. If you are looking for a particular type of game, enter, for example, "best card games on iPad."

*Figure 9-15: **You can search on either your computer or your iPad for opinions and reviews of games.***

Back in your iPad, open the App Store, and do searches on games in general, free games, and then on particular types of games. For example, Figure 9-16 shows a search on "Solitaire." In what follows I'll describe two games that I think are fun to play and well crafted, as examples of the many that are available.

Figure 9-16: **For most popular games, there are many alternatives to choose from.**

Solitaire

The ancient card game Solitaire has been on computers since the earliest PCs and Macs and on the iPad since the first one. If you do an iPad App Store search on Solitaire, you will see a number of Solitaire games by different creators. One that I like is the free version by Finger Arts. It does have ads, but they are across the bottom of the screen, so they are not very intrusive. You can get an ad-free version for $2.99 (as of summer 2013).

You can choose the look of the cards by tapping that option on the bottom of the screen and make other settings by tapping **Options** on the right. You can also jump right in and begin playing by clicking **Play**, choosing a difficulty and the number

of cards to draw. At that point you can tap the card deck on the middle right to begin play.

Mahjong

Description

The addictive power of Mahjong, multiplied by 1001.
Containing 1001 unique Mahjong stacks in one, beautifully crafted package, wrapped together with 8 slick themes, over 40 lovely backgrounds and 5 extraordinary tile sets this is a stunning Mahjong package.

This is an ancient Chinese game where you try to use up all the tiles by matching them. You tap first one tile and then a matching tile and the two disappear, allowing you to see and work with other tiles. The 1001 Ultimate Mahjong version of this game is free, but has some in-app purchases you can make. To me, the free version of the game without additions plays very well and is as addictive as ever.

When the game first opens, you are asked to choose from many different initial layouts of the tiles. You also can tap **Options** and choose from a number of tile sets, backgrounds, and themes, as well as set the volume. Upon choosing a layout, the game is created and you are given a number of pointers about the playing area, how to play, and several sets of options. Note in particular the Family Tiles where you don't try to match the same tiles, just the same family. Work from the top down and the edges in. It is truly addictive.

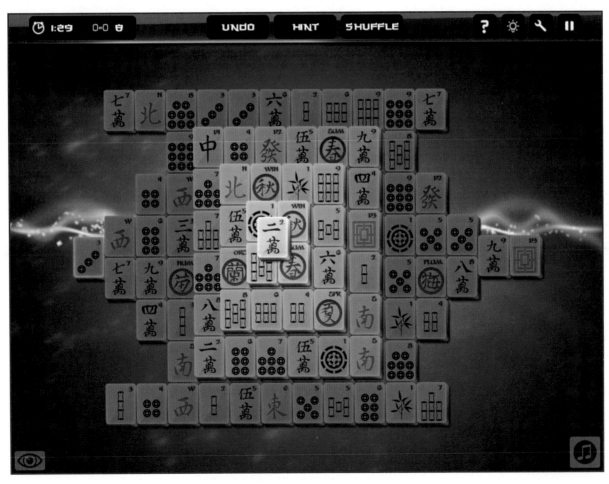

⏩ Explore the Game Center

It is difficult for me to understand that the Game Center is not where you go to play games. You play games by starting them from the Home screen. Game Center is where you keep track of how well you are doing and, most importantly, connect with others that play the same games that you do and challenge them

to play against you. The Game Center helps you connect with other players, keeps track of the accomplishments of you and your opponents, and tells you about other multiplayer games.

1. From the Home screen, tap **Game Center**. If you have never used Game Center before, you will be asked to enter your Apple ID and password and select a nickname. The Game Center will open as you see in Figure 9-17. If you installed the games discussed earlier, that will be reflected in the center Games bubble.

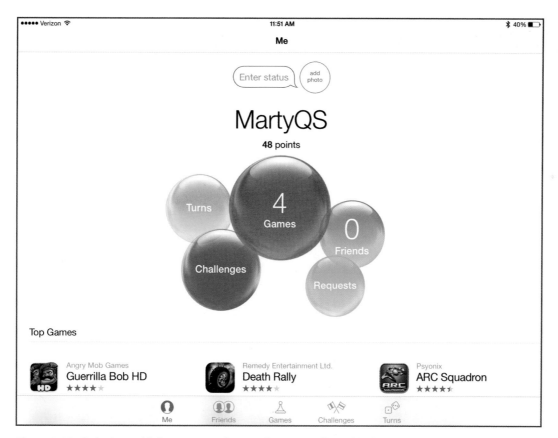

Figure 9-17: *Only the multiplayer games that you have are reflected in the Game Center.*

2. Tap **Add Status** to add any comment you want your game-playing friends to see and then, if you want, add a photo of yourself.

3. Tap the **Games** bubble to display the multiplayer games you have downloaded and some recommendations for others.

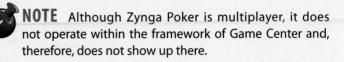

NOTE Although Zynga Poker is multiplayer, it does not operate within the framework of Game Center and, therefore, does not show up there.

4. Tap one of your games to view your and your friends' statistics. Tap your statistics and tap **Share** to share results with others and ask them if they want to play using Messages, Mail, Twitter, or Facebook. The appropriate message blank will open. Add an addressee and any comments you want, and then tap **Send**.

QuickQuotes

Paul Kukuk

I have the first-generation iPad, 16GB version with Wi-Fi and 3G cellular. I purchased the 3G model thinking we would use cellular Internet when Wi-Fi was not available. Since my wife and I each have iPhones, I soon discovered that the ongoing cost of two phones, each having data plans, plus an iPad with a data plan incurred more communication costs then we could justify. Therefore, we dropped the iPad data plan and only use Wi-Fi. This does not require a contract and may be canceled and restarted if we plan extended travel where we want cellular data.

For me, the iPad, like all Apple products, "just works." It is intuitive to use, has a long battery life, and never crashes or freezes. I can store an amazing amount of information on the iPad, including photos, music, and documents.

I am a bit of a photographer and enjoy editing photos on my iPad. There are many third-party apps for editing photos and video. The newer version of the iPad has a camera and can use Apple iPhoto and iMovie apps, which are excellent to edit photos and video. I use iMovie on my iPhone to create and edit movies by dragging video clips and photos along with a music track from iTunes. I then transfer the finished video/slideshow to my iPad. If I had a current-model iPad, I would use it for movie creation. The large screen is wonderful to show photos and video to family and friends.

I try a number of inexpensive or free apps and if they don't suit my needs, I can delete them and reinstall them later if I choose, without paying a second time. I have many of the same apps on my and my wife's iPhones and the iPad. Apps, once purchased from the App Store, can be used on all of our devices.

My grandchildren enjoy playing games, listening to music, and looking at photos on my iPad. Children quickly become bored with games, so the free ones, or at most 99-cent games, are entertaining with little expense and can be removed when the children are no longer interested.

I have gotten books from my local library, purchased books from iTunes and other sources, and have downloaded many free books from various sites. These have given me an opportunity to read classics at no cost. The large iPad screen is very easy to read, even in the dark. The font size and type can be changed to suit my comfort level.

I found I needed a car charger and a set of noise-canceling headphones to allow me to use the iPad. This makes Skype calls much more convenient and of higher quality.

I use both Netflix and Hulu to stream movies both on the iPad directly and, with an Apple TV adapter, to a big-screen TV.

I also use the iPad to check weather, stock prices, as a calculator, for word processing, and spreadsheets. Apple's word processing and spreadsheet apps are excellent and inexpensive.

The size and portability of the iPad are a large benefit over sitting in front of my computer. I can relax in a living room chair, on the deck, or in my car or RV, and do nearly anything that previously required sitting at my computer, using a mouse and keyboard.

QuickSteps to...

▶▶ **Enable Accessibility Features**

▶▶ **Review Accessibility Features**

▶▶ **Consider Other Accessibility Features**

▶▶ **Protect iPad Information**

▶▶ **Protect the iPad Itself**

▶▶ **Protect Yourself**

▶▶ **Set Up iCloud**

▶▶ **Use iCloud Backup**

▶▶ **Use iTunes Backup**

▶▶ **Update Your iPad**

▶▶ **Maintain Your iPad**

Chapter 10

Accessing, Securing, and Maintaining Your iPad

The iPad has many settings to customize it the way that works best for you, a number of which you have already seen in earlier chapters. In this chapter we'll look at other settings that may help you to more comfortably use the iPad, to protect it and you, to back up the data on your iPad, and to update and maintain your iPad.

USE YOUR IPAD COMFORTABLY

To fully use your iPad, it must be comfortable for you. You must be able to, as best as possible, understand what your iPad is displaying and saying, and to interact with it. To do this, the iPad has a number of accessibility features to assist your use.

Figure 10-1: The iPad has an extensive list of accessibility features.

▷▷ Enable Accessibility Features

You can enable the iPad's accessibility features, shown in Figure 10-1, either from the iPad itself or from a computer attached to the iPad.

Enable from the iPad

From the Home screen, tap **Settings | General | Accessibility**.

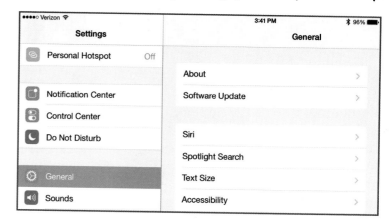

Enable from a Computer

1. If you don't already have iTunes on your computer, open a browser on the computer, go to apple.com/itunes, and click **Download iTunes**.

2. When the download is complete and you have iTunes running on your computer, turn on your iPad and plug it into your computer.

3. In iTunes on your computer, click *your* **iPad** in either the upper right or in the column or sidebar on the left (see Figure 10-2).

4. Scroll through the right pane to the bottom and click **Configure Accessibility**. A list of accessibility features will open.

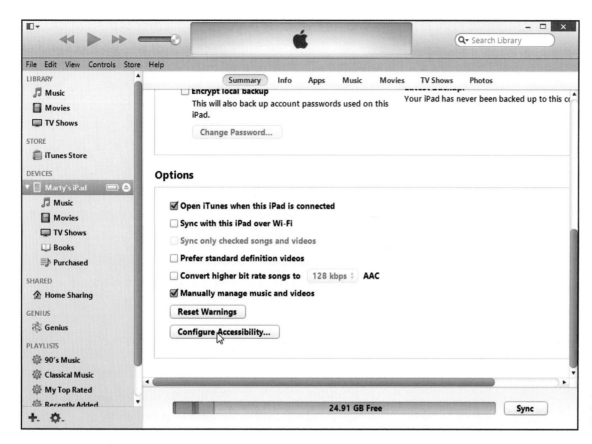

Figure 10-2: *Some of the iPad's accessibility features can be enabled from iTunes on your computer.*

iPad Accessibility Shortcut

You can set up a quick shortcut on your iPad to enable one of the accessibility features by triple-pressing the Home button.

Set this up from the list of accessibility features by doing the following:

1. Scroll to the bottom of the list of accessibility settings and tap **Accessibility Shortcut**.

2. Tap the accessibility features you want to turn on with this shortcut.

▷▷ Review Accessibility Features

The iPad's accessibility features provide a wide range of support for vision, hearing, learning, and mobility. If you are finding any discomfort or difficulty in any of these areas, look over the following sections to see if any of them can be of assistance to you.

VoiceOver

VoiceOver provides a verbal description of what is on the iPad's screen. This allows you to hear a confirmation of what you tap or drag your finger over on the screen. The language you hear is the one that you select in **Settings | General | International | Language And Region Format**, although not all languages are supported. This feature works whether you have Mail, Safari, Calendar, or other built-in apps active on the screen. (Some apps that are not built in—ones that you have to download— may also work with VoiceOver, but not all of them.)

To turn on VoiceOver (see Figure 10-3):

Tap **Settings | General | Accessibility | VoiceOver | VoiceOver**.

VoiceOver redefines the touch properties of the iPad's screen so when you tap an item, you hear a description of it instead of activating it. You must double-tap an item to activate it. Dragging a finger around the screen allows you to hear whatever is under your finger. If Speak Hints is turned on, which I recommend, you are also told what you can do with the item you tapped or moved your finger over. There are a number of special gestures that VoiceOver uses to facilitate using your iPad. If you want your iPad to:

- **Activate an item**   Double-tap it.
- **Speak an item**   Tap it or drag your finger over it.
- **Speak and activate an item**   Hold a finger on an item and tap anyplace on the screen with another finger.
- **Speak the next or previous item**   Swipe to the left or right.
- **Speak all information beginning from the top of the screen**   Swipe up with two fingers.
- **Speak all information beginning from the current position**   Swipe down with two fingers.
- **Speak additional information about an item**   Tap with three fingers.
- **Speak the first item on the page**   Tap at the top of the page with four fingers.
- **Speak the last item on the page**   Tap at the bottom of the page with four fingers.
- **Stop speaking the current item**   Tap with two fingers.
- **Go to the next or previous page**   Swipe to the left or right with three fingers.
- **Scroll the page up or down**   Swipe up or down with three fingers.

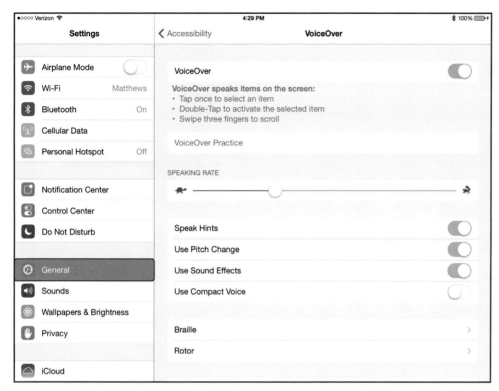

you know whether an accessibility feature is helpful to you. If you have only a marginal need, you may be tempted to give up on it.

Zoom

Turning on Zoom magnifies the entire screen, initially by 200 percent. Once Zoom is turned on, you will see only a portion of the original screen images, but the contents are much larger; text, photos, menus, and commands are all magnified. (I can't show an illustration of this because the screenshot only shows the normal screen without magnification. Turn on Zoom and see it for yourself.) By default, when you turn on Zoom or go to a new screen with Zoom turned on, you are automatically placed in the top-middle area of the screen. To move around and see the rest of the original screen area, you must use a three-finger drag and then revert to a one-finger drag to go to additional screens outside the original screen area—normal gestures are unaffected. The new commands that are available with Zoom include:

Figure 10-3: VoiceOver gives you audible corroboration of what is on the screen.

- Turn on Zoom by tapping **Settings | General | Accessibility | Zoom | Zoom**.
- When Zoom is turned on, temporarily turn it off and back on again by double-tapping the screen with three fingers.
- Increase or decrease the level of magnification by double-tapping, and on the second tap, do not lift your fingers,

It will take a while to get used to VoiceOver, but Apple gives you several tools to help you with it, including putting a rectangular box around what it is speaking about; providing a practice screen; playing sound effects, such as a sound when you change pages; providing phonetic feedback; and using pitch changes. There are also special VoiceOver commands for use with Safari, Maps, and both the onscreen and Bluetooth keyboards that you can read about in the Apple *iPad User Guide*. The key is to keep at it until but either drag them up to increase the magnification or down to decrease it.

- Move around the area of the original screen by dragging with three fingers.

Colors and Contrast

The iPad's accessibility features include two options: Invert Colors and Increase Contrast. These options may make it easier to see and read what is displayed on the iPad's screen. (Once again, I cannot take a screenshot of this. You'll have to try it for yourself.) Turn on these features and try them out:

- Turn on Invert Colors by tapping **Settings | General | Accessibility | Invert Colors**.

- Turn on Increase Contrast by tapping **Settings | General | Accessibility | Increase Contrast | Increase Contrast**.

Speak Selection and Auto-Text

You can have your iPad speak aloud selected text even when VoiceOver is turned off in two situations:

- Select text and tap **Speak** to have the selected text spoken to you by tapping **Settings | General | Accessibility | Speak Selection | Speak Selection**.

- Have the iPad speak automatic corrections and suggestions, such as spelling and capitalizations, by tapping **Settings | General | Accessibility | Speak Auto-Text**.

Larger Type and/or Bold Text

You can have your iPad enlarge type, independent of Zoom, in apps that support Dynamic Type, such as Alerts, Calendar, Mail, Messages, and Notes, or make all text bold, both with the objective to make it easier to read.

- Turn on Larger Type by tapping **Settings | General | Accessibility | Larger Type | Larger Dynamic Type**, and dragging the slider to the size you want.

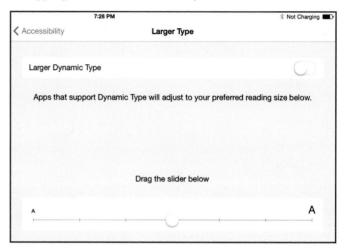

- Turn on Bold Text by tapping **Settings | General | Accessibility | Bold Text | Continue**.

Reduce Motion

The way objects move on the screen, such as alerts, can be reduced to make them easier to see and recognize.

- Turn on Reduce Motion by tapping **Settings | General | Accessibility | Reduce Motion | Reduce Motion**.

Hearing

The iPad provides several features to support hearing impairment.

- Turn on Subtitles and Closed Captioning for those videos that support it by tapping **Settings | General | Accessibility | Subtitles & Captioning | Closed Captions + SDH**, tapping **Style**, and tapping a style.

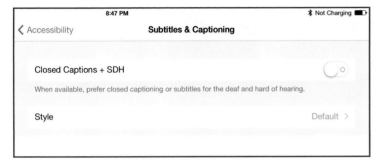

- Combine both the left and right audio channels and feed the result evenly to both ears by tapping **Settings | General | Accessibility | Mono Audio**.

- Adjust the balance between the left and right audio channels by tapping **Settings | General | Accessibility** and dragging the Hearing slider to the left or right.

Guided Access

To make the iPad easier to learn, you can temporarily restrict all activity on the iPad to a single app and:

- Control which features in the app are active.

- Disable areas of the screen that aren't related to the desired activity.

- Disable all of the iPad's hardware buttons except triple-pressing the Home button.

To use Guided Access:

1. Tap **Settings | General | Accessibility | Guided Access | Guided Access**.

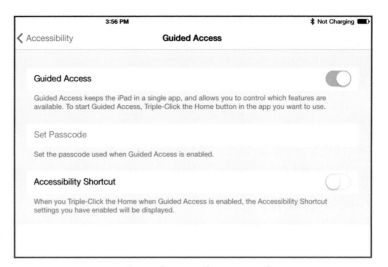

2. Tap **Set Passcode** and enter the passcode you want to use twice.

3. Open the app you want activity restricted to and press the **Home** button three times. A set of controls will appear at the bottom of the screen. (I can't include a screenshot of these controls because the use of the buttons is restricted.)

   a. Using your finger, draw a circle around the controls and areas of the screen you do *not* want used.

   b. Tap **Hardware Buttons Options** and tap **Sleep/Wake Button** and/or **Volume Button** to restrict their use.

   c. Tap the **Touch** button so it is on (has a green background) to *allow touch* in the areas of the screen that have not been restricted in Step 3a. When the Touch button is off, touch is prevented on the entire screen.

   d. Tap the **Motion** button so it is on (has a green background) to *allow* the screen to go from landscape to portrait and vice versa.

4. When you are ready to start the restricted use, tap **Start** in the upper-right corner. The app screen will only be usable within the confines of the restrictions you have set.

5. When you want to temporarily stop restricted use, press the **Home** button three times and tap **End** in the upper-left corner of the screen.

6. To permanently turn off Guided Access, tap **Settings | General | Accessibility | Guided Access | Guided Access**.

Physical Control

The iPad provides several features that help you use it even with limited physical ability:

- **Switch Control** allows you to use an adaptive accessory to select items on the screen by sequentially highlighting the items, which can then be selected. There are a number of options for customizing the highlighting and use of the accessory. Turn on Switch Control by tapping **Settings | General | Accessibility | Switch Control | Switch Control**.

- **AssistiveTouch** allows you to use your iPad when you have limited range of motion or you are using an adaptive accessory. Turn on AssistiveTouch by tapping **Settings | General | Accessibility | AssistiveTouch | AssistiveTouch**. When you turn on AssistiveTouch, a new button appears on the screen that looks like an onscreen Home button. When this control is touched, a menu appears that allows you to tap **Home** to replace pressing the Home button; tap **Device** and tap other icons to replace the Lock button, change the volume, mute sound, and rotate the screen; tap **Siri** to begin a conversation; and tap **Favorites** to define and use new gestures that perform selected tasks.

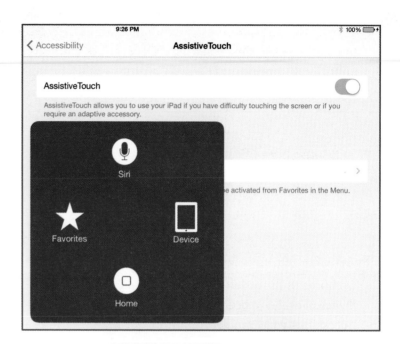

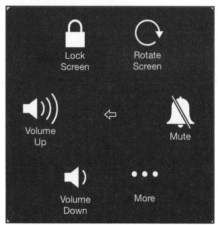

▷▷ Consider Other Accessibility Features

There are other features on your iPad in the normal set of items that you can use to assist your use of the device. Among these are Siri, Text Size, and Sounds.

Use Siri and Dictation

As you read in Chapter 6, Siri can help you reduce the use of the keyboard for many functions on the iPad, such as opening apps, writing notes, asking the time, taking a picture, asking where you are, adding a reminder or appointment, and many others. Also, using the dictation capability within Siri can assist in writing. See Chapter 6 for the details on using Siri and dictation.

Text Size

As you read earlier in this chapter, one of the iPad's accessibility features includes turning on larger type. This same capability is found in General Settings | Text Size. There is no difference between the two—just two places to turn on the same feature.

Sound Volume

From the Home screen, tap **Settings | Sounds** to set the loudness and sounds used for ringtones and alerts to make them clearer and more auditable, as shown in Figure 10-4.

- Drag the slider to the right to make ringtones and alerts louder.

- Alternatively, tap **Change With Buttons** to use the buttons on the side of the iPad to raise and lower the ringtone and make alert sounds louder or softer in the same way these buttons are used with music.

- Tap one of the ringtones or alerts and then choose and tap a sound to both hear and choose it as the new sound for the event.

SECURE YOUR IPAD AND YOU

In the reality of the world today, there are a lot of actions that can harm an iPad and can harm you using an iPad. To counter these threats, there are a number of steps you can take for both your iPad's safety as well as your own. There are three elements of iPad protection: protection of the data on your iPad, physical protection of the iPad, and protection of you from being hurt by anything you do on the iPad.

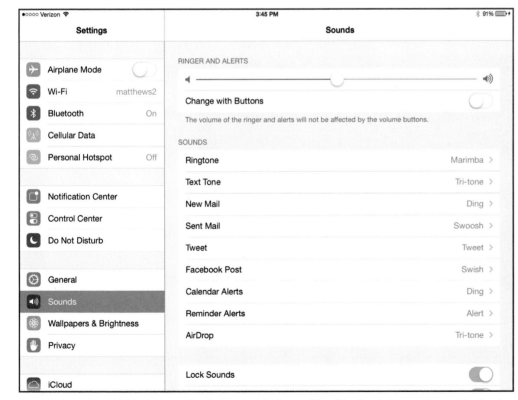

Figure 10-4: Identifiable ringtones and alerts can help you identify what is happening on the iPad.

Protect iPad Information

The iPad gives you several ways that you can protect the information that is stored on it. The first and most obvious way is to lock the iPad either after a period of inactivity or when you shut it down. The second is to require a passcode when you first start it or when you unlock it. You can also restrict access to just some of the information on the iPad or to its apps.

TIP While you can take a number of steps to protect the information on your iPad, the simple truth is that if you want to totally protect information from falling into the wrong hands, don't put it on the iPad.

Auto-Lock

By default, your iPad automatically "goes to sleep" when you don't use it for a period of time or you press the Sleep/Wake button. This turns off the screen and some internal functions, but you can still listen to music and get messages and alerts. To wake the iPad, you must either press the Sleep/Wake button or the Home button. When you do that, you will get a message: "Slide To Unlock." At this point, you can add a passcode for further protection. See "Enable a Passcode" later in this chapter.

You can determine the amount of time with no activity before Auto-Lock takes effect by tapping **Settings | General | Auto-Lock** from the Home screen and tapping one of the alternatives.

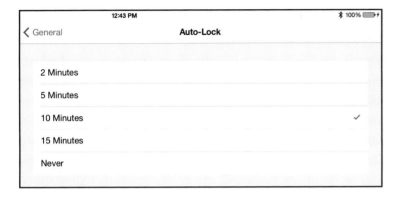

Cover Lock

When you use an enabled iPad cover or case, such as Apple's iPad Smart Cover or iPad Smart Case, and turn on the setting, the iPad will automatically go to sleep or wake when you close or open the case or cover. To adjust the setting, tap **Settings | General | Lock/Unlock**. (Do not tap Lock Rotation or Auto-Lock—scroll down to Lock/Unlock.)

Enable a Passcode

Locking and unlocking your iPad does no good without a passcode to prevent use of the iPad and access to its data when it is locked. To turn on a passcode, tap **Settings | General | Passcode Lock | Turn Passcode On** and then enter and re-enter a passcode.

By default, the passcode is a simple one consisting of four numbers. The iPad, though, gives you the option of turning off the simple passcode by tapping **Settings | General | Passcode Lock | Simple Passcode** and allowing you to enter a more complex passcode of uppercase and lowercase letters, numbers, and special characters.

You can extend the length of time after the iPad goes to sleep before the passcode is set so if you wake the iPad within that time you do not need to enter the passcode. Tap **Settings | General |**

Passcode Lock | Require Passcode and tap the length of time you want to use.

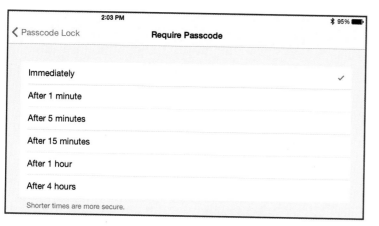

Set Restrictions

The iPad allows you to restrict access to certain apps and games, restrict certain content and access to features, and disallow changes in certain areas. This is more for the protection of younger users than for security purposes, but it's still valuable. To set up restrictions, tap **Settings | General | Restrictions | Enable Restrictions**, and then enter and re-enter a Restrictions passcode. The Restrictions page will open, as shown in Figure 10-5.

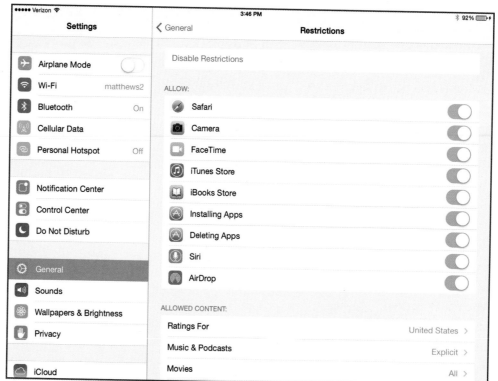

Figure 10-5: The iPad makes it easy to control the content for young users.

Initially, all features, functions, and apps are allowed, so to restrict their use, you need to turn them off. To disallow:

- Certain apps and app-related functions, tap the option under Allow to turn it off.

- Certain types of content for particular types of media, tap the media under Allowed Content and then tap the type of content to disallow.

- Certain actions in related areas, tap the area or app under either Privacy or Allowed Changes and tap the actions to disallow.

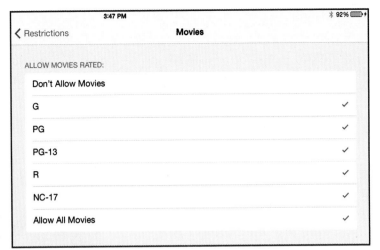

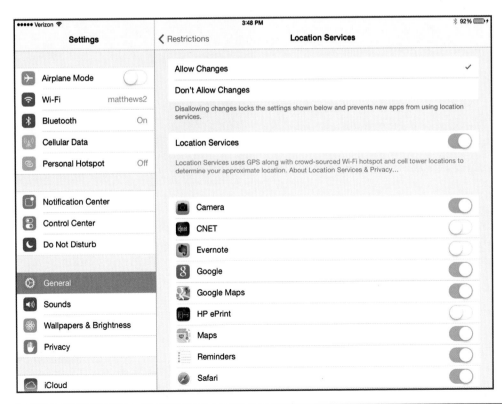

- Certain types or functions of games to disallow them.

 TIP Only a few apps are listed in the Allow list, but to prevent the use of others, uninstall them and do not allow new apps to be installed.

 NOTE When you disallow access to an app, its icon is simply removed from the Home screen.

Protect the iPad Itself

The iPad, being small, light, and attractive, is easily lost or stolen. A lot of its protection is just common sense: You keep track of it, you don't leave it lying around, and you don't advertise that you have it. But even with the best intentions, bad things happen. To counter this, the iPad has two features: Find My iPad and Erase Data.

Enable Find My iPad

Find My iPad uses iCloud to locate your iPad *if* it is turned on. You, of course, need to have an iCloud account first. See "Set Up iCloud" later in this chapter. Once you have turned on Find My iPad, you can:

- See on a map where your iPad is
- Play a sound and display a message on it
- Remotely lock it using a passcode
- Erase all of your data, apps, and settings

To enable Find My iPad and test it:

1. After setting up iCloud, turn on Find My iPad. From the Home screen, tap **Settings | iCloud | Find My iPad | OK**.

2. To locate your lost iPad, on a computer, open a browser and go to iCloud.com.

3. Type your Apple ID and password and press **ENTER** or **RETURN**. If requested and desired, click **Install** (possibly twice) to install the iCloud Web App. Click **Done** when you are finished installing iCloud.

4. Click **Find My iPhone** or possibly **Find My iPad**. If requested, type your iCloud password and you will see a map with green marker(s) indicating where your iOS devices are.

5. Click **Devices** in the upper-left corner. Click your iPad. Options for finding your iPad will appear.

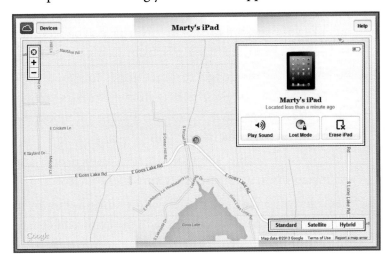

6. Click **Play Sound**. An Alert message will appear on your iPad and play an alert sound, which in this case is a bell ringing.

7. Click **Lost Mode**, enter a phone number (yours or a trusted friend) for the person who found your iPad to call about it, and click **Next**.

8. Accept the default message to display with the phone number on your iPad or make any change you want, and then click **Done**. Your message and phone number will appear on your iPad and then your iPad will shut down and lock.

9. As a final and last desperate step to take when you think your iPad has been stolen, click **Erase iPad**, and, if you really want to do it, click **Erase**. All data, apps, and settings will be removed.

CAUTION! Consider the warning message before erasing a missing iPad: "*An erased iPad cannot be located or tracked.*"

Erase All Data

You can automatically erase all data on your iPad after ten failed attempts at entering a passcode. This prevents someone who is trying to guess your passcode from accessing your data. To turn on this feature:

From the Home screen, tap **Settings** | **General** | **Passcode Lock**, enter your passcode, and tap **Erase Data**.

 TIP Unless you have an infallible memory, it is important to write your passcode down, especially if you have enabled Erase Data, and then store the paper you wrote it on in a safe place.

▷▷ Protect Yourself

The iPad is a great device, allowing you to do many things on the Internet and directly on the iPad. Some of the things that you can do have the possibility of harming your reputation and harming you financially, psychologically, and in very rare circumstances, even physically. The chance of harm is low, but it is real and you need to take measures to protect yourself. The most important is to be prudent and use good common sense.

- Be very careful of emails that ask you for money or for something like your bank account number, your Social Security number, or especially any password. *Never give your passwords out for any reason.* If you get email that looks like your bank or brokerage or other organization and it asks for your user name, password, or other personal numbers, *do not give it out* and report it to the bank or other organization. This is called phishing, and it is an attempt to acquire personal information by pretending to be someone or some organization they are not.

- As I said in the discussion of Facebook in Chapter 9, consider carefully before giving out information about yourself. Some information on Facebook you must give out, like your age, but no one says you have to be accurate, and you can prevent anyone else from seeing it.

- Remember the old adage: If something is too good to be true, it probably is. Consider carefully the offers you get and understand as much as possible what the other person is gaining through the transaction.

- As much as possible, shop and interact with people and organizations that you are fairly sure are reputable.

- Consider getting a credit card with a limited amount to use on the Internet. Also, use a credit card, not a debit card that can immediately draw money out of your checking account. Credit cards also often have more protections against misuse than a debit card does.

- Check prices. Amazon.com is often, but not always, a good source for low prices on many products, but in any case, check several sources before making a big Internet purchase.

- Be careful about the cables you plug into your iPad and the chargers you plug it into. The extra cables and chargers from Apple will cost a little more than alternatives you see on the Internet, but you know they will work and are safe. My experience with third-party cables is that they don't always work and, in rare instances, they can be dangerous. In my mind, it is better to spend a little extra and get Apple cables and chargers.

USE ICLOUD

iCloud is an Internet service provided by Apple that allows you to store information "on the cloud," which is, in reality, on computers known as servers belonging to Apple. If you sign up for iCloud, the information on your iPad is manually or automatically sent over the Internet to these servers. This allows you to keep a copy, or "backup," of your information so if something happens to your iPad you will not lose it. This includes the apps, music, and books you have purchased, as well as the mail, contacts, Photo Stream, calendar, reminders, documents, bookmarks, and notes that you have created. The iCloud also allows you to share, and therefore access, the information you have backed up with your other iOS devices such as an iPhone or iPod and with your computer, and it is what facilitates Find My iPad. The connection between iCloud and your iPad or other devices is through Wi-Fi, so you must have a Wi-Fi connection to use iCloud.

⏩ Set Up iCloud

You may have set up iCloud when you first set up your iPad and, therefore, already have an iCloud account. If so, jump to the next section, "Use iCloud Backup"; otherwise, set up iCloud now. It is very worthwhile to back up your iPad data, and it is free.

To set up iCloud, make sure you have a Wi-Fi connection to the Internet. With that:

1. From the Home screen, tap **Settings | iCloud**. If you haven't already set up iCloud, a form to do that will appear. Enter your Apple ID and password and tap **Sign In**.

2. Tap **OK** or **Don't Allow** to allow iCloud to use the location of your iPad or not. Only if you allow this can you enable Find My iPad. The iCloud settings will appear, as you can see in Figure 10-6.

3. Tap the On/Off button for the services that you want iCloud to back up in addition to the default items of your purchased apps, songs, and books; your Camera Roll; settings; app data; screen setup; and messages. The first six items, from Mail to Notes, are obvious and you simply back them up or not.

You might ask, "Why wouldn't I want to back up everything?" The only reason not to is because you have a limited amount (5GB) of free storage on iCloud (you can, of course, buy more—10GB costs $20 a year).

4. Tap **Keychain** to turn on the ability to store passwords and credit card information in an encrypted form so that only you can read it. Neither Apple nor anyone else without your iPad and passcode can read the information that is stored.

If you choose to use the iCloud Keychain, you must enter your Apple ID password and then choose whether you want to use your iPad's passcode as your iCloud security code or create a new code. You then must enter either your current passcode or a new code, which must be re-entered. Next, you must enter a telephone number that can receive text messages (called SMS or Small Message Service messages), which is used to verify your identity when using your iCloud security code. Finally, after tapping **Next**, you must once more enter your Apple ID password.

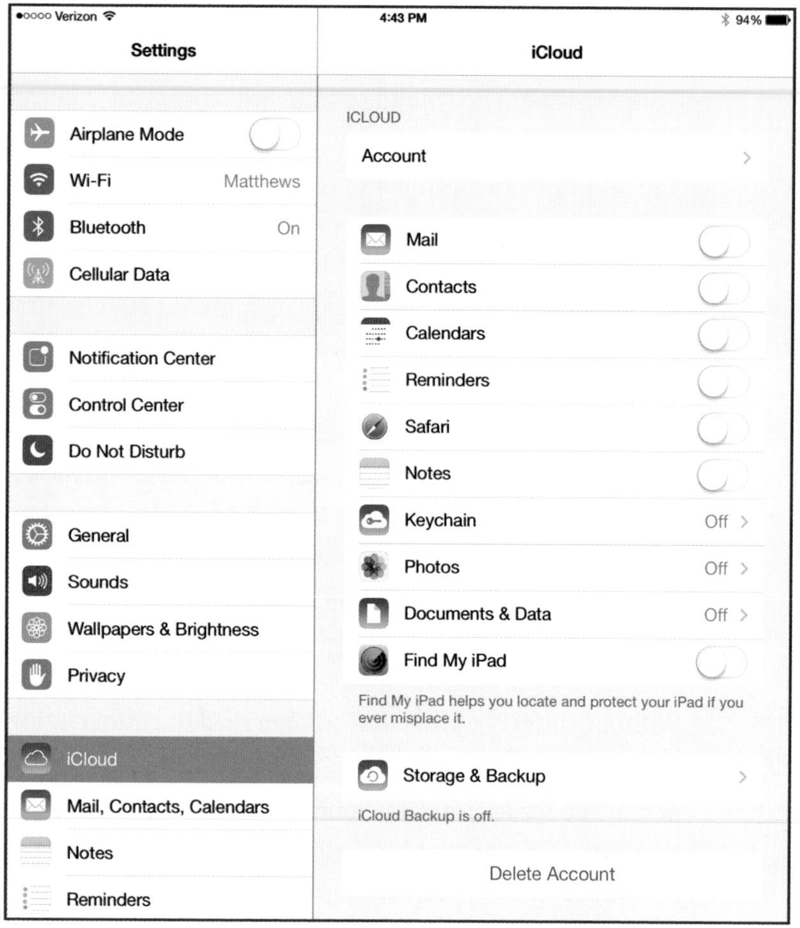

Figure 10-6: *The iCloud settings let you determine which of the major functions of the iPad are backed up.*

NOTE When you store items in the iCloud Keychain, the information is encrypted, meaning it is transformed into an unreadable format that cannot easily be deciphered, if at all. During the encryption a key is generated that only you, or someone with your passcode, will be able to use to read the encrypted information as if it wasn't encrypted.

5. If you choose to store documents and data from various apps, you also have the choice of whether to use cellular data when Wi-Fi is not available. This provides for the backing up of word processing, spreadsheet, presentation, and similar documents and data.

See the discussion of using iCloud with Photo Stream and Photo Sharing to share your photos in Chapter 8, and see the discussion of Find My iPad earlier in this chapter.

▷▷ Use iCloud Backup

iCloud Backup automatically makes a copy of your account on Apple servers of the music, apps, and books you have purchased, as well as the contents of your Camera Roll, settings, app data, messages, and screen contents and organization. Also, if you have enabled any of the items in Figure 10-6, these will be backed up. Once you have set up iCloud as described in the previous section, iCloud Backup is turned on by default, although you can change that. When your iPad is locked, meaning you are not using it, but you are connected to a power source and have Wi-Fi available, iCloud will automatically connect to your iPad and copy items it hasn't previously backed up on Apple servers.

Manage iCloud Backup

With iCloud Backup turned on, backups happen automatically without any intervention by you. Your information is backed up on a periodic basis, and you can see when, both on your iPad and on your computer, your iPad is connected to it. iCloud settings allow you to see how much of your iCloud storage you have used (the first 5GB is free), buy more storage, see how the

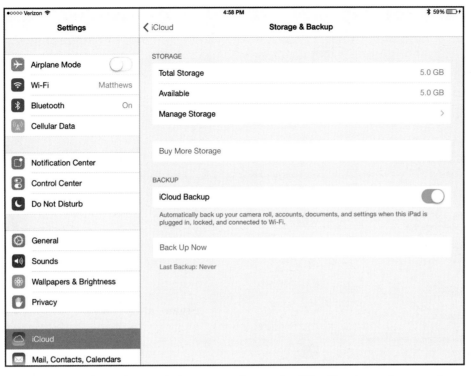

Figure 10-7: You do need to watch the amount of space that iCloud is using and manage how that space is being used.

storage is being used, turn off or on iCloud Backup, see when the last backup was done, and do one now, as you can see in Figure 10-7.

1. To access iCloud Backup's management settings, tap **Settings | iCloud | Storage & Backup | Manage Storage | *your* iPad | Show All Apps** to see what is included in your iCloud backup, as shown in Figure 10-8.

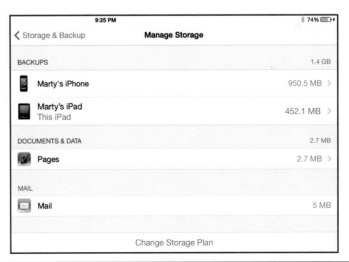

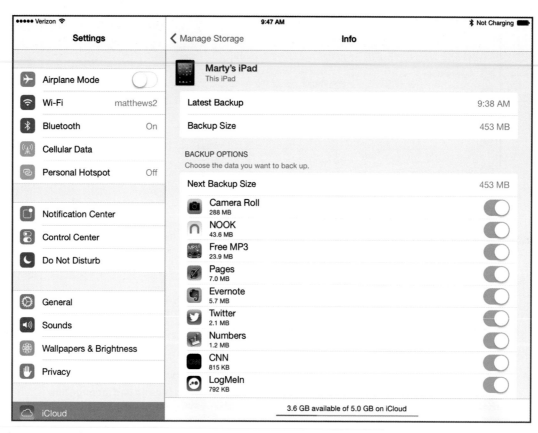

Figure 10-8: The iPad gives you a good facility for managing what is backed up with iCloud.

2. Go through your apps and turn off the ones that you don't want backed up. Some apps, like the Kindle and Nook readers, also store your purchases on their site and do not need to be stored on iCloud. Other apps may not be worth storing. On the other hand, if you are not using very much of your iCloud's free 5GB of storage, it doesn't make any difference.

3. When you have the backup options the way you want them, tap **Manage Storage | Storage & Backup | Back Up Now** to do a current iCloud backup.

TIP To buy more iCloud storage, tap **Settings | iCloud | Storage & Settings | Manage Storage | Change Storage Plan** and select the storage plan you want to buy.

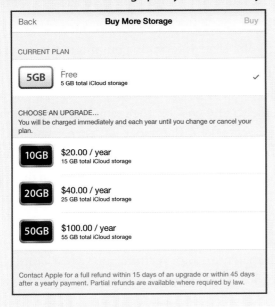

2. Go through the iPad setup as described in Chapter 1, except that on the Set Up Your iPad screen, tap **Restore From iCloud Backup**. Enter your Apple ID and password and continue through the setup.

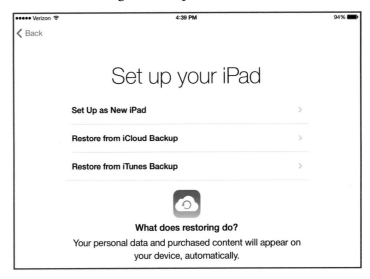

Restore from an iCloud Backup

Should you need to restore your iPad and you have had iCloud doing automatic backups, it is very easy and should restore your iPad to its last backup. To do that:

1. From the Home screen, tap **Settings | General | Reset | Erase All Content And Settings**, enter your passcode if you have enabled one, tap **Reset** twice to confirm that you want to do that, and enter your Apple ID password (see "Reset Your iPad" later in this chapter). The iPad will erase itself, reload the operating system (iOS), and start the iPad setup.

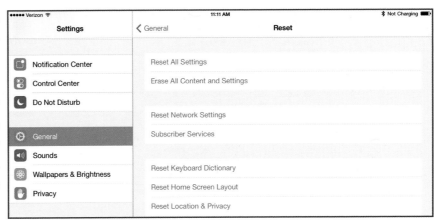

3. Choose the backup—normally, the latest is what you want to use. You will see the Restore From iCloud screen that will show you the progress of the restoration. Then the iPad will restart or "reboot."

4. After restarting, you will get a message that the update has completed. Tap **Continue**.

5. Enter your Apple ID password. After reading a message about Find My iPad in iOS 7, tap **Continue**, create a passcode, tap **Get Started**, and enter your Apple ID to sign in to iCloud.

Restore Completed

Your iPad was restored successfully. There are just a few more steps to follow, and then you're done!

Continue

Use Keychain

Once you have set up iCloud Keychain, you will receive a query each time you use a password or a credit card as to whether you want to store the password and/or credit card in iCloud Keychain.

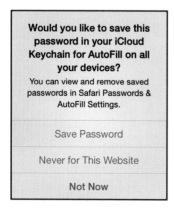

Would you like to save this password in your iCloud Keychain for AutoFill on all your devices?

You can view and remove saved passwords in Safari Passwords & AutoFill Settings.

Save Password

Never for This Website

Not Now

Use iTunes Backup

In addition to iCloud Backup, which is discussed in this chapter, you can use iTunes on your computer to back up your iPad on the computer. To do that:

1. Plug your iPad into your computer. If iTunes on the computer does not automatically start, start it.

2. Click your iPad in the left column sidebar. (If you don't see the sidebar and possibly the menu bar, click the black and white rectangle in the upper-left corner and click **Show Menu Bar**. In the menu bar, click **View | Show Sidebar**.)

3. If it isn't already selected, click **Summary** in the top of the right pane to open the summary and backup controls for your iPad, as you can see in Figure 10-9.

4. Under Backups, click **This Computer | Encrypt Local Backup**, enter and verify a password, and click **Set Password**. The backup will begin and show you its progress.

When the backup is complete, you will see today's date and the time under Latest Backups. From that time on, your iPad will be automatically backed up to your computer, but you will see that the automatic iCloud backup is now disabled. You cannot automatically back up to both iCloud and your computer. You can manually back up to your computer and still automatically back up to iCloud. Click **Back Up Now** under Manually Back Up And Restore.

Figure 10-9: Backing up through iTunes on your computer is a little more cumbersome than wirelessly backing up to iCloud.

UPDATE AND MAINTAIN YOUR IPAD

Like any computer, it is important to keep your iPad updated and maintained so that it performs at its best for you.

Update Your iPad

Update means that you are using the latest version of the iPad's operating system (iOS), which controls everything that the iPad does outside of an app, and iOS does a lot to support apps. Updates to iOS contain both fixes to problems ("bugs") in the current version, as well as improvements to it. Finally, new apps, both Apple's and third-party, often require the latest version of iOS. I strongly recommend that you periodically check on and install new iOS updates. Quarterly is a good schedule to use.

1. From the Home screen, tap **Settings | General | Software Update**. If your software is up to date, you will be told that.

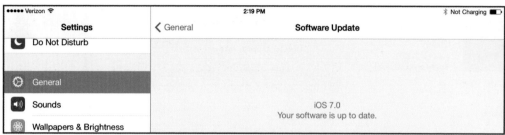

1. From the Home screen, tap **Settings | General | Reset**. You will see seven options for various levels of resetting:

2. If a new version of iOS is available, you will be given the option to install it. Tap **Install Update** and enter your Apple ID password. The update will take place. You will see its progress.

Reset Your iPad

Resetting your iPad clears it of various levels of information, returning it, as the given level, to the condition that it existed in when you first took it out of the box. This can be helpful in several situations, the most drastic being when the iPad has been corrupted for some reason and you need to have it completely restored.

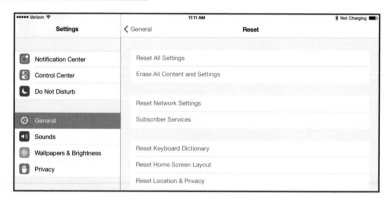

 CAUTION! Resetting your iPad makes permanent changes to your iPad and, depending on the level of resetting that you do, you can do anything from simply rearranging the Home screen to totally erasing all content and settings, including all purchases (apps, music, videos, and books); all data; and all contacts, messages, calendar entries, messages, notes, and mail. *It is strongly advised that you do a complete backup to your computer and to iCloud before doing any of the major resetting.*

- **Reset All Settings** returns all settings and preferences to their factory settings. No changes are made to your information on the iPad, like mail, messages, contacts, and photos.

- **Erase All Content And Settings** totally removes everything that has been added to the iPad since it came from the factory, including all your purchases and data and all settings.

- **Reset Network Settings** disconnects you from all Wi-Fi networks you have joined and removes some VPN (virtual private networking) settings.

- **Subscriber Services** removes you from subscriptions you have by requiring you either to resubscribe or to enter a new authorization key.
- **Reset Keyboard Dictionary** erases all custom words you have entered into the spelling dictionary.
- **Reset Home Screen Layout** restores the Home screen to its original or factory layout.
- **Reset Location & Privacy** turns off all the location and access permissions you have given apps.

2. Tap the level of restoration that you want to do; enter your passcode, if you are using one; and, if asked, enter your restrictions passcode. Read the warning or explanation about what you are about to do, and tap **Reset**, if you, in fact, want to do that. Depending on the level, you may be requested to enter your Apple ID password and once more tap **Reset**.

 NOTE Resetting and restoring are related, but are not the same thing. Resetting returns some or all of the iPad to its factory settings. Restoring often begins with resetting and then restores a backup to give the iPad the settings and content it had at the time of the backup.

Maintain Your iPad

Maintaining your iPad involves taking care of it and, when they arise, fixing problems with it.

Take Care of Your iPad

Your iPad, like any electronics with a glass screen, is fragile. You don't drop it on a hard surface, you pack it carefully when traveling, and you are careful not to spill coffee on it. There are also several proactive things that you can do for your iPad:

- Get and use a protective case for it. This was briefly discussed in Chapter 1, but if you don't have one, do an Internet search for "iPad cases."
- Get and install a protective film covering for the screen. They are not easy to install and it is hard to eliminate all the bubbles, but the effort is worthwhile to prevent the screen from being scratched and possibly broken.
- Use Apple cables and power converters. While they cost more than third-party replacements, they are guaranteed to work with your iPad and not cause a problem.
- Use only a soft cloth to clean the screen. *Do not use any glass cleaning products!*
- Do not use your iPad in dirty, dusty, or smoke-filled environments.
- Do not plug anything into your iPad that isn't made specifically for the iPad.
- Use common sense.

Fix Problems with Your iPad

Again, as with any electronic device, no matter how well you treat it, things happen. Most commonly, apps are not behaving as they should, but sometimes it is more than that. Here are some steps to work through to see if you can fix your problem.

1. Turn your iPad off by pressing and holding the Sleep/ Wake button on the top-right corner until you get **Slide To Power Off** and then swipe that. Leave the power off while doing Step 2.

2. If you have any suspicion that the iPad battery is low, plug the iPad into a direct power outlet, not into another device. Let the battery charge for at least 15 minutes before going on and leave it plugged in.

3. Restart the iPad by pressing and holding the Sleep/Wake button until you see the Apple logo. In many cases, these first three steps will fix most problems with apps.

4. Some apps have settings that allow you to just reset the app. Check by tapping **Settings** | *app* and look for Reset. Tap it.

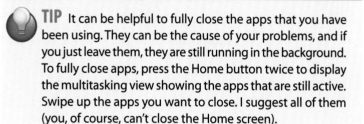 **TIP** It can be helpful to fully close the apps that you have been using. They can be the cause of your problems, and if you just leave them, they are still running in the background. To fully close apps, press the Home button twice to display the multitasking view showing the apps that are still active. Swipe up the apps you want to close. I suggest all of them (you, of course, can't close the Home screen).

5. Do a basic reset of the iPad in which nothing is removed or changed by simultaneously pressing and holding the Sleep/Wake button and the Home button until you see the Apple logo. This will fix a number of other problems.

6. If the problem is with connecting to iTunes on your computer, try restarting iTunes and then restarting your computer. Also, make sure the Universal Serial Bus (USB) cable is in good shape and well connected.

7. Do a complete restore from an iCloud or iTunes backup as described earlier in this chapter in "Restore from an iCloud Backup." Be sure to use Erase All Content And Settings in the reset stage. If nothing has worked to this point, Step 8 is the only alternative.

8. Take your iPad to an Apple store or an Apple-accredited repair location. It may be that the Genius bar may do the trick, or you will need hardware repair.

The good news is that the iPad is amazingly tough and resilient. To paraphrase Timex, it takes a licking and keeps on computing.

QuickQuotes

John Nelson "Seattle 'Puter Tutor"

I love the iPad, its lightness, quickness, and portability. I take it everywhere; it is an extension of me. I use the iPad for many of the functions I used to do on a computer; still, it's a very different tool. I don't try to get it to do everything my computer does—it can't. But what it does, it does very well. The iPad is an almost transparent interface between me and the information I want.

The one thing I do most on my iPad is keep notes and to-do lists in Evernote. I have lists of the day's tasks, family birthdays, activity logs, resource lists, technical instructions, notes I clip from the Web, plans for remodeling projects, and much more. With Evernote, everything I type on the iPad automatically appears on my home computer, and vice versa. As a senior, with a senior's unpredictable memory, Evernote is probably my favorite app—nothing gets lost!

Another app I find invaluable is Zite, which is a selective news aggregator. I can choose the categories of news I want, and it will scour the entire Internet and collect articles on those subjects. I can also add keywords, and it will group the articles on those words. And it learns as I use it exactly what I like and what I don't.

Planetarium is an app that shows me an image of the entire night sky above me. I hold the iPad upside-down above me, and Planetarium correctly orients itself to my time, location, and exactly where I am looking. It shows me the night sky with names and information about the planets, stars, and star groupings I'm seeing. It also allows me to look at stars and planets on other dates and times so I can see their movement.

I do a lot of Google searching during my classes to keep ahead of my students, and during lunch and other free times I read news and other items; or if I'm especially brain-dead I just play Solitaire. I often keep my iPad near me during dinner to look up items that come up in conversation.

Index